MiGs
OVER NORTH
Vietnam

MiGs

OVER NORTH

Vietnam

The Vietnamese People's Air Force in Combat: 1965-1975

ROGER BONIFACE

HIKOKI
PUBLICATIONS

This book is dedicated to the Vietnamese people
and the heroic pilots of Vietnam

First published in 2008 by
Hikoki Publications Ltd
1a Ringway Trading Est
Shadowmoss Rd
Manchester
M22 5LH
England

Email: enquiries@crecy.co.uk
www.crecy.co.uk

Project Editor: Robert Forsyth
Production Management: Chevron Publishing Limited
Colour profiles ©: Tim Brown
Maps ©: Adriel Yap

Chevron Publishing wishes to thank Jerry Scutts for his assistance
in the preparation of this book.

ISBN-13: 9 781902 109053

Printed in China

Contents

Acknowledgements

It took a tiny army of people to help me write this book and this acknowledgement is only a modest recognition of their assistance.

First and foremost, I must thank Robert Forsyth of Chevron Publishing, for taking this work from total obscurity to being published in this magnificent form. Robert Forsyth has been a great believer in telling the story from the 'other side'. His various works on the Luftwaffe such as the history of JV 44 – 'The Galland Circus' (a seminal piece of authorship) lies testimony to this. I, like all the Vietnamese people and their aircrew, owe him a great debt.

I must thank the Ministry of Foreign Affairs of Vietnam for allowing me the opportunity to visit Vietnam and conduct my research. Once in Vietnam, those working in the English section of the foreign press ranks made every effort to assist me in translations. Without their assistance this book would have never been written, as many visits and interviews had to be arranged in a relatively short time.

I must also thank all those at the Vietnamese News Agency who helped me beyond the call of duty in acquiring photographs of the period. Many photographs had to be reviewed in detail in order to make sure that all data was as correct as possible, such as the names of airfields, units, etc.

I must mention Miss Ngo Thi Kim Dung of the VPAF Museum who is a walking encyclopedia on the VPAF. She shared every piece of information with me and made sure that no detail was left unexplored. We spent some hours together just going over pilot photographs.

I will never forget how Nguyen Minh Tam of the B-52 Museum in Ha Noi went through the details of the Linebacker raids with me and described to me events that had yet to be published. I could write a book just on my meeting with him.

The debt this book owes to Nguyen Van Minh of the Army Historical Branch is great. He contributed a great amount of detail about the training and selection, and basic ideology behind VPAF pilot selection of the time. It was through him that I managed to understand the ideological motivation behind the pilots and their actions.

I am also grateful to Le Thanh, the painter, who gave accounts of what it was like to experience the bombings in December 1972. I was impressed by his knowledge of the period and how he brought home the realities of those days when he showed me the wreckage of a B-52 still lying in his garden.

No book of this nature can ever be written without obtained first-hand accounts from the pilots. I was indeed very fortunate to obtain interviews with Pham Nook Tan, Nguyen Nhat Chieu and Nguyen Van Bay. These three pilots were in action throughout the war and not only distinguished themselves as fighter pilots but as first-class leaders and tacticians. The opinions and experiences they related to me became the element that gave this work its efficacy and validity. For me, these men reflected the composite thoughts and ideals of the VPAF – they were there and lived the history.

I must give special thanks to Pham Ngoc Lan for helping me through the draft of this book during times when he was pressed with more urgent duties. He never once tried to influence this book in any way, but always gave impartial advice so as to inform a reader rather than mislead.

Help also came from the United States of America, especially from the Air University Library at Maxwell AFB. I must give special thanks to Terry Hawkins, Marlowe Peters, Diana Simpson and Gene Johnson who gave their valuable time in assisting me to obtain data on VPAF ranks and US loss and victory rates over Vietnam between 1962 and 1973.

I would like to extend my gratitude to Jeremy Morris, a retired US Navy Captain, and James B. Souder, a retired US Navy Commander. Both of them were F-4 pilots in Vietnam and they contributed directly to the information concerning the air combat on 26 October 1967, when Jeremy Morris was credited with a MiG kill. They were also instrumental in obtaining information about the combat on 27 April 1972.

This book has also given me the opportunity to know Dr. Istvan Toperczer, whom I regard as a leading light on any detail of the VPAF. He freely contributed photographs and advice to me and gave me encouragement when it might have been easier to give up.

The National Library of Singapore played an important part by making certain that that my pieces of information from America got to me and by working overtime to ensure that all liaisons with The Air University Library in went smoothly. I must specially acknowledge the professional work that Ms. Rokiah Mentol and Mr. Rajendra contributed on my behalf.

I also owe a debt to Mr. Adriel Yap, a graduate student from the National University of Singapore, who did a great job on the maps you see in this book. His professional attitude is a fine example to older hands like myself.

I must not forget Mr. Alvin Lee of Singapore who produced hundreds of negatives for this work without ever complaining that I was paying him so little!

My good friends Stewart and Heidi Lee, together with Professor Larry Francis, all assisted me in ways that helped this book immeasurably. Special thanks go to Stewart for designing and formatting the charts in the book.

I must not forget Francis from Hobby Focus and those at the Orchard Store (Singapore's oldest model shop) who allowed me use their books like a library yet not actually buy anything!

Although there were many who assisted me in this book I must take sole responsibility for any inaccuracies and omissions that may arise. A special thanks to Lisa Alford and Sue Steel for listening to me discuss VPAF fighter tactics and contribute constructively.

Also to Helen Nash and Sue Whately for answering the phones when my editors called for me and Julie Witty for inspiration.

Also, I must thank Mark Nelson of Chevron Publishing who has made much with little. I believe that without his advice and creativity this work would have been undermined by my shortcomings.

Last but not least to my family for all their support especially to Kathryn for her total support and Sophia for all the typing.

RB, April 2008

A Tribute from a Vietnamese

All human beings living on this planet always praise their own kind; all love their country – their beloved motherland – as holding the right view. People around the world always strive to live in peace and in friendship, regardless of how poor and difficult the place where they were born. All peoples take pride in their histories, roots and the achievements of their ancestors.

So whoever breaks this pursuit of happiness and this desire for a peaceful life by occupying foreign land, should not be surprised when there is retaliation. People do this to protect their national integrity and will fight to the last drop of blood.

For me, a Vietnamese, a fighter for the revolution who was brought up by the Communist Party and President Ho Chih Minh, living to fight for my ideal was a natural reaction to what was taking place around me.

I fought to protect my sacred nation of Vietnam for the happiness of my people and my motherland. My country was attacked and destroyed by outsiders too many times in the past. I fought to liberate the south of Vietnam and, like all my comrades, devoted every sinew of my thoughts and energies to achieve that goal. That is why we made light of our great sufferings, took courage and fought bravely beyond the call of duty against the enemy. We defended our country because we had inherited in our blood the will to fight on until the finish, a tradition passed on to us by our ancestors.

Using a few to defeat a more numerous enemy, taking justice to defeat cruelty.

Major General Pham Ngoc Lan (retired), Ha Noi, 3 April 2000

Preface

When I first became interested in the air war over Vietnam, I (like others who were interested in the subject) read books written from the American point of view, as these were the only ones that were available. This was not a problem at first since all information was new and interesting.

Then, as legendary figures like Nguyen Van Coc, Nguyen Van Bay and Colonel Toon began to be mentioned in these accounts, my interest in the North Vietnamese pilots began. However, as I tried to find out more about these mysterious figures who flew the MiGs, I discovered that the total information available on them did not amount to a single page in any book. So early in 1994 my quest to write this book began. I was warned by those who knew better that my goal was 'nearly impossible' and how right they were!

When I seriously began to put my information together in 1999, I realized that I was looking at 'another war', where opinions and events were completely different from what I had read previously.

Through the help of many Vietnamese, I have been able to look at documents hitherto unknown outside Vietnam and I managed to discover some 'truths and myths' about the air war over North Vietnam. I was given the opportunity to speak to some of the leading pilots of that period, such as Pham Ngoc Lan, Nguyen Nhat Chieu and Nguyen Van Bay, who very graciously gave their time to speak to me about their wartime experiences. I felt very honored because this kind of interview had never been granted to any foreigner until that time.

Apart from the fascinating stories and accounts they had to contribute, I was very surprised at their complete modesty and humility. All of them were amazed that anyone could be interested in what they had done – '... After all, we only flew the MiGs,' was their common answer. General Pham Ngoc Lan was even kind enough to read through a draft of this book and gave me commentaries on the stories of the combats. (The extent of his help even involved him taking time off on the first day of the lunar new year to do some work on this book. In Vietnam the first day of the lunar New Year is a private time that is usually only shared with one's family.)

The experience of writing this book has shown me that there are contradictions built into the subject, not only concerning the factual details of the war but also about the Vietnamese people themselves. In some ways their attitudes resembled the 'stiff upper lip' emotions of Royal Air Force pilots of World War II. This is very different from the generally accepted view of the time that the Vietnamese were unemotional people who lacked many 'Western' feelings (such as individual thought) because they were Asians and, even worse, because they were Communists. Many of the Vietnamese people I met were not hard-core Communists, but merely viewed Communism as a vehicle that reflected their growing nationalism. When a more capitalist and democratic form of life was thrust upon them by the USA and the West they rejected it as matter of pride and stubbornness.

This ability to show their nationalism by not liking to be told what to do is very similar to the Anglo-Saxon mentality that was put to good use in the Battle of Britain. In many ways the pilots who fought in the Vietnam War were doing no more or less than the average RAF pilot did in 1940. It would not be incorrect to say that the reports and stories in this book relate, in effect, about the 'Battle of Vietnam'.

Another contradiction that became apparent to me is how the West perceived the Vietnamese and their approach to air-to-air tactics. The American fighter pilot, by and large, viewed himself as an individual, but nearly all USAF and USN pilots relied very heavily on pre-planned manoeuvres and tactics in nearly all situations. The emphasis on teamwork was very high, so high that many North Vietnamese pilots believed that American fighter and bomber tactics were very predictable, yet American tactics mostly succeeded because of numerical advantage rather than any innate superiority. This view is not new and was also noticed by Saburo Sakai, the great Japanese ace of World War II.

On the other hand, most North Vietnamese pilots were given strict scenarios to follow in every combat and these were usually obeyed by 'rookie' pilots. However, a large number of North Vietnamese pilots developed their air-to-air tactics 'on the spot', flying with great instinct and unpredictability. Such a scene was clearly shown when Nguyen Van Bay and Vo Van Man shot down an American F-105: whilst in a combat scenario with American fighters they were using the experience of rice-pounding from their childhood. In the main, fighter tactics were discussed between individual squadrons and the results often differed widely. Furthermore, pilots who flew together nearly always came from the same areas of Vietnam: this feeling of solidarity and community had a major influence on the pilots and their approach to tactics.

It is also interesting to note that the American definition of 'teamwork', by and large, meant following a specified pattern, as in a football game where each person keeps a certain position and performs fixed tasks. However, the North Vietnamese viewed teamwork as the ability to read another pilot's mind in combat situations, because all situations were different.

The pages that follow offer an account for the first time based upon the information currently available about what it felt like to be on the 'other' side.

Roger Boniface 2008

VIETNAM is 1,500 miles long. It hangs at the outer edge of Southeast Asia and looks like a dragon, with its head spreading around the city of Ha Noi. The dragon's slim neck runs from Vinh to Da Nang; the main body covers the coastal flats, the tribal highlands and the Mekong Delta; its tail curls into the Gulf of Siam some 225 miles north of Malaysia.

Because of its position south of China and close to its volatile neighbours, Khmer (formerly Cambodia), Laos and Thailand, Vietnam has been under constant threat. All of these states have, in the past, exerted policies of annexation or demanded tribute from the Vietnamese. The most notable of these were the Chinese conquest in the early 15th century, the French annexation in the 19th century, and finally the Japanese occupation during World War II.

Modern Vietnamese nationalism was born in the early 20th century when a wave of anti-colonial feelings developed in Southeast Asia. Under French rule the Vietnamese suffered very severe economic and racial discrimination, making political independence vital. Communism was seen as the perfect vehicle to end many centuries of foreign domination and abuse. The Vietnamese had witnessed how easily the French were defeated by fellow Asians (the Japanese). This made the Vietnamese realize that the French were not all-powerful and that they could therefore be overthrown.

During the period 1930 to 1945, a leader called Ho Chih Minh emerged as the most prominent leader and spokesman for many Vietnamese. He became instrumental in pushing for independence. Before long his status was similar to that of Mohendas K. Gandhi in India: he was affectionately known as 'Uncle Choo'.

Ho Chih Minh (he who is enlightened) was born in 1890 in Nghe An Province in central Vietnam. He was instrumental in the founding of three different Communist parties: the French Communist Party in 1920 (while living and working in France in the years following World War I), the Indochina Communist Party in 1925, and finally the Vietnamese Communist Party (the Viet Minh) in 1941.

On 20 September 1945, he declared the independence of Vietnam from French colonial rule – a move that the departing Japanese did little to stop. The French were in no mood to give up their lucrative colonies in Indochina so easily, but sought initially to negotiate. However, by August 1946 the Paris talks that were supposed to smooth over the problem had failed totally, and the Viet Minh and the French were at war.

After waging a very successful guerilla campaign, Ho was confident enough to proclaim, on 14 January 1950, the founding of the Democratic Republic of Vietnam. On 7 May 1953, the French were thoroughly beaten at the battle of Dien Bien Phu, leading to the signing of a truce on 20 July 1954, thus ending the First Indochina War.

During the 1950s he tried to rationalize his military resources and began to create the embryos of the Vietnamese Air Force and Navy. All forces were based on western models and the Air Force was no exception.

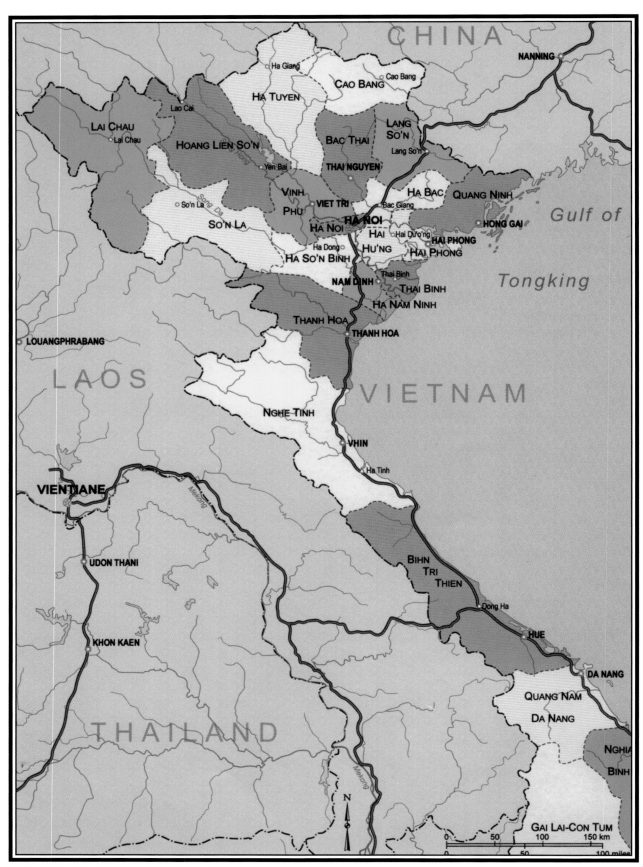

The Provinces of Vietnam

A brief history of the North Vietnamese People's Air Force (VPAF)

ON 9 March 1949 Ho Chih Minh passed a decree that a committee be set up to study the feasibility of creating an air force for his country. The Ministry of Defense established an Air Force Council to draw up plans for this new air force, based initially on the French system. The Council had specialist advisors from Japan and Germany.

The first group of 30 student pilots was given less than four hours theoretical instruction. These budding pilots were then given practical flying lessons in a Tiger Moth and a French-made Fieseler Storch.

By 1955 the Ministry of Defense decided to upgrade its existing military structure and established the groundwork for a modern air force. The primary objective was to modernize all the former French and Japanese airfields and make them operational once again. The Airfield Research Council was set up to assist the General Staff in identifying any logistical problems and to give specialist advice. The three main airfields of any value in North Vietnam were Cat Bi, Do Son and Kien An. The French gave up control of these airbases by 15 May 1955, in accordance with a truce agreement signed in Paris. They were quickly reconstructed and airfields at Gia Lam, Vhin, Dong Hoi, Lang Son, Lao Cai and Tien Yen were also added to the reconstruction programme.

In March 1956 the first batch of 110 student pilots were sent overseas. One group of thirty students, under the command of Pham Dinh Cuong, underwent transport and light bomber training. A second batch of 30 student pilots under the leadership of Dao Dinh Luyen was earmarked for fighter pilot training. A third group of students was given helicopter training in the Soviet Union.

By the end of 1956 the Ministry of Defense formed the Flying Club of the Civil Aviation Department at Cat Bai Airbase. The Chinese assisted in the setting up and construction of the first aviation training school in North Vietnam, known as the No.1 Training School. Soon after this, the No.2 Training School was established in Gia Lam. However, at this time the training programme covered only non-flying courses such as meteorological knowledge, signal programs and other ground support functions. However, by 1957 flying experience with the MiG 15 was added to the training programmes.

With the introduction of jet fighters such as the MiG 15 and MiG 17, many of the runways had to be extended and two new airfields were created at Do San and Cao Bang. By the end of 1958, the VPAF had 44 reconstructed and new airfields under its control.

Thus, by the start of 1959, a network of airfields existed which covered the whole of North Vietnam. The main airbases at Gia Lam, Vhin and Dong Hoi protected Ha Noi and the surrounding area. The airfields at Na San, Dien Bien, Lai Chau and Lai Cai covered the northwest. The northeast came under the protection of the airfields at Cat Bi, Kien An, Do Son, and Tien Yen. The new airbases at Lang Son and Cao Bang covered the north of the country.

On 24 January 1959 the Air Force Office was created and placed under the command of Dang Tinh. This office controlled both military and civil aviation matters. In addition, in the same year the first batch of Soviet-trained pilots returned. Also, the first air transport regiment was formed, formally called the 919th Air Transport Regiment. By the end of 1959, the Air Force Training School could train its own pilots to fly sophisticated

A MiG 15UTI. Trainers such as 'Red 2618' were always in short supply. Most VPAF pilots entered combat with insufficient flying hours. (Vietnamese News Agency)

propeller-driven aircraft such as the Yak 18 and the MiG 15 jet fighter. However, advanced jet training was still carried out primarily in China and the Soviet Union.

In 1960 a batch of 52 pilots under the command of Nguyen Nhat Chieu and Pham Ngoc Lan was sent to the Soviet Union for conversion to the MiG 17 air superiority fighter. A further group of 30 pilots also underwent MiG 17 conversion training at the Chinese airbase at Son Dong. To supplement this, another 70 pilots received helicopter conversion training and another batch of 200 students underwent ground support training in China.

By December 1962 the Soviet Union had supplied the VPAF with at least 40 fighters, 36 of these being MiG 17s, and a small number of two-seater MiG 15 trainers.

On 3 February 1964, the Deputy Defence Minister, General Hoang Van Thai, signed an order creating North Vietnam's premier fighter group, the 921st 'Sao Dao' Fighter Regiment (Trungst Doan Quan Tiem Kich 921). This regiment became active a few weeks after this date when the support facilities at Noi Bai were completed. The first operationally trained fighter pilots arrived from the Soviet Union soon after February 1964.

Within a span of 15 years the North Vietnamese had evolved their air arm from a 'paper air force' to one that would cause many problems to the greatest air force the world had ever seen.

'Red 101' was a Zlin -226 trainer aircraft attached to the 910th Training Regiment. Nearly all Vietnamese pilots trained in the early years flew in this type. Dinh Ton was among this famous few. (Author)

1 The Gulf of Tonkin Incident

ON 24 July 1964 three US F-102 interceptors were deployed to Da Nang, which is only 240 miles from Vhin. This movement was codenamed 'Operation Candy'. However, the real shooting war in the air can be traced back to the Gulf of Tonkin incident where the US destroyer USS *Maddox* was allegedly attacked by North Vietnamese torpedo boats on 2 August 1964. A second alleged attack, which seems unverifiable, was used by the Johnson administration as good enough cause to widen the conflict and he ordered an attack on North Vietnamese boat bases at Quang Khe, sixty miles inside North Vietnam. The aircraft carriers *Ticonderoga* and *Constellation* launched their air armada on 7 August 1964. The force, estimated at 64 aircraft, included F-8 Crusaders, A-4 Skyhawks, A-1 Skyraiders and F-4B Phantoms. The force hit and destroyed petrol, oil and lubricant facilities in Vhin. The Americans hailed the punitive raid as a success, despite losing one Skyraider and one Skyhawk, resulting in Lieutenant L. E. Alvarez remaining a prisoner for eight years.

In response to the raid, the Viet Cong shelled Bien Hoa, about 18 miles north of Saigon, destroying five Canberra B-57 bombers. The American policy at that time was to punish North Vietnam for any acts of insurgency carried out by the Viet Cong, but at this time the regime in Ha Noi had little control over the Viet Cong in the south. So, to escalate the situation even further, on 9 and 10 December, USAF Skyraiders hit the provinces of Quang Tri and Quang Binh in North Vietnam. The effects of these punitive raids were threefold on the North: firstly, it made them despise the Americans even more; secondly, it brought the Communist regime in Ha Noi closer to the Viet Cong (thus creating a self-fulfilling prophecy) and thirdly, it gave the North good cause to speed up the acquisition of new jet fighters (from allies such as China) and increase their training programmes and recruitment moves.

The North Vietnamese were also stepping up their preparations by planning and building more airfields and increasing pilot training. Their pilots had started to fly more after their return from training in China; all pilots had increased their flying time by a third in a matter of a few months. The North Vietnamese also soon realized that the Americans kept to very predictable routes to and from their targets. In fact, the Americans continued this habit until the end of the conflict, which aided the North Vietnamese considerably. For example, if an attack came from Udorn, then the American aircraft would fly over Northern Laos and swing southeast and attack Ha Noi. If an attack came from Khorat, then the formation would either go towards Ninh Binh (60 miles south of Ha Noi) or the formation would divide into two formations just before the Thai border, going on to bomb Ninh Binh and Ha Noi simultaneously: this pattern was especially popular during the 'Rolling Thunder' campaign.

Aircraft taking off from aircraft carriers would hit the 'neck' of Vietnam above the 17th parallel, a 200-mile stretch from Vhin Linh to Vhin. The VPAF would be rendered further unwitting assistance from the Americans since their reconnaissance aircraft would fly over a target before it was hit. The VPAF did not intercept any American aircraft with MiGs below the 20th parallel as all its limited strategic areas were north of that. It is not surprising that the main MiG bases were found along those routes, in and around the Ha Noi and Haiphong areas.

and interceptor units. These different elements would be controlled by a central ground control command.

Even as late as August 1965 many in the North Vietnamese high command still did not have a clear plan to counter any B-52 attack on Ha Noi. Their intercept tactics were only developed in a piecemeal fashion, based on observation of the rather predictable American flight patterns. Many like Commander Luyen Dao Dinh (one of the first trained pilots of the VPAF) secretly feared that the Americans would vary their attack patterns in time, but his fears were to be unfounded.

President Johnson started his new term in office, January 1965, by initiating a debate about pulling out of Vietnam. Many Americans did not want to waste lives and money in another 'Asian War'. However, there were other parties who did not want to be seen to be 'running away'. In addition, those in the aircraft and arms industries would profit because of the increased orders and sales, with the area of conflict providing a welcome opportunity to try out the latest military hardware. Ultimately, an interventionist policy was chosen and President Johnson gave the order for air strikes against North Vietnam, codenamed 'Flaming Dart'. By 7 March 1965 this became known in history as 'Rolling Thunder' and air-to-air combat over North Vietnam was born.

A photograph taken from the USS Maddox (DD-731) during her engagement with three North Vietnamese motor torpedo boats which allegedly opened fire on her in the Gulf of Tonkin on 2 August 1964. The view shows all three of the boats speeding towards the Maddox. The outcome of the incident was the passage by Congress of the 'Southeast Asia Resolution' (better known as the Gulf of Tonkin Resolution), which granted Johnson the authority to assist any Southeast Asian country whose government was considered to be jeopardized by 'communist aggression.' The resolution served as Johnson's legal justification for escalating American involvement in the Vietnam Conflict. Recent declassified NSA documents state that the Maddox fired first on the motor torpedo boats. (U.S Navy)

The VPAF knew that victories in the air were of huge significance because of the great psychological and political impact. It would give the North Vietnamese people confidence and belief that the regime in Ha Noi could protect them even from an enemy as powerful as America. Therefore, the Communist leaders realized that to get the first 'kill' was of the utmost importance. Their main long-term strategy was to make North Vietnam the 'killing skies', just as Cambodia would be known as 'the killing fields' in later years. In time, American pilots would describe the skies around Ha Noi as 'Hell'.

By early 1965 aid from China and the Soviet Union was increasing at a steady pace with MiGs and surface-to-air missiles known as SA-2s (or SAMs) arriving, amongst other equipment. The North Vietnamese based their ground defence system on the Soviet model, where long- and short-range radar was used in combination with an observer corps working in tandem with anti-aircraft

This AN-2 Colt 'Red 02103' was operated by the Pham Nhu Can squadron of the 919 Regiment. This aircraft is credited with the destruction of 2 US vessels and it also damaged a US radar base in Laos. This type was used extensively between 1961 and 1962.

2 'Rolling Thunder'

THE first raid of 'Rolling Thunder' was carried out on 2 March 1965, with US B-57s, F-100s and F-105Ds directed to bomb the ammunition depot at Xom Dong, about 40 miles northeast of Vhin. The dumps were hit and sustained heavy damage, but the price was five aircraft lost – two F-100Ds and three F-105Ds to anti-aircraft units.

Meanwhile the North Vietnamese pilots waited for the day that they would enter combat for the first time and they did not have to wait long. On 2 April, the pilots were briefed about their tactics and told that as soon as the weather and opportunity was conducive, they would make their historic flight. A young pilot called Pham Ngoc Lan was one of those selected and he recalls, 'We were quietly confident at the time and did not have any fear of the Americans, although we respected their experience and more modern equipment.'

The following day, all eight MiG 17s from the 921st Fighter Regiment were armed and fueled whilst their ground radar tracked the Americans towards the rail bridges at Ham Rong. The pilots were put on alert (the first such occasion of many); they walked to their MiGs and waited at cockpit readiness. The pilots of the intercept flight were Pham Ngoc Lan, Phan Van Tuc, Ho van Quy and Tran Minh Phuong. The covering flight pilots would be Pham Giay and Tran Han. At 0940 hours the scramble order was given and all pilots strapped themselves in and took off to make history. The covering flight took off first, then the intercept flight took off a minute later at 0948 hours, leaving Noi Bai air base (about three miles northwest of Ha Noi) and heading for Thanh Hoa, about 100 miles south of Ha Noi. Following the instructions they were receiving from ground control; the MiGs flew low, out of reach of the American

short-range radar and safe from any trigger-happy SAM unit.

Their intended targets were only 30 miles away, just 20 minutes flight time after take-off. The four intercept MiGs flew in a modified four-finger formation, with Ngoc Lan in the leading MiG. Tran Minh Phuong, a little higher on his right, was flying in the No.4 position. Phan Van Tuc in the second MiG was flying to Ngoc Lans's left, with Van Quy flying very close to Van Tuc's right in the third MiG. When the pilots had visual contact they could see the American aircraft were already busy bombing the Ham Rong Bridge: the MiG pilots radioed in their co-ordinates and instantly were given the order to intercept. All four pilots then accelerated and pulled up to gain height and then dived on the American aircraft from above, making contact over the Tao Bridge (three miles from Ham Rong).

The bridge itself was being attacked in pairs by F-8 Crusaders. The first pair in the intercept flight was vectored to the unsuspecting F-8s: soon Ngoc Lan (in Red 2310) attacked two F-8s on his left. Van Tuc was first to fire and he saw hits. At that moment Ngoc Lan cut diagonally across Van Tuc's MiG. He closed in and waited until the reticule had covered the shape of the F-8: when he was less than 400 yards, distant he pressed the trigger for a series of short bursts and felt the recoil of three heavy cannon scream from his MiG 17 and rip into the American aircraft, causing it to explode. It crashed near the river gate of Ba Lat near the Thai Binh River. All the other pilots had witnessed this kill.

With this victory he is credited with making Vietnamese aviation history. However, there was more history to be made in another part of the sky. Here two MiGs of

MiG 17F 'Red 2310' takes off on a sortie with Pham Ngoc Lan at the controls in April 1965. (Vietnamese News Agency)

Nguyen Hong Nhi scored eight confirmed kills as a 921st FR pilot. All his kills were made on the MiG 21, the first on 14 March 1966. (Vietnamese News Agency)

the intercept flight saw an American aircraft on their right and dived to attack. As Van Tuc was closer to the American, flight leader Ngoc Lan cut behind his wingman and told him to go for the kill (this switching of roles became common in the VPAF). Then Van Tuc applied full power and fired a three-second burst at the American aircraft, seeing evidence of hits as the F-8 flicked to one side and then crashed into the ground – there was little chance of the American escaping at such a low level.

Then all the MiGs received the order to return to base before they ran out of fuel. Unfortunately, Ngoc Lan had lost contact with the other pilots because his compass had broken down and he was now critically short of fuel. Under normal circumstances it would not have been any problem to reach any of the bases around Ha Noi. However, Ngoc Lan was familiar with the geographical features of the Ninh Binh area because they had trained there for many months for this attack. He had to find his way back on visual recognition alone. He reduced speed and lowered his MiG to an altitude of 8,000 feet to maximize the 200 litres of fuel left in the tanks (only a few minutes' flying time). A few moments later he could see the Duong River and Ha Noi in the distance. By now his plight was being carefully followed by ground control, who ordered him to bale out. Heroically, Ngoc Lan refused to leave his aircraft and kept faith with the trusted MiG,

hoping to find a landing place and thus save the valuable aircraft. Then, without warning, the engines ceased functioning. When recalling this moment, Pham Ngoc Lan commented, '…when I was observing for a place to land… the engine stopped functioning then vibrated to life again, but it made a sound like an exhausted bird trying to see the sky for the very last time.' He radioed ground control that he was going to make an emergency landing, as by now the MiG was descending fast, but Ngoc Lan kept it stable by pushing his pedals and pulling in the stick, preparing for a crash-landing. He selected the Duong River for his landing, but disastrously, at the point of no return, he saw a small sampan in his path, with the boatman covering his face, obviously expecting the worse. At the last second Ngoc Lan managed to pull the MiG up and he flew past the sampan, missing it by a few feet. Then the MiG nosed into the water and it began to zigzag on the surface like a giant dolphin, throwing the pilot about in the cockpit like a rag doll. Ngoc Lan remembered this well as he recalled, 'The collision was terrible, as I was pushed up and my helmet banged against the top of the canopy and then my forehead hit the steering rod, and things became dark.'

He did not how long he was unconscious, perhaps as long as thirty minutes, but when he recovered and opened the canopy to look around he saw the unexpected. A group of Vietnamese militia had surrounded his aircraft, pointing guns at him, believing that an American aircraft had been shot down.

MiG 17 F, 'Red 2310', as flown by Pham Ngoc Lan after running out of fuel following his interception of a US aircraft on 3 April 1965 in which he became the first VPAF pilot to shoot down an enemy aircraft. The MiG made an emergency landing along the Duong River. This view shows the formidable armament of one 37 mm Nudelman N-37 cannon (40 rounds total), two 23 mm Nudelman-Rikhter NR-23 cannons (80 rounds per gun). (Vietnamese News Agency)

1:72 Scale

MiG 17 F, 'Red 2310', of the 923rd Fighter Regiment, Kien An, as flown by Pham Ngoc Lan during his engagement with US fighters on 3 August 1965, in which he made the first VPAF air-to-air kill of the war. Pham Ngoc Lan also flew 'Red 2304' in his early missions.

Principal VPAF Airbases

Although Ngoc Lan had identity papers on him, he decided not to take any chances: he left his pistol on the wing of the MiG and called out for help. Receiving no answer he walked on to the wing of the MiG to observe any damage. Ngoc Lan was also aware of another problem: as he recalled, 'My native town is Dien Ban district in the south and my accent might make our people think I was a Saigon regime pilot.' Luckily the village elder appeared on the scene and all was explained as the MiG was covered up by the militia. Within minutes, a helicopter had arrived to collect North Vietnam's first aviation hero.

All three other pilots managed to land safely at Noi Bai amidst wild celebrations. The VPAF claimed two F-8s shot down without loss to themselves. The Americans admitted to losing one F-105 to ground fire and one more damaged, but none to MiGs. The North Vietnamese attached so much value to this victory that they made 3 April a public holiday known as Air Force Day! The VPAF pilots used up 686 rounds of ammunition, of which 526 were 23 mm and 160 were 37 mm shells, to shoot down two American aircraft.

4 April was to turn out to be very eventful for both sides, possibly more so than the day before. By all accounts visibility on the day was bad as there was fog and the sky was overcast. However, American reconnaissance flights were observed flying over the Thanh Hoa district. The North Vietnamese knew that their targets would be the rail bridges and the electrical works in Thanh Hoa itself. Furthermore, the Americans had not completed the job the day before so it was highly likely they would be back. The American attack group consisted of 79 aircraft, 46 F-105s armed with 750-pound bombs and ground-to-air missiles. Cover was provided by 21 F-100s (Super Sabres) , four of which carried cannon used to destroy MiGs and AIM-9 (Sidewinder) air-to-air missiles. Against this, the VPAF could muster eight MiG 17s. The intercept flight consisted of Tran Hanh, Pham Giay, Le Minh Huan and Tran Nguyen Nam. The covering flight consisted of Pham Ngoc Lan, Tran Hung, Ho Van Quy and Tran Minh Phuong. When the order to scramble came, the covering flight took off at 1022 hours, with the intercept flight following a few minutes later as all eight MiGs headed for Thanh Hoa. As usual, they flew low over the countryside in two loose, four-finger sets, moving in a zigzag pattern that resembled the movements of a snake.

A signed photograph by Pham Ngoc Lan (right) with Tranh Hanh. The gun camera film shows a shared kill of a F-8 Crusader on 3 April 1965. (Vietnamese News Agency)

(This type of flying made North Vietnamese pilots name their MiGs 'snakes.') The intercept flight had to wait for ground control to give them the all-clear before they increased power and climbed almost vertically to attack. The Americans were using their F-100s as escorts to cover the area along the Song Chu estuary in front of the F-105 fighter-bombers. After only eight minutes the MiGs had visual contact with the Americans and this was confirmed by ground radar. Due to general inexperience, the covering flight attacked the escorts instead of the fighter-bombers. At that point the F-100s were commencing their bombing run on the bridge: it was then that the MiGs realized their error (but too late) and broke into two pairs.

One of the MiGs went after the fighter-bombers at full speed, giving the Americans no time to react. At the same moment, Tran Hanh and Pham Giay were closing in on a F-105 (known as a 'Thud') and before the American knew what had happened, the MiGs were there. Tran Hanh fired a quick burst at close range and the Thud crashed immediately in a ball of flames. Whilst attacking another pair of F-100s, Le Minh also started firing and saw hits on a Thud, whose pilot quickly turned his aircraft to escape but crashed soon afterwards. The intercept flight flew straight into the Super Sabres and hit them head on with guns firing, but the MiGs missed their targets: in a flash the Sabres flew past the MiGs and a turning battle started. The MiGs, being more nimble, proved more than a match for the Sabres until more MIGCAP Sabres joined in and the inexperience of the North Vietnamese pilots began to show. Soon a Sabre got behind a

Pham Ngoc Lan showing how a MiG 17 could turn on its back and dive for the deck to break off an engagement with American fighters. (Vietnamese News Agency)

A pioneer pilot of the 921st FR, Le Minh Huan scored two kills (one shared). The last was an F-105 downed over Ham Rong on 4 July 1965. He was killed in action the same day. (Vietnamese News Agency)

MiG (possibly Tran Nguyen Nam) who then made a vertical dive, but took cannon hits: amazingly, he managed to pull up at the last moment and broke away from the combat zone. The outnumbered North Vietnamese tried to save themselves by breaking away from the scene, although this left the intercept flight lower down at the mercy of the Sabres. Another MiG, flown by Tran Hanh, escaped from the pursuing Americans by turning and weaving until the Americans gave up: he later had to make an emergency landing west of Nghe An because he had taken cannon hits from the Sabres. All pilots survived, with only two MiGs lost. The MiG pilots claimed three F-100s and another was shot down by anti-aircraft units. Curiously, the Americans did not claim any confirmed kills on this day but their records do show the loss of three F-100s shot down and two pilots lost.

The North Vietnamese pilots in this action obviously did not keep to strict discipline and may have got carried away with the previous day's success. Taken within the context of their very limited experience, the North Vietnamese 'rookies' did well but overconfidence might well have been the reason for unnecessary losses. Therefore, on 5 April Ho Chih Minh sent the 921st FR the following message: 'You have fought bravely and shot down the American aircraft ... Don't be conceited with your victories and do not let yourself be stopped by difficulties on the way.' Such over confidence was a problem that was never totally eradicated in the ranks of the VPAF.

On 9 April 2nd Lt. G. Terrence M. Murphy and Ens. Ronald J. Fegan scored the first confirmed kill of the war when they destroyed a MiG 17 with an AIM-7 Sparrow missile.

On 17 June four MiGs of an intercept flight met a flight of four F-4B Phantoms which shot down two MiG 17s with Sparrows, making them the first US Navy kills. The MiGs fell around the Thanh Hoa region.

The F-4 had begun to make its presence felt because it was a state-of-the-art, long-range fighter, more advanced than either the MiG 17 or the MiG 21. It could carry two pilots and operate from land bases or from carriers and had a top speed of 1,485 mph, faster than a MiG 21 and twice as fast as a MiG 17. It could also carried four AIM-7

Sparrow and four AIM-9 Sidewinder air-to-air missiles. The early F-4s did not carry any guns and this was viewed as a serious shortcoming in close quarter air combat. Nevertheless, by the end of the war F-4s claimed to have shot down 145 MiGs for the loss of 52 of their own (US figures).

During the same action Le Trong Long and his wingman shot down an F-4 in a head-on pass over Nho Quan, about 60 miles south of Ha Noi, which made the fifth kill for the 921st FR. Another F-4 kill over the same area, on the same day, could not be credited to any individual pilot.

26 April marked a notable occasion when the Americans first used F-4 Phantoms flying in bomber formation to lure MiG s into a trap – on this occasion the F-4s that were flying over Cao Bang province. Only two MiG 17s from the 921 FR were scrambled to intercept this formation. Nguyen Hong Nhi and his wingman Nguyen Danh Kinh spotted the eight 'bombers' and dived in to attack – just at the critical moment the eight F-4s started to break into pairs and assumed their fighter roles. By now the MiG pilots had discovered that it was a trap, but it was too late. Both MiGs broke in different directions to save themselves but this only reduced their chances of survival, as they were unable to support each other. Hong Nhi decided to keep holding his dive, hoping to escape, but when he was less than 4,000 feet from the ground two F-4s closed in on him and fired two missiles. Hong Nhi instinctively pulled his MiG left but one of the missiles hit his tail and broke the aircraft into two halves. With seconds to spare, Hong Nhi pulled the parachute lever and baled out over the Yen Bai area. This encounter would teach the future ace an invaluable lesson when confronted with a similar scenario. Never the less, he had to spend nearly a year in hospital because of the injuries he sustained. His likely victors were Major Roland W. Moore and Jr/1Lt James F. Sears of the 389 TFS/366 TFW.

The VPAF restricted its intercept missions for the rest of the year, choosing instead to keep the Americans busy with its SAMs and anti-aircraft units. The mere possibility of MiGs and SAMs in an area would force the American aircraft lower down into the 'weeds' to run the gauntlet of Vietnamese anti-aircraft units. The Americans scored their last two victories of 1965 in July when F-4s shot down two MiGs using AIM-9 missiles.

By the end of August 1965 the VPAF had lost ten pilots killed, with fourteen MiGs lost

in combat operations, but claiming more than thirty five American aircraft shot down, nine of these being F-4 Phantoms. By September the VPAF had activated its second fighter regiment: the 923rd Fighter Regiment or 'Peaceful Sit' and was initially based at Kep, about 40 miles northeast from Ha Noi. Its responsibility was to take over the eastern sector of North Vietnam including Haiphong. By the end of the conflict this unit would claim to have shot down 703 American aircraft.

On 20 September the Americans attacked the storage facilities in Ha Noi. The intercept flight consisted of Pham Ngoc Lan, Nguyen Doc Do, Tran Van Tri and Nguyen Nhat Chiew. This mission required the intercept flight to make contact with the Americans before the latter reached their

Nguyen Nhat Chieu celebrates a kill in front of 'Red 2217'.
He downed his first F-4 Phantom on 20 July 1965 near Nha Nam. Nhat Chieu finished the war with six kills.
(Vietnamese News Agency)

Pham Ngoc Lan, Hanh Tran and Phan Van Tuc all flew MiG 17 'Red 2014' on sorties. The aircraft is seen here undergoing maintenence from technicians. (Vietnamese News Agency)

targets. The confidence of the VPAF pilots was still very high. They flew low as usual to Cot Ngah (about 20 miles north of Ha Noi) where the flight made visual contact and obtained clearance from ground control for the attack. At once they climbed to about 16,000ft and got behind the F-4s: before the Americans could take evasive measures the MiG flight split into two. Ngoc Lan with Nhat Chieu as his number 2 singled out an F-4. Within seconds of gaining the initiative, Ngoc Lan began firing with all his cannon. Nhat

Chieu started to fire a split second later and immediately saw hits. He continued firing as he closed in on the F-4, obtaining continual strikes, and the F-4 was seen to fall and crash. This was Nhat Chieu's first victory. Meanwhile Ngoc Do and Van Tri chased the escaping F-4s and F-105s as far as the Yen Tu mountains, then turned for home, leaving the SAM missiles do their worst.

November 6 saw four pilots share victory over an attack helicopter over Hoa Binh, 45 miles southwest of Ha Hoa. The pilots

A MiG 17 Fresco A 'Red 2517' of the 923rd FR returns to Kien An after a sortie in 1965. The sense of a 'People's Air Force' can be seen from the crowd approaching to greet the pilot. (Vietnamese News Agency)

'Red 4228' of the 921 FR was an early MiG 21PF, which had a braking parachute, housed in the port side of the fuselage section forward of the ventral fin. (Vietnamese News Agency)

involved were Tran Tan, Nguyen Nhung, Pham Ngoc Lan and Tran Minh Phuong, flying only their fourth mission. They soon identified a target flying under thick cloud cover – it turned out to be a US helicopter trying to rescue American pilots. Nguyen Nhung and Ngoc Lan flew down through the cloud cover and with three short bursts Nguyen Nhung shot down the first-ever helicopter kill for the VPAF.

With that action, both sides closed their air-to-air accounts for 1965. The VPAF had entered 156 'dogfights' and scored ten victories, with four probable kills, losing about 14 MiGs and ten pilots killed. The VPAF would have received about 30 trained pilots and another 30 MiGs by the year's end, although only about 25 MiGs were ever available for combat missions at any one time. The number of radar sites now numbered about 47, mainly situated around Noi Bai, Kep and Bac Mai. The Americans had lost 46 F-4s (13 to MiGs and 33 to anti-aircraft units and SAMs). They reacted by stationing 18 squadrons, consisting of 660 aircraft, against 30 or so MiG 17s.

The fighting came to a pause because of a halt in bombing that lasted for 37 days and that officially came to an end on 31 January 1966. These pauses in bombing were supposed to make the North Vietnamese feel grateful that the Americans were not bombing their country: the expectation was that they would start to 'behave themselves' by not supporting the Viet Cong. That may well have been the American political position, but from a military point of view the US used the time to replace its men and materials. This also united the North Vietnamese even further and brought

them closer to the Viet Cong as allies. The American policy of attrition meant that to achieve a 3:1 kill ratio, a 10:1 combat ratio had to be sustained against the VPAF.

Because the VPAF did not encounter American aircraft, this lull was used to familiarize the many new pilots with their aircraft. The MiG 21 was about to enter service and the North Vietnamese knew they would have a fighter that could match the F-4 in top speed.

3 February 1966 saw Lam Van Lich from the 921 FR shoot down two attack helicopters about 50 miles southwest of Ha Noi, making these the first kills for the VPAF in 1966.

On 4 March the 923rd Fighter Regiment participated in its first combat mission. The flight consisted of eight aircraft, with the intercept flight being made up of Tran Minh Phuong, Nguyen The Hon, Phan Thanh Chung and Ngo Duc Mai. They intercepted American aircraft at 1600 hours over Phu Tho, 60 miles northeast of Ha Noi. When the order was given, the MiG 17s were in perfect position behind and above the Americans. They were given orders for just one pass, as SAM missile units were numerous in the area. Phan Thanh Chung led the flight of four MiGs in a finger-four pattern: as pilot of the leading aircraft he fired from 1,000 yards, but due to the extreme range he saw no hits. He fired early, hoping the Americans would drop their tanks and take on the MiGs, leaving the fighter bombers unescorted. If this was accomplished, then the mission would be a success. Duc Mai, flying as Phan Thanh's wingman, did not fire on his intended target until he was about 80 yards from an F-4. He then pressed the firing button and

Nguyen Nhat Chieu (extreme right) with unidentified members of his squadron. 'Red 2310' can be seen in the background. (Vietnamese News Agency)

immediately he could see cannon strikes on the enemy aircraft. By the time he had closed in to less than 45 yards range, the F-4 filled his gun sights. He gave his victim another burst of gunfire and saw the entire plane disintegrate in mid-air. The flight flew through the American formation and prepared to return to base – the whole intercept action had taken less than two minutes. However, it was not completely over, because when they prepared to land they were 'jumped' by American fighters, but the enemy broke off the attack without achieving any success. All the MiGs landed safely. The Yen Bai and Pho Tho areas proved a killing ground for F-4s, as MiGs shot down at least fourteen American aircraft during the war in that vicinity.

At noon on the same day, VPAF radar picked up an unmanned drone flying at an altitude of 59,000 feet in Quang Tri province, apparently making its way to Ha Noi. The central ground control unit calculated that the drone would fly along Highway 1, south of Ha Noi, and would return by the town of Che in Quang Ninh province. In response, Nguyen Hong Nhi of the 921st FR was ordered to scramble in a newly delivered MiG 21PFL (Red 4242). When 'pilot 201' (each VAPF pilot was given a flying number) had reached an altitude of 26,000 feet and was traveling at 600 mph, he was vectored to fly a full 180 degrees over Bac Giang to bring him behind

the drone. Within minutes Hong Nhi was 35 miles behind the drone and he then dropped his long-range tanks to began his attack run. A few minutes later, he was at an altitude of 30,000 feet, 20 miles behind his target. The distance was cut to 18 miles, then 12 miles, as Hong Nhi began to climb and accelerate to Mach 1 speed. When Hong Nhi had reached the same altitude as the drone, he turned on his internal radar and immediately picked out his target on his screen. At this point he switched on his heat-seeking ATOLL missiles and waited until he heard the locking tone that was the signal to fire. When the drone was 1,000 yards away and closing, Hong Nhi fired his missile, feeling it drop from its underwing rack, to fly like an arrow towards its target. He saw the missile go straight into the exhaust of the drone, causing it to bank to its left and dive straight into the ground. When Hong Nhi landed there were great cheers, as this was first drone kill and a first kill for the new MiG 21PFL.

The North Vietnamese also scored their first night victories when Nguyen Hong Nhi shot down an unmanned drone on 3 February.

On 26 April the 923rd FR intercepted F-4s escorting an EB-66, which was an A-3 Skywarrior used to jam North Vietnamese radar before a strike over North Vietnam. The VPAF successfully intercepted this escort, resulting in Ho Van Quy claiming two F-4s

MiG 17Fs belonging to the second squadron of the 921st FR under the command of Nguyen Nhat Chieu. The MiGs are in air superiority grey with wing undersides in natural metal. Visible here are 'Red 2215', 'Red 2217', 'Red 2253' and 'Red 2115'. (Vietnamese News Agency)

MiG 17 F, 'Red 2215', of the 921st Fighter Regiment, 1966   *1:72 Scale*

shot down, with another damaged over the Bac Sen and Vin Mit areas, although with the loss of one MiG 17. The Americans had to abort the escort because the EB-66 was forced to return to base prematurely. On the same day the Americans claimed to have shot down the first MiG 21 of the war when Major Paul J. Gilmore and Lieutenant William T. Smith reported having shot down a MiG 21 using AIM 9 missiles. The North Vietnamese do not have any records of a MiG 21 intercept at this time and the 923rd FR who covered this area still flew MiG 17s in combat missions at that time. This raises the possibility that Major Gilmore may not have shot down a MiG 21 on that day, but a MiG 17 instead.

On 5 June, MiG 17s from the 923rd FR shot down two F-8 Crusaders without loss to themselves. On 9 June , MiG 21s from the 921st claimed two F-4s shot down (these being the first kills by MiG 21s). On June 21, the intercept flight of the 923rd FR shot down a reconnaissance aircraft, with each of the four pilots (Phan Thanh Truong, Duong Truong Tan, Nguyen Van Bay (who would claim seven kills) and Phan Van Tuc, being given credit for a complete kill. A convention started with the 923rd FR from this date that the whole intercept flight would be awarded a full kill for every victory. The North Vietnamese did not draw any real distinction between full kills and shared kills. This

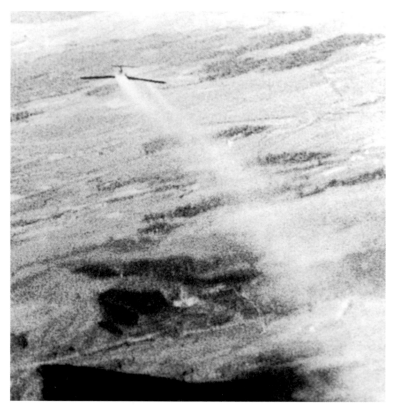

Olds as commanding officer of the 8th Tactical Fighter Wing. Colonel Olds was a very experienced tactician who had scored thirteen victories over the *Luftwaffe* during World War Two: he was to add four MiGs to that tally in Vietnam and would play a key role in the war against the MiGs, being one of the instigators of 'Operation Bolo' (see Chapter 5).

To beef up the VPAF's small fighter force a further 30 pilots were received by front line units, 13 of them being posted to the 921st FR: these pilots were used as a reserve pool owing to their lack of flying time, but by December 1966 eight of them would have seen combat. The remainder were posted to the 923rd FR to fly the MiG 17.

sharing of a kill by a whole squadron of four pilots happened at least on eighteen occasions until 19 November 1967, when this custom died out. This seemed peculiar to the 923rd FR and the reason appears to have been two-fold: firstly, to increase teamwork and play down the individual nature of claiming kills; secondly, to artificially increase North Vietnamese kill rates to enhance morale. However this was never a generally accepted policy.

June 1966 was a busy month for the VPAF pilots because by the end of the month they had made twelve intercepts, shooting down eight American aircraft, although only four pilots could claim outright kills.

By the end of June the Americans claimed four MiG 17s shot down, with two pilots killed. The Americans had been using Cambodian MiG 17s to learn the weaknesses of the Russian fighter and to study the limits of its flight envelope. American success against the MiG 17 improved from the end of 1966 but this can be attributed mostly to the increasing odds used against the VPAF with straightforward attrition taking its toll on the smaller air force. The Americans also made personnel changes that created a more aggressive stance against the VPAF.

On 1 July, Lieutenant General William W. (Spike) Momyer appointed Colonel Robin

On 7 July, two MiG 21s from the 921st FR shot down an F-105 with an ATOLL air-to-air missile. The Thud crashed 40 miles northwest of Ha Noi. Tran Ngoc Xiu was credited with this relatively rare kill by an ATOLL missile (VPAF pilots interviewed claim about 40 per cent of all kills were made by missiles). At this stage, the MiG 17 pilots started to indulge in dogfights with American aircraft; the former were growing in confidence all the time as they could constantly turn inside the faster F-4s and use their cannon to lethal effect from close range. The MiG 21s would use their superior speed and dive on the Americans from higher altitudes. The VPAF would use both the MiG 17 and the MiG 21 against the Americans, using both techniques in unison by catching the Americans in what can only be described as a diving and turning 'sandwich'.

On 11 July, Vu Ngoc Dinh and Dong Van Song of the Intercept flight shared a victory over an F-105 using such turning tactics. The Thud was seen to crash near Phu Hien, 60 miles northwest of Ha Noi. Phan Than Truong claimed one American aircraft downed on 13 July: the following day, Ngo Duc Mai confirmed he had shot down an F-8 crusader (the wreckage was found in the An Thi

1:72 Scale

MiG 21F, 'Red 3072', from the 923rd FR. The topsides were painted in dark green with brown irregular spots. The bottom of the fuselage and wing undersides possibly in matt black. The drop tanks remained natural metal with the stars in the usual six positions. There is suggestion that these paints were sourced from Soviet stocks used for military vehicles - hence they took on a warn and faded appearance very quickly as reported by surviving pilots.

district). By the end of July, the Americans shot one MiG 17 and two MiG 21s, taking their total to 20 MiG kills since April 1965. The VPAF claimed 24 American aircraft shot down, seven of them F-4 Phantoms, giving the VPAF a kill ratio of 1.2 to 1 in their favour.

On 22 August 1966, the aircraft carrier *Independence* launched an air strike on the Phu Long Bridge on Highway 5. The attack force was headed by four F-8 Crusaders; another group of twenty A-4 Skyhawks flew slightly behind, with an escort of six F-4B Phantoms and another four Crusaders at the rear of the formation.

Ground control picked up this incoming raid and scrambled four MiG 17s from the 923 FR. The pilots involved were Nguyen Van Bay, Tran Triem, Vo Van Man and Phan Van Tuc. The MiGs took off from Gia Lam and flew at a height of 6,500 feet along the Red River intending for a head-on attack. When the American formation was less than three minutes from contact, Van Bay ordered his squadron to increase speed to 500 mph and widen their flying formation to present less of a target to the escorts. When visual contact was made all the MiGs dropped their long-range tanks and attacked the A-4 fighter-bombers. Instantly the Skyhawks broke in all directions and a frantic dogfight began. Tran Triem managed to get on the tail of an A-4 and shot it down with cannon fire from close range, whilst Van Tuc and Van Man both shared in the destruction of another A-4 seconds later.

Before long the 14 escorts joined in the fray, shooting missiles at the MiGs from long range, hoping to break up their formation and kill them individually. This tactic of 'divide and kill' was known to the VPAF pilots, who tried desperately not to get separated. Both Van Man and Van Tuc managed to dive to safety, which left Van Bay and Tran Triem to fend for themselves, although by now both MiGs had to evade missile after missile. When four missiles came at them simultaneously, both MiGs had to break into opposite directions to evade certain destruction. Van Bay dived for the deck at full throttle thinking that his wingman would do the same. However, two Crusaders flew in front of Tran Triem, who then decided to attack them. He managed to get behind the second Crusader, but could not get a shooting angle as both American fighters started to turn in an arc, thus reducing speed and forcing Tran Triem to do the same. As Tran Triem began to be overcome by target fixation, a third Crusader suddenly appeared behind him and fired four missiles, killing him instantly in a ball of flame.

The death of Tran Triem was a great loss to his squadron, as he was much liked: he had been a school friend of Nguyen Van Bay. The thought of revenge was never far from the latter's mind after this loss.

The 923rd FR was on standby again on 5 September, when the pilots on duty were Nguyen Van Bay (Red 3065) and Vo Van Man (Red 3567). The Americans had been busy the whole day, starting from 0700 hours, when

12 US Navy aircraft attacked a bridge in Ninh Binh. At 0900 hours, 16 F-105s and F-4 Phantoms attacked the town of Moc Chau. The Americans returned after breakfast and bombed the power plant in Hai Phong with 12 A-4 Skyhawks. To round off the day, the USAF returned at 1330 hours with 16 F-105s and F-4s and attacked the railway yards in Yen Bai.

The VPAF knew that the Americans nearly always attacked up to four times a day with the Navy mounting two attacks and the USAF responsible for the other two, so some thought it unlikely that any more attacks would be made as the enemy had already used his quota! However, the intelligence section of the VPAF believed that the attacks, so far, were only pinpricks and because it was still only 1400 hours another attack was likely, so all MiGs remained at readiness. By 1545 hours the day had turned clear with little cloud cover: this made the possibility of an attack very much on the cards and, indeed, within minutes an American formation was picked up by radar, flying at a height of 5,000 feet at a distance of 160 miles. When the formation size was defined as medium to large, the VPAF commander Nguyen Van Tien ordered Van Bay and Van Man to scramble at once. However, as many at the 923rd FR did not believe an attack was likely, both Van Bay and Van Man had taken off their flying equipment and needed about four full minutes put on their gear and run to their MiGs.

The American formation was divided into three groups, with the second and third groups about seven miles behind the lead group. The VPAF radar units soon realized that the two escorting groups consisted only of two aircraft each, with most of the lead group comprising bombers.

The chief radar operator on the day, Le Thanh Chon, recalled, 'The Americans used a small number of fighter escorts on that occasion because they did not expect us to be prepared for another attack that day.' It did not take long for the VPAF to figure out that an hour's time difference separated the US carriers and Ha Noi time, so the US bombers would only have one hour before sunset when they had to return (the time was 1520 Ha Noi time at this stage). Therefore, Ha Noi could not be the target but the area round Phu Ly certainly might be.

Van Bay was instructed to fly on a heading of 190 degrees, at an altitude of 3,500 feet and at a speed of 550 miles mph, and to head for the bombers. However, it was soon realized that because of the late take-off, the MiGs could not be vectored to intercept the bombers before they bombed Phu Ly, so they were vectored towards the Crusaders instead. Because the two groups of escorts were far apart they could not support each other in a fight – both Van Bay and Van Man knew that for the first time the odds would be even!

When contact with both sets of fighters was only minutes away, Van Bay ordered his wingman not to drop his tanks until the signal was given (this was to maximize combat time). For most of the time both pilots said little to each other – it was thought in the VPAF that these two men had an almost telepathic understanding of each other's intentions. At this stage ground control cut out all instructions to the MiGs and let them dictate the combat – a privilege only granted to a few pilots.

When Van Bay felt the time was right, he ordered Van Man to increase to full power and drop his tanks. They could see the black contrails made by the F-8 Crusaders in the distance as they went in for the kill. By now, the two opposing sets of fighters were flying in a head-on collision course. However, before the worst happened, both Crusaders broke to their left and flew into a cloud, obviously hoping that the MiGs would do the same so they could ambush their opponents by flying in a half circle, getting inside the MiGs' turn and then shooting them down. The hunter-like instincts of Van Bay made him fly around the cloud and position his MiG where he felt the Americans might appear. All this time Van Man placed his MiG slightly below that of Van Bay because he knew that his leader would attack the second Crusader, which was flying higher than its own leader. This would give Van Man a clear shot at the Crusader leader, who was flying lower. When both Crusaders appeared from the cloud Van Bay increased his speed and closed in the second aircraft, which seemed to be weaving about trying to cover his leader. Van Bay wanted both fighters, so he had to kill the second Crusader first. As he closed to less than 400 yards he could still see his target weaving to left and right. He waited until it swerved to its right and as the Crusader entered his gun sight he fired a short burst, but the cannon shells fell short. He then quickly adjusted his firing line and when the Crusader seemed to level off for a split

A popular figure in Vietnam, Nguyen Van Ba (left) was the only VPAF pilot to claim a kill in a piston engine aircraft. He achieved this on 15 December 1965 when he shot down a C-123 in a Trojan T-28 No.963. (Vietnamese News Agency)

second, he fired a second burst – all six of his 37mm shells and 16 of the 23 mm shells tore into the Crusader, killing the pilot, and the F-8 plunged into the ground. This kill made Van Bay the first ace of the Vietnam War, with five victories.

The kill had happened so quickly that the leading Crusader had not noticed the demise of his wingman. Van Bay recognised the chance to down the leader as well and become the first VPAF pilot to shoot down two American aircraft in a single sortie. However, he slowed down and allowed his wingman to move in front to take this kill while he acted as wingman. Almost instantly Van Man accelerated in front, closing in so closely on the F-8 that he could see the rivets on its fuselage. When he was less than 100 yards away he fired a burst, which brought belches of black smoke from the Crusader and he had to break quickly to escape collision with the burning aircraft. The Crusader fell earthwards in pieces, but luckily the pilot managed to

eject. With this success Van Man had become the second ace of the war, less than a minute after Van Bay achieved this feat.

This was 13 days after the death of Tran Triem and both VPAF pilots felt that they had avenged the loss of their comrade.

An Ilyushin Il-14, transporting men and equipment to Laos in the support of the Pathet Lao insurgency in the late 1960s this Il-14 may have belonged to the 919th Air Transport Regiment. (Vietnamese News Agency)

3 A victory from rice-pounding tactics

THE VPAF pilots were by now facing the grim reality that every combat against a more numerous foe required not only large slices of luck and skill, but also good team work. The combat reports of four pilots from the 923rd FR clearly show this.

The Americans had stepped up their operations for most of 1966 and in May of that year they began to use pilotless drones (first recorded on 14 May): the purpose of these craft was to spy on the North Vietnamese positions and missile sites which were their main targets.

19 September saw the transfer of four MiG 17s belonging to the 923rd FR from Gia Lam to Kien An (near Hai Phong). The four pilots were headed by the famous Nguyen Van Bay (Red 3065) who had four victories by this date. The other members of the flight were Luu Huy Chao (Red 3071) and Vo Van Man (Red 3067), who had three victories each at this time, and Do Van Hoang, a novice pilot (Red 3069). This was the most successful flight in the entire VPAF at that time with twelve kills to its credit, so the downing of a drone took a very high priority!

The four MiGs left Gia Lam at 1600 hours and were instructed to fly near ground level to evade detection by American radar. The movement of these MiGs were further cloaked when two MiG 21s joined Van Bay's flight, flying at the same heading but at a higher altitude to give the Americans the impression that it was only a reconnaissance flight. When Van Bay and his flight landed at Kien Ann the MiG 21s returned to Gia Lam.

This flight was given preliminary instruction on the drones' known flight patterns. However, all preparations to shoot down drones were put on hold when, at 1400 hours on 21 September, the flight was put on alert: an American formation was approaching from Thailand and was crossing Laos, heading for the old city of Hue where they would be re-fuelled in mid-air by large KC-135 tankers. The VPAF tracked this formation closely and by 1430 hours, the Americans were flying northwards in a single formation that stretched for more than 75 miles. By this time Van Bay and his comrades were put on a stage two alert. The Americans flew towards the Chinese island of Hainan: they would then fly towards what the VPAF ground control designated a 'checkpoint', which would indicate their final target, but which target would it be? If the checkpoint was Hon Gai, the target would be Phu Lai. If it was Tien Yen (more inland), then it would be Dap Cau. The VPAF had only seven minutes to determine the target before it was too late.

Eventually Hai Phong was projected as the target because the drones were last seen over this area and because of the analysis of the head ground controller, Le Thanh Chon. He later recalled, 'It was my opinion that the final checkpoint would be Hon Gai because the American formation was flying at an altitude of 11,200 feet. This was higher than our 37 mm anti-aircraft defenses could reach. I therefore reasoned that Bac Giang was to be the target because it is 60 miles from Bac Ninh district, giving the Americans enough time to organize their formation for a raid.'

At 1450 hours, the scramble order was given and Van Bay and his flight took off into a sunny afternoon. The flight was directed to Vinh Bao at an altitude of 4,800 feet. By now the MiGs were spotted by American radar so Van Bay changed his heading to due north to avoid American interceptors. The American formation had unexpectedly changed its direction towards Hai Phong. The attack aircraft had by now split into two large

A row of silver MiG 17Fs at Kep in 1966. 'Red 2014' has the IF antenna, which suggests a late production Fresco A. Other aircraft in the line are 'Red 2410', 'Red 2018', 'Red 2114', 'Red 2310' and 'Red 2510'. (Courtesy Toperczer)

formations and Van Bay was now trailing them along the line of Highway 5. When the MiGs were only 23 miles from contact, Huy Chao had to abort owing to engine trouble. The small band of three MiGs continued with its mission. Nguyen Van Bay was now flying head-on against the American F-105 and he made a 30-degree bank to increase his shooting angle. By now the American fighters had released their long-range fuel tanks and were heading towards the MiGs.

When the MiGs were in visual contact with the Americans, both Van Bay and Van Man were surprised to see only two F-105s instead of a large formation. Van Bay and Van Man speeded up for the kill when two more leaf-green F-105s appeared from beneath them. The inexperienced Huy Hoang, flying his first combat mission, became separated from the two leading MiGs and he ended up as the target for an F-105 which rapidly closed in and was about to fire. Only seconds later, Van Bay saw white tracer spit from the American aircraft as he warned Huy Hoang, 'Missiles - 69, break, break!' The warning was too late: one of the missiles hit Hoang's MiG and it went into a deadly downwards spiral. Both Van Bay and Van Man looked on with horror at the 'rookie' pilot and shouted for Hoang to take to his parachute, but Hoang had been knocked out by the impact of his head hitting his gun sight. Luckily for Hoang, he regained consciousness and hit his parachute button and its white mushroom shape appeared below, to the relief of the other two. There was little give or take by either side, so Van Bay was concerned to make sure that Hoang was not shot at whilst in his parachute and only began to take evasive action when he saw that his comrade had landed safely. The

likely victor over Hoang was Lt. Fred A.Wilson, Jr., from the US 333rd TFS.

Unfortunately, a group of F-4 Phantoms, led by Lieutenant-Colonel Risner (the Korean War ace with eight kills) had now joined the 'party' and Risner wanted to add to his score. The sky was now filled with American aircraft and there seemed little hope for survival for the two remaining MiGs.

A useful tip that had been picked up in previous engagements was that all American fighter aircraft gave out white puffs of smoke before a missile fired: this was the so-called charging-up period. If a MiG pilot took evasive action when a missile was being charged up, he stood a good chance of getting away before the missile left the rails of his adversary's launch bay.

Nguyen Van Bay recalls, 'I knew that they wanted to kill me so I was determined to bring one of them down with me.' The American F-4s and F-105s had been chasing the MiGs around for three minutes without success. Both MiGs tried to bring the fight to lower altitudes (less than 3,000 feet) as both Bay and Man felt their numerical inferiority could be countered by the shelter afforded by the Yen Tu mountain range nearby.

Nguyen Van Bay realized that the F-4s were lining up and firing at the MiGs in an orderly queue and before long they would both be dead. At that moment he remembered that, when they had pounded rice in the fields as children, any break in the rhythm of the leader would cause everyone to lose their momentum and stop pounding. 'This might work with the F-4s,' he thought.

An F-4 began to dive on Van Man (who was flying to Van Bay's left) and began to level off to fire his missiles: this was when an

F-4 was most vulnerable because it had to maintain level flight in order to fire a missile. At this moment, he told Van Man, 'Remember rice-pounding: the Phantom is going to pound you. Turn around when I give the signal,' and Van Man immediately realized what Van Bay meant.

To take advantage of this 'Achilles heel' in the Phantom's defences, Van Man would have to wait a few seconds before the white puffs appeared and he turned to face his attacker. Just when the Phantom was about to fire, Van Bay warned Van Man, who quickly swung his MiG 17 around and fired a short burst into the nose of the Phantom,

causing it to crash. The other Phantoms lost their rhythm and ceased firing. Then an F-105 (flown by Lt. Karl Richter of the US 421nd TFS) fired two missiles at Van Man, which exploded near his MiG causing it to smoke badly. By some miracle Van Bay managed to protect his comrade by drawing the Americans away from him, but by now he was very low on fuel, with only 300 litres showing on the guage. Van Bay decided to land near a small village at the foot of the hill. When he lowered his undercarriage he would be at the mercy of the Americans but, as he hoped, his pursuers gave up because of the danger of crashing into the hills.

The whole combat had taken over eight minutes. Most combats rarely lasted over two minutes and the stresses and strains on the VPAF pilots were immense as every second of those few minutes required superhuman strength and concentration.

This combat has been narrated in detail to give the reader some idea of what VPAF pilots had to face in nearly every mission they flew. This VPAF victory also showed how a simple strategy learned in the rice fields of Vietnam was used to shoot down a Phantom, the most advanced fighter of its day. It also saved two pilots' lives.

The VPAF claimed seven US aircraft shot down by MiGs from October to December 1966, five of them F-105s. The Americans claimed seven aircraft shot down during the same period, two of them being An-2 light transport aircraft (the only two claimed in the war).

A group of unidentified pilots stretch their legs anxiously before a sortie early in the war. The MiG 17s are in air superiority grey livery. (Vietnamese News Agency)

A line-up of MiG 17Fs attached to the 921st FR. 'Red 2014' may have been flown by Tranh Hanh on 3 April 1965. (Vietnamese News Agency)

'Another view of 'Red 2014' being prepared for a sortie. This aircraft may also have been flown by Pham Ngoc lan. (Vietnamese News Agency)

A MiG 15UTI from the 923 FR takes off on a training mission. 'Red 3033' is in a very weathered dark green camouflage with silver canopy. These unorthodox colours were applied at unit-level and tended to weather very quickly. (Vietnamese News Agency)

1:72 Scale

MiG 21F, 'Red 3020', flown by Ngo Duc Dao, Nguyen van Bay (the younger). He was killed in this aircraft when he was with the 923 FR. This aircraft is commonly associated with the legendary 'Colonel Toon'. No stars on lower wings.

MiG 21F, 'Red 3020' in another guise. This time in dark green, and possibly brown, with heavy weathering. (Vietnamese News Agency)

4 The December Massacres

THE worst day suffered by the Americans was 2 December 1966, later described as 'Black Friday'. On this day F-105s were to hit petrol, oil and lubricant facilities at Phuc Yen, less than 20 miles northwest of Ha Noi. For the US pilots concerned, this was the most dangerous task in the world and was known as a 'trip to the outskirts of Hell'. Moreover, for eight of the crews it would be a one-way ticket to death or captivity. The F-105Ds came from the 388th Tactical Fighter Wing based at Karat (Thailand) and the escorting Phantoms came from 12th Tactical Fighter Wing based in Cam Ranch Bay (South Vietnam).

When the aircraft came close to the target there were no MiGs in sight, and for good reason as the North Vietnamese were waiting for the Americans with the highest density of SAMs yet pitted against their enemy. The Americans flew into an ambush and suffered accordingly: first an F-4C was hit by a SAM (both pilots ejected), next an F-4C was hit by another SAM while flying as high cover – the crew ejected. A few moments later an F-105 was hit by SAM (killing the pilot), then another F-4C was hit by anti-aircraft fire (crew ejected). A fourth SAM downed a Navy F-B 'Black Knight'. The next success was an A-4C Skyhawk. Then in quick succession an A-4C (kill no. 7) and a Phantom (kill no.8 but the crew ejected) were destroyed by SAMs. The main reason for this success was that the Russians had began supplying the North Vietnamese with as many SAMs as were requested. The North Vietnamese merely swamped the American formation with a barrage of missiles.

14 December 1966 would turn out to be a very special day for the VPAF, with similar impact to Black Friday. It began when a large American formation made up of 40 aircraft was tracked heading for VPAF targets near Ha Noi. The formation consisted of 24 F-4C Phantoms and 16 F-105s from the Udon airbase in Thailand. Just before entering North Vietnamese airspace, the American formation split up into three groups, all flying at different altitudes. The F-4s would fly at the highest altitude hoping that they would draw the MiGs into combat. Those flying at the lowest altitude would try and fly below North Vietnamese radar and the rest would turn on their ECM equipment and jam North Vietnamese radar systems.

By 0800 hours the 921st FR were put on standby. Nguyen Van Coc (flying Red 4213) and Dong Van De (flying Red 4212) prepared to meet this raid. They were the two most promising pilots of their regiment. Dong Van De was the first ever home-trained MiG 21 pilot.

At about 0815 hours, the scramble order was given and the head ground control officer, Le Thanh Chon, vectored them towards the American formation. He recalls, 'I led Van De's squadron to fly along the course of the Lo River because they could take advantage of the geographical features of the Tam Dao mountain range. This route would have made it very difficult for them to be picked up by American radar.' The two MiG 21s were to fly at an altitude of 4,800 feet and cruise at a speed of 600 mph. This route would give the MiG 21s a chance to attack from the west with the sun at their backs: this would make visual identification of the American formation very much easier. VPAF pilots believed such an attack would increase their chances of a kill by at least 50 per cent.

On this day luck was with Van De and Van Coc as they closed to within 50 miles of the American formation and were still not detected. The MiGs were flying at an altitude

Two MiG 17s take off from a VPAF base on an interception.

of 19,200 feet, when Van De instructed Van Coc to move over to the right and cover him in the attack. This was because the American formation would appear on their left and Van De would have a clearer field of fire.

When the American formation was 20 miles away, the VPAF pilots were ordered to drop their long-range fuel tanks and increase their speed. Nguyen Van Coc was first to make visual contact when he reported, '212, enemy at heading 030 degrees, 12 miles away – there are four groups making a line towards the mountains ahead.' At this point Van Coc was flying a little higher and behind his squadron leader. This approach would give him an opportunity not only to cover Van De but fire at the enemy if the chance arose.

A minute before contact was made, Van De reported, 'Cuu Long (ground control), all enemy aircraft are bomb-carrying F105s...attacking now.' Then Van Coc replied, '213 also attacking now.' Ground Control replied, '213, attack and then return to base immediately, heading 360 degrees.'

From a height of 6,000 feet higher than the Americans, both MiGs dived on the F-105s at supersonic speed. The American formation had by now spotted the fast-approaching MiG 21s and began to drop their bombs and break in all directions like branches of a tree.

Van De in the leading MiG waited until the distance between him and an F-105 was down to 1,300 yards. He could see the fighter-bomber almost fill his gun sight and then calmly pressed the firing button. In an instant he could see his missile climb like an arrow in front of his MiG. His aircraft was by now travelling in excess of 380 feet per second, creating great pressures on his mind and

body, but he retained enough control to pull up at the last moment to prevent himself crashing into his prey. The heat-seeking ATOLL missile flew straight into the exhaust of the F-105, causing a yellow-flamed explosion, which made Van Coc report cheerfully, '212 has scored a victory... it's burning! Its burning! It's burning! A good kill.'

By this time, future ace Van Coc had also targeted an F-105, fired a missile at it and, in his own words, '... like a fist, knocked it out of the sky.' Ground observers described it as 'burning like a torch' in the blue sky above Vinh Phu.

The escorting F-4s were flying ahead of the formation and were unable to respond in time. Other F-4s were attacking the surrounding airfields and they also were not in any position to defend the fighter-bombers.

The two victorious pilots regrouped and awaited instructions to return to home base. From a distance Van Coc could see the American formation flying in disarray, some F-105s heading home at full speed and other F-4s flying to 'rescue' the F-105 from the MiGs and making long dark trails of black smoke in the sky. After a few minutes the F-105s regained their composure and returned to formation, as they believed the 'MiG threat' had left them.

The astute Van De noticed an unguarded blind spot to the right of the F-105 and decided to attack again: this would be the last thing the Americans would expect because VPAF fighters were not known to have attacked a formation twice. Furthermore, both Van Coc and Van De could

Vu Ngoc Dinh and Nguyen Hieu discussing fighter tactics in front of a MiG 21 PF. (Vietnamese News Agency)

not believe their luck when the F-4s had still not made any radar contact with them. 'Have the F-4s not turned on their radars today?' thought Van De. Seconds later, ground control heard him report, '212 attacking now.

They decided to dive on the Americans again and screamed down on the unsuspecting F-105s. As Van Coc was later to record, 'We came like sharp swords from nine layers of clouds at the throat of the enemy.' The MiGs were traveling at 950 mph, with Van De in the lead aircraft targeting the third F-105 in the second group of aircraft to his right. The speed of the dive forced Van De to stabilize his MiG by pushing hard with his pedals: when the F-105 was within range, he fired his second missile and saw it crush the target. In an instant Van Coc shouted out, 'It's burning! 212 has shot a second aircraft down.'

Loud cheers also went up in the ground control station as they were then ordered to fly to an altitude of 25,000 feet at a heading of 020 degrees.

The MiGs departed the scene as quickly as they had arrived. The F-4s were unable to catch them because using their superior speed to chase, the MiGs would use up all their supplementary fuel after only four minutes flying at full speed. The eight closest F-4s then resorted to firing all their missiles at

long range in the hope of hitting the MiGs, but these missiles merely exploded harmlessly as Van De and Van Coc escaped. The F-4s gave up their chase when they reached the edges of Lake Ba Be.

The action was remarkable not only because Van De was able to score a 'double' American kill, but also because he did it on his first combat sortie. To add to the achievement, this was Van Coc's first kill on his first combat sortie. For his actions Nguyen Van De was given two medals of honour from Ho Chih Minh. During the same ceremony Ho Chih Minh similarly honoured Nguyen Van Coc, and both pilots were made 'Heroes of Vietnam'.

As their combat experience increased, the VPAF pilots were able to change from a two-aircraft attack pattern to the finger-four attack pattern, in which four MiGs would fly like an outstretched hand. This pattern, which was universally used, enabled all four MiGs to cover the blind side of their comrades' aircraft. The VPAF would sometimes use a three-ship formation (similar to the *Luftwaffe's Rotte* grouping in World War Two) in order to blood young pilots in action. Such a three-aircraft formation was used on 17 December. At 1000 hours, a large American formation was heading towards the industrial area of Dong Anh. Once their

Squadron leader Nguyen Nhat Chieu (back row, second from right) and his ground crew members. 'Red 2014', a MiG 17 Fresco C can be seen in the background. (Vietnamese News Agency)

The entire 921st FR is seen here in a line-up. The first five MiG 17 Fresco Cs are in air superiority grey. The ninth MiG, 'Red 2027', and the eighth are in natural metal. (Courtesy Toperczer)

route was confirmed as Ha Noi, three MiG 21s of the 921 FR were put on standby. On this occasion the pilots were not novices but Nguyen Hong Nhi who had six kills, Vu Ngoc Dinh (four kills) and Nguyen Danh Kinh (three kills). At 1030 hours the squadron was scrambled and directed to fly low over Hoa Binh to evade American radar and Vietnamese SAMs.

Within minutes of take-off Nguyen Hong Nhi was given permission to intercept a formation of 12 F-4s. Acting on instinct, Hong Nhi decided to delay his attack and within moments he spotted the bomb-carrying F-105s, his primary targets. The three-ship formation required one MiG (Hong Nhi) to act as bait and draw the F-4s away from the F-105s.

When the F-4s spotted Hong Nhi heading for them, they turned towards him and momentarily abandoned the bombers. The two other MiGs, flying behind the lead MiG, then attacked the unguarded F-105s. By this time the F-4 pilots realized they had been wrong-footed and they decided to turn back to cover the F-105s, but by now both Ngoc Dinh and Dinh Kanh had each targeted two F-105s and shot them both down with missiles. All three MiGs departed the scene by diving for the deck, leaving the American formation in disarray. This was the first of many occasions that the three-ship formation was used with great success.

By the end of 1966, the Americans had lost 451 aircraft in the war and 111 F-10s were shot down over North Vietnam in just a single year. Other casualties included forty-two F-4s lost in combat, twelve claimed by MiGs. The VPAF lost twenty two MiGs and thirty pilots killed to American aircraft. The Americans claimed they had downed thirty-one MiGs.

A very clean looking MiG 17 Fresco C, 'Red 2837', being refuelled for another sortie at Gia Lam in 1965. (Vietnamese News Agency)

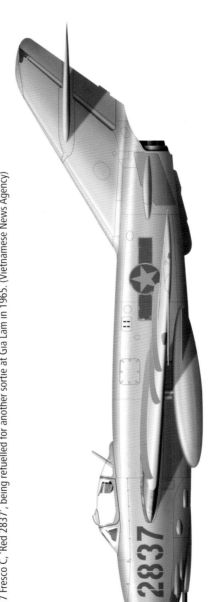

1:72 Scale

MiG 17 Fresco C, 'Red 2837', Gia Lam, 1965.

'MiG 21PF, 'Red 4527', was based in Yen Bai and was attached to the 921st FR. The pilot was Nguyen Van Nghia who scored five kills and is seen here talking to his ground crew circa 1967.

MiG 21PF, 'Red 4527', Nguyen Van Nghia, 921st FR, Yen Bai, ca. 1967

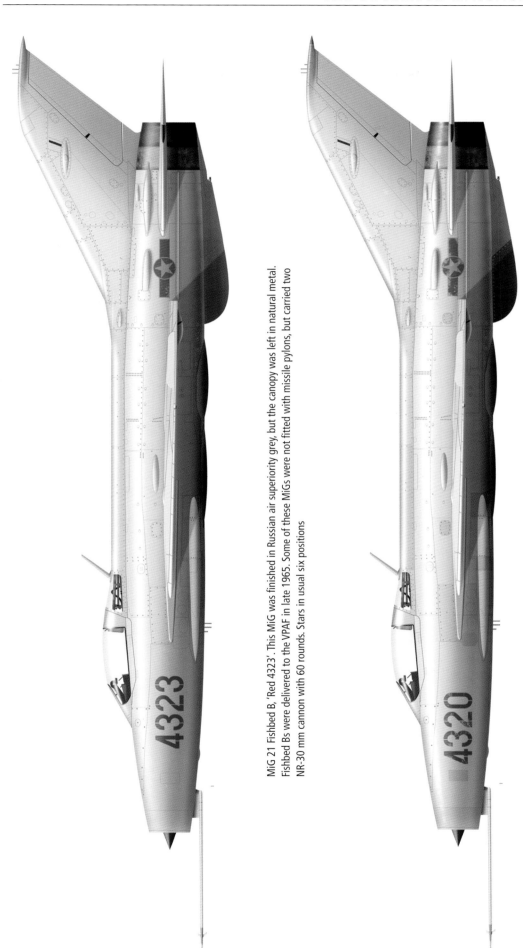

MiG 21 Fishbed B, 'Red 4323'. This MiG was finished in Russian air superiority grey, but the canopy was left in natural metal. Fishbed Bs were delivered to the VPAF in late 1965. Some of these MiGs were not fitted with missile pylons, but carried two NR-30 mm cannon with 60 rounds. Stars in usual six positions

MiG 21 F-13 'Red 4320'. Built at the Zavod Factory in Russia for export, it had no autopilot. Delivered to the VPAF in 1966. This aircraft was flown by Nguyen Hong Ni when he downed a Firebee on 14 March 1966. Stars in usual six positions.

5 'Operation Bolo'

THE air war over North Vietnam would escalate even further in 1967, with both sides experiencing significant victories and losses. The Americans, still smarting from the Black Friday massacre, were planning a massacre of their own. This was to be known as 'Operation Bolo' and was conceived by front line pilots with the advice and assistance of Colonel Robin Olds, commander of the US 8th Tactical Fighter Wing: the objective was to bring down MiGs in large numbers.

In the morning of 2 January, the F-4s would fly over North Vietnamese airspace imitating the flight characteristics of F-105s (the fighter-bombers) to entice the North Vietnamese defences into sending large numbers of MiGs to intercept them. The F4Cs were all equipped with the ECM pods that would make them appear as F-105s on radar. The bait was taken and the MiGs were sent into this 'Phantom trap', resulting in the Americans claiming a MiG 21 shot down. Colonel Olds and Lt. Charles Clifton claimed a second MiG with an AIM-9 (Olds would eventually score four kills in the war). The MiGs could claim no American aircraft shot down this day but the Americans admitted to losing a F-4 to ground fire. This would prove to be the most one-sided air-to-air combat of the war, if American reports are to be believed.

The North Vietnamese admit to losing five MiG 21s on this day with none of their pilots being killed. The official North Vietnamese records show and no pilots were reported killed until 6 January. If American reports are believed completely, then it would be highly unlikely that eight MiGs would have been shot down without a single casualty. Therefore the North Vietnamese figures seem closer to the truth.

On 5 February 1967, an F-4 was shot down, as was another F-4 the following day.

These kills could not be confirmed or credited to any pilot.

The Americans started to hit airfields by this time and Ha Noi was targeted more frequently. On 24 April, more than twenty American aircraft attacked storage facilities. The VPAF scrambled eight MiG 17s from the 921st FR. The covering flight and intercept flight both made contact. The first flight consisted of Vo Van Man, Nguyen Ba Dich, Nguyen Van Bay and Nguyen The Hon. The flight was only allowed one firing pass: its members attacked the American aircraft from abeam, then broke away, claiming two F-4s shot down, (both kills were shared by these four pilots.) The second flight claimed another F-4 shot down over Pha Lai on the eastern tip of Vietnam, less than 20 miles from the Chinese border. The victorious flight consisted of Mai Duc Toai, Luu Huy Chao and Hoang Van Ky.

The interesting points to note about these flights are the lack of MiG 21s in the missions, possibly due to excessive losses. The victories were 70 miles apart (unusual for MiG kills) and the North Vietnamese effort was spread very widely over a large area as both intercepts were made from aircraft from the 923rd. On the same day in response, American F-105s destroyed a further fourteen MiGs on the ground when they hit Hoa Lac airfield. The US Navy claimed another two MiG victories when they shot the VPAF fighters down as they attempted to take off from the old Japanese airfields at Kep: Nguyen Van Kham was killed in this conflict.

On 25 April the Americans attacked Ha Noi and Haiphong. They had presidential approval to hit North Vietnamese airbases. As a result the North Vietnamese had to make more intercepts or shuffle their MiGs between different bases but, as most of them were in and around Ha Noi and Haiphong, this was of limited value. The only base the Americans never attacked in any numbers (it was officially never attacked) was Gia Lam in Ha Noi, which served as the international airport, but the VPAF did not have the benefit of historical hindsight! A flight of four MiGs consisting of Mai Duc Toai, Le Hai, Luu Huy Chao and Hoang Van Ky shot down an F-105 over Gia Lam.

The Americans also made simultaneous attacks against rail and harbour targets at Haiphong. The MiG 17s of the 923rd FR were called upon again to intercept. Although the pilots made only a single pass, they achieved three victories, bringing their individual scores for Nguyen Van Bay, Nguyen The Hon, Ha Ban and Nguyen Ba Dich. The North Vietnamese kill tallies for some pilots may well have been higher, but due to their tactic of hit-and-run it would be impossible to determine which pilot actually delivered the 'killer blow' in any one combat so the system of sharing the kills between pilots seemed to be only logical under the circumstances.

Only by late April did MiG 21s appear again on the scene after the losses on 2 January. By April 1967 the 921st FR had to stand down for four months and re-equip with new MiG 21s and pilots. Although the VPAF suffered only one pilot killed by April 1967, most VPAF MiGs were not operational, due to low serviceability and lack of spare parts. It should also be noted that the VPAF was very much smaller than its opponents realized, as it never had more than 40 MiGs on standby at any one time. The MiG 21s made their return in style on 30 April by shooting down two F-105s, both Nguyen Ngoc Do and Nguyen Van Coc scoring victories. On the same day Le Trong Huyen and Vu Ngoc Dinh claimed an F-105 each. For that day, Captain T.C. Lesan claimed a MiG 17 downed, using 20 mm cannon.

Nguyen Nhat Chriu and Pham Ngoc Lan Taleen photographed early in the conflict. Both pilots wear leathers similar to their World War Two 'predecessors'. They have remained friends for over fifty years.

These dark green MiG 17Fs were referred to as 'snakes' because they flew in a weaving pattern similar to the movement of a snake before intercept missions.

1:72 Scale

Chinese made Shenyang J-6, 'Red 3002'. The Chinese markings were painted over with VPAF markings. Most MiGs were painted at the first opportunity after delivery. This MiG belonged to the 923rd FR. Stars in usual six positions.

A single-barrel 14.7 mm anti-aircrcraft gun (left) used by the Luong Yen self-defence unit, which shot down an F-111 on 22 December 1972 using only 19 shells. (Author)

In the immemorial manner of the fighter pilot, Ngo Duc Mai shows how he scored his latest kill. Behind is 'Red 2087'. Duc Mai downed an F-4 Phantom near Yen Bai on 4 March 1966. He finished the war with at least three kills.

'Red 2231' and 'Red 2315' were early production Fresco Cs. These aircraft appear extremely fresh and may be newly delivered aircraft.

'MiG 17 F 'Red 2231'. *1:72 Scale*

Ngo Duc Mai (three victories) and Nguyen Hieu view a map before a mission in early 1967. (Vietnamese News Agency)

Dang Ngoc Ngu (KIA 8.7.72) was one of the few pilots to score during the 'Rolling Thunder' Campaign and Linebacker Raid period. He may well have flown in more combat sorties than any other VPAF fighter pilot. (Vietnamese News Agency)

Camera gun view from an F-105 Thunderchief of a MiG 17 presumerably chasing another Thunderchief near Ha Noi. Combats rarely lasted more than a minute or two – if not seconds, so to have captured this fleeting moment was a rare occurrence.

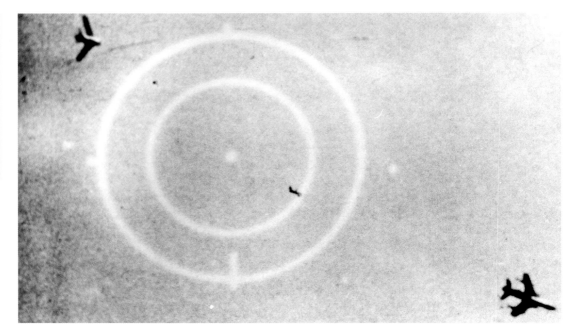

A MiG 17 caught in the camera gun of an F-105 Thunderchief. The MiG 17 although much slower than its US adversaries was very nimble and, in the right hands, a superb dogfighter.

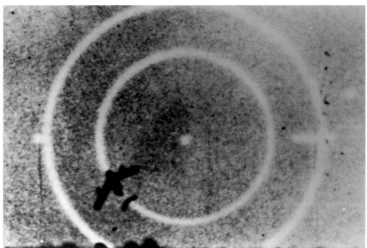

A clear view of a MiG 17 evading a US fighter at relatively low altitude where its manouerability excelled. A distinctive feature of the MiG 17 in plan view is the long wing fences. This MiG has also been camouflaged and wears quite large national insignia positioned very close to the wing tips.

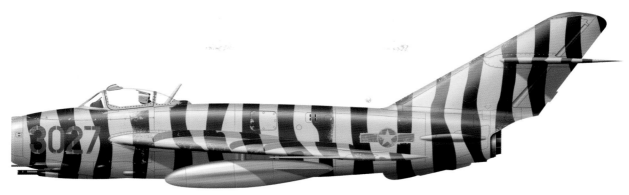

1:72 Scale

MiG 21F, 'Red 3027', from the 923rd FR. This MiG was in dark green with blue zebra stripes on fuselage and wing upper surfaces. The aircraft were painted this way for special over-water operations. The aircraft carried stars in all six positions.

Two MiG 17 Fs landing at Kien Ann airfield, circa 1965. Both have been camouflaged in two tone greens. (Vietnamese News Agency)

Radar sites such as this were responsible for tracking US raids over Ha Noi and Hamhong during the Vietnam War. This particular site is the one that tracked the first ever US raid over the Ham Rong bridges in March 1965.

1966 US Air Force reconnaissance photographs showing North Vietnamese Air Force MiG 17 jets parked in protective shelters at Phuc Yen airfield north-west of Ha Noi.
(Jerry Scutts)

A 1967 US Air Force photograph captures a MiG 21 in flight over rice paddy fields near Ha Noi.
(Jerry Scutts)

A US Air Force photograph shows a SAM-2 missile in flight after it had been fired upon a US Air Force Phantom RF-4C near the Red River area of Ha Noi in August 1967. The missile went onto hit the Phantom.
(Jerry Scutts)

6 High Stakes!

THE month of May usually brings clear weather and skies over Vietnam and 1967 was no exception. The Americans aimed to use this good weather to hammer home their air superiority to the VPAF.

The reality of the situation was that, under the protection of two anti-aircraft regiments and four SAM units, the VPAF was taking the initiative and pushing south. This was a time when both sides started to raise the stakes. The Americans continued to bomb Ha Noi and Haiphong and the VPAF's airfields were now targeted with increasing regularity. May 1967 would see one of the fiercest air battles of the entire Vietnam War.

The US F-D Phantom entered service in May; it carried the 20 mm M61 Vulcan cannon attached via an external pod; the cannon could fire 6,000 rounds per minute and would give the F-4 an edge over the MiG 21 in close combat.

Two MiG 17s from the 923rd FR were sent further south under the protection of two anti-aircraft regiments and four SAM units. When American air activity was observed, four more MiG 21s were sent to Tho Xuan, about 30 miles west of Thanh Hoa.

Smarting from the loss of three MiGs downed in the 4th Military District, the VPAF took the offensive on 7 May, when two MiG 21s from the 921st FR were alerted. Nguyen Van Coc and Dong Ngoc Ngu took off from Tho Xuan to intercept an American formation. The covering flight of MiG 21s (flown by Nguyen Dang Kinh and Nguyen Van Lung) were a few minutes before them. The MiGs survived a scare when they were fired upon by friendly anti-aircraft units nearby - the anti-aircraft crews were extremely nervous, being this far south. The weather conditions were poor and, to make things even worse, the intercept flight nearly shot down the covering flight! By now the MiGs were flying in heavy cloud and did not receive much assistance from ground control. Just before the MiGs aborted the mission they were vectored onto an incoming American formation. When they got above the formation, Ngoc Ngu spotted two F-4s flying ahead of the main group, about eight miles to his left. The F-4s kept flying low into the clouds and so a game of cat and mouse began. Somehow Ngoc Ngu lost contact with the F-4s, so he was forced to return due to shortage of fuel.

Meanwhile the fuel situation was no better for Van Coc: he had dropped his fuel tanks prematurely owing to the abortive attempt to shoot down the covering flight. He was about to follow Ngoc Ngu when he spotted the F-4s flying at 4,000 feet dead ahead. He remembers his heart pounding as he maneuvered behind the trailing aircraft. When the gap closed to 800 yards, he let fly both missiles. After a few pulsating seconds he could see the missiles curve into the F-4 and explode, bringing the American warplane down into the sea near My Yen.

On 12 May 1967, a flight of MiG 17s intercepted a large formation of American aircraft over Hoa Lac, 25 miles west of Ha Noi. The 923rd FR pilots attacked in two separate flights, the first one comprising Cao Thanh Tinh, Le Hai, Ngo Duc Mai and Hoang Van Ky. They could see the smoking F-4s from a distance and were given the order to make a single firing pass. As they had done many times in the past, all four MiGs flew in tight formation and hit the American formation from astern, all pilots firing their sixteen cannon in unison, spitting a shower of death on the Americans. To their great satisfaction, the three US aircraft fell out of the sky as if a big hand had pulled them down. The intercept action was over in seconds so there was no time to confirm any crashes, and all the MiGs landed safely. The pilots were given credit for downing three F-4Cs. Later over the Yen Lac area, a similar pass was made by three MiG 17s of the 923rd FR, downing an F-4C and an F-105: the successful pilots were Duong and Nguyen Van Tho. The 921st FR also downed an F-105 over Van Yen (about 30 miles north of Ha Noi): Le Trong Huyen and Dong Van Song flying MiG 21s shared this kill. SAMs also accounted for three more aircraft that day. On the debit side a MiG 17 of the 923rd was shot down by an F-105, although happily the pilot ejected to safety. This day turned out to be one of the most successful days for the VPAF during the whole war.

The weather was good for the whole month of May 1967 and for the successful pilots it was a dream come true. As an American pilot put it, 'Contact with the MiGs was almost daily. We had some damn good battles during the month of May.' Nguyen Nhat Chieu recalls, 'May 1967 was a time I flew combat missions up to two or three times a day.' The Americans claimed seven MiGs downed: Major James A. Hargrove and Lt. Stephen H. Demuth could lay claim to being the first crew in an F-4 to down a MiG with 20 mm cannon. The 923rd FR lost eight MiG 17s to the Americans, decimating the unit. However, they continued to make intercept missions, despite their squadron's lack of new aircraft and low serviceability. On 14 May the 923rd FR lost three more MiG 17s to F-4Cs, with two of them taking close-range hits from cannon fire.

On 19 May (Ho Chih Minh's birthday), a flight of four MiG 17s intercepted F-4s 25 miles southwest of Ha Noi. The VPAF downed two F-4s over the Hoa Binh district, with Phan Thanh Tai and Nguyen Huu Diet each claiming an F-4C destroyed, but losing four of their own to the Americans. The drain on the 923rd FR continued, but the point was that they still kept coming, and continued to shoot down American aircraft. The Americans would never get total control of the air against the tiny VPAF.

The senior officers of the VPAF recognized that the 923rd FR was doing more than could normally be asked of any one unit during this period. The award of a regimental banner from Ho Chih Minh was received with great pride.

20 May saw Colonel Olds scoring his second and third kills on this day, making him the top American scorer in Vietnam at that time. In reply Dang Ngoc downed an F-4 on the same day over Ha Noi (the VPAF MiGs would shoot down sixteen American aircraft over the city by the war's end). This was the last air-to-air claim made by both sides in May.

The VPAF was still very cautious in com-mitting their forces in the south as they were stretched out very thinly, but the main prize of shooting down a B-52 bomber still eluded them. They also knew that if this goal was ever to be reached they had to become more ambitious. However, such ambition had its price. On 23 May a flight of MiG 21s that were trailing a bomber lost one of its number to a TALOS surface-to-air missile fired from an American warship. The pilot, Dinh Van Ha, was killed instantly as his MiG flew straight into the ground in the Vhin area. He was the thirty-seventh aircrew killed in combat in 1968 and it was still only May!

During May 1968 the Americans claimed twenty-three MiG 17s and five MiG 21s shot down. This would represent about 55 per cent of all MiGs supplied to the VPAF for the whole year. However, the North Vietnamese have officially admitted to losing six pilots killed in combat during May. The number of VPAF pilots lost and the American claims do not sit well together as it is unlikely that 79

Le Hai, a great dogfighter, scored all of his six kills (possibly seven) in a MiG 17 when with the 923rd FR. He downed his first F-4 Phantom on 19 November 1967. (Vietnamese News Agency)

Nguyen Nhat Chieu celebrates with his engineer after a victory very early in the war. (Vietnamese News Agency)

per cent of the MiG pilots shot down during May managed to bale out safely. Nevertheless, American claims before 1970 tended to be more accurate than after 1971. In response, VPAF MiGs shot down eight American aircraft.

By the end of May the VPAF had undertaken over 470 sorties, made over 200 intercepts and taken part in 34 dogfights. The heavy attacks on airfields made nine of them unserviceable, leaving only Gia Lam (Ha Noi), Phuc Yen (northwest of Ha Noi), Kep (40 miles northeast of Ha Noi), Hoa Lac (20 miles west of Ha Noi), Kien An (10 miles southwest of Haiphong) and Tho Xuan (90 miles south of Ha Noi).

The VPAF was suffering high loss rates in terms of men and equipment. Although there was a pool of pilots to take part in combat missions, the gradual loss of experienced crews from January to May 1968 meant that pilot capability was falling fast. Furthermore, many MiGs were grounded due to a lack of spare parts and of trained ground technicians available to keep the squadrons anywhere near to strength. At times only four serviceable aircraft were available for intercept missions. Even though new aircraft were being delivered all the time, they took too long to be assembled, never replacing the aircraft lost in combat. There were a number of technical 'advisors' from Cuba and the USSR (number unknown), but the results show they were not enough. The VPAF had to stand down all its squadrons for a five-week period from 1 June. The MiGs only intercepted EB-66s, aircraft used for radar jamming and detection.

By mid-July, the VPAF was starting to intercept American aircraft once again and by the 11th of the month, Dong Van Song and Le Trong Huyen teamed up again to share their second kill when they brought down an A-4 Skyhawk with a single firing pass over a group of four F-8s and twelve A-4s. The A-4 crashed in Hai Duong, about 35 miles west of Haiphong. Five more American aircraft would be shot down over this area during the war: a main highway that connects Ha Noi and Haiphong goes through the Hai Duong area and the Americans were trying to cut transport links between North Vietnam's largest cities.

On 17 July, a flight of two MiG 21s downed an F-8 over Lang Chanh (50 miles northwest of Thanh Hoa), Nguyen Nhat Chieu scoring his second victory twenty-two months

after his first. Two MiG 21s from the 921st FR, piloted by Nguyen Ngoc Do and Pham Thanh Ngan, shot down another F-4. During June and July the MiGs only claimed three American aircraft and lost eight in return (five of these to 20 mm cannon). The VPAF had been building up its forces and was preparing to intercept American formations in larger numbers (as high as 20 MiGs as on 23 August).

A MiG 21 flown by Dong Van Song was shot down by Sidewinder missiles from two F-4 Phantoms. Van Song managed to bale out but sustained injuries that kept him in hospital for some time. His likely victors were Lt. Guy H. Freeborn/1Lt. Theodore R. Bongatz and Lt. Commander Robert C. Davies/Lt. Commander Gayle O. Elie from VF-141/CVW-14. Both sets of pilots were credited with the destruction of a MiG 21. These claims appear to be correct as Bui Dinh Kinh was killed in a MiG 21 that very day.

On 23 August 1967 the VPAF intercepted American formations in the largest numbers of the war. The VPAF tracked about fifty aircraft approaching Ha Noi from Laos. Ground control put ten MiGs on standby whilst the formation was being tracked, making for either Ha Noi or Haiphong. When the target was ascertained, the MiGs were scrambled at 1345 hours. The plan was for the lead flight (of two MIG 21s) to gain altitude and attack the Americans from above: the second flight of eight MiG 17s was to attack the Americans from the sides, forcing them into a turning combat called a 'furball' by the American pilots. The MiG 21s got visual contact at 1451 hours and received the order to attack. Their pilots were Nguyen Van Coc and Nguyen Nhat Chieu, the two most experienced pilots of the 921st FR. They started their dive, each taking an aircraft in his sights. Nhat Chieu fired his ATOLL at an F-8 and saw a flash as the missile hit its target, causing it to explode. Van Coc fired his missile a moment later, downing an F-4 with his ATOLL.

By now all the American aircraft had realized what was going on and had regrouped to take on the two MiGs. Nhat Chieu missed with his last missile and began to do an 'Immelmann' through the clouds. He then dived on the Americans, firing his 20 mm cannon. At that very moment Van Coc, who was trying to shoot at the same F-4, was hit by his own flight leader: he had to break away and was ordered to land as he was

'MiG 17F, 'Red 2011', flown by Ngo Duc Mai, as preserved today. (Vietnamese News Agency)

Ngo Duc Mai scored three kills as a 923rd FR pilot. The first of these was an F-4 Phantom on 4 March 1966 near Yen Bai. On 12 May 1967, he shot down the American MiG expert, Colonel Norman Cagadix. The author has been unable to confirm that Colonel Cagadix was ever shot down or that he ever flew combat missions over Vietnam. (Vietnamese News Agency)

1:72 Scale

MiG 17F, 'Red 2011', 923rd FR. May 1967

Nguyen Dang Kinh downed six US aircraft flying the MiG 21. (Vietnamese News Agency)

losing power all the time and was now down to 50 per cent thrust. Both their victims crashed in Nghia Lo, about 70 miles northwest of Ha Noi. This was Nhat Chieu's third kill and Van Coc's second victory. The covering flight of MiG 17s was not given the order to attack over Nghia Lo because SAM units were tracking the American formation. When the formation was nearing Ha Noi, the MiG 17s finally received the order to make a head-on attack. On the first firing pass, the four MiG17s hit two American F-105s and all four pilots shared both kills. (The pilots concerned were Cao Thanh Tinh Le Van Phong Nguyen Van Phong and Nguyen Hong Diep.) Their kills were seen to fall in Phu Yen, just north of Ha Noi. A fifth F-105 kill over Phu Yen could not be confirmed. The Americans claimed one MiG 17 shot down by a F-105 piloted by Lt. David B. Waidrop. This operation was a success as the Americans had to abandon the mission.

On 17 August the American attacks on the airfields continued, reducing the combat effectiveness of the VPAF: to counter this and improve their intercept times, the VPAF fighter units were moved to non-operational airfields. These satellite airfields were closer to the routes taken by the Americans. This strategy made it harder for the MiGs to be hit on the ground as they were spread out more thinly, (the Royal Air Force used a similar approach during the early stages of the Battle of Britain.) On the debit side, two MiG 17s downed an F-105 on 24 August, but no pilot could claim the kill. The number of sorties fell by 66 per cent from July to September 1967 when compared to the activity during the peak of Rolling Thunder in April and May 1967.

Nguyen Hong Nhi shot down a reconnaissance F-4 on 30 August over the Thanh Son and Moc Chau district.

Further attacks were aimed at the airfields at Kien An, Cat Bishop Lac and Kep. Despite this, the VPAF kept a very low profile in September. Nevertheless, Nguyen Ngoc Do and Pham Thanh Ngan got in some useful target practice when they each shot down a reconnaissance drone. The Americans could not put in any MiG claims for September.

Nguyen Hong Nhi added to his growing reputation on 10 September when he and Nguyen Danh Kinh intercepted another reconnaissance F-4 that was supporting an American formation which had just bombed Viet Tri. Ground control directed Hong Nhi's squadron to fly at low level, heading due south, for Phu Ly. After they had entered the Hoa Binh area they soon spotted two RF-4 Phantoms. When the F-4s spotted the MiG 21s they dived to low altitude and ran for home. Hong Nhi, using his height advantage, soon gained on the F-4s and shot down one of them with an ATOLL missile, making it nose-dive into a stream.

At 0400 hours on 26 September, an A-6 fighter bomber from the carrier USS *Saratoga* flew low under VPAF radar and raked the airstrip at Kep, but by noon the airstrip was made operational by clearing away a 200 feet strip of runway to allow MiGs to take off in single file. By 1000 hours the skies were clear and all set for an American attack. The pilots from the 921st FR braced themselves for action.

At 1030 hours, the order to scramble was given and Nguyen Hong Nhi and Dong Van Song took off to intercept formations of American F-4 Phantoms. Hong Nhi and Van Song had flown with each other many times before. However, for Van Song luck had not always been on his side as he had been twice shot down and hospitalized. Nevertheless, he had two kills to his name by this time. On this occasion, they were immediately ordered to fly due west, Van Song flying slightly behind and above his squadron leader, as he had done many times before.

Ground control was an invaluable ally in directing MiGs to their targets but contact was always kept to a minimum because at this stage of the war the Americans had begun to use similar radio frequencies to the VPAF to voice tap their instructions: this assisted American radar operators to attain very good fixes on the exact whereabouts of all MiGs. However, experienced pilots such as Hong Nhi used only minimum contact with ground control because they were exempt from the usual strict ground control direction – he could fight his own fight.

When the American formation was 30 miles from contact, Hong Nhi was informed that the formation consisted of two groups with twelve F-4 Phantoms in each. When the

MiGs had reached an altitude of 14,500 feet, flying at 700 mph and 20 miles from contact, Hong Nhi was informed that one group of twelve F-4s was behind him and able to sandwich him if he attacked the front group. The decision to attack was left to him.

For safety Hong Nhi and Van Song climbed to 19,000 feet and then saw a group of twelve F-4 Phantoms flying in finger-four patterns. They were flying in tight formation, with four aircraft in each pattern and were about 6,000 feet below him. Because they had the height advantage, Hong Nhi decided to attack the last four F-4s. He knew that only a quick kill would bring success as, in the distance, he could make out the black trails of the second formation closing in on them. Time was of the essence!

Hong Nhi then turned his MiG over and began to dive at the F-4s at full speed. As he closed in on his prey he could see the F-4s just drop their bombs in the jungle below and break into six equal groups. Obviously this was a trap! The F-4s had behaved like fighter-bombers but were now reverted to their fighter role. The VPAF pilots realized that not only were they outnumbered 6 to 1, but also 24 to 1 in terms of missiles, as each F-4 carried four missiles to their two. However, Hong Nhi was still confident that some of the Americans would make mistakes and create a chance for a kill. In his dive he saw two F-4s breaking left, then right, in a zigzag manner and he decided to attack this pair. The second F-4 in this pair was now nearly in his firing sights. When his missiles had locked in on the exhaust of his prey, he fired. The missile homed neatly into the exhaust of the F-4, causing fire to engulf the entire length of the aircraft as it crashed into the ground.

Within seconds of this kill Van Song fired his missile at the lead F-4, destroying it in mid-air. Both pilots reported excitedly, 'It's burning …. we have shot down two F-4D Phantoms.' They then both dived to low altitude and flew back home.

This feat was unique, as Hong Nhi had become the first pilot to down two American aircraft in a single mission, and to do this twice. By the end of 1967 he would down six American aircraft with air-to-air missiles. It is interesting to note that the Americans admitted only to losing three aircraft to missiles in the entire war!

15 October saw Nguyen Van Coc score a kill in a surprise attack on an F-4 near Bac Ninh (north of Ha Noi), bringing his total to at least three kills, with others being shared.

On 25 October, Nguyen Huu Tao, in a lone-wolf attack, shot down an F-105 near Ha Noi by diving through the clouds, using a hit and run technique favored by many North Vietnamese pilots.

During October, when the VPAF started to increase its number of sorties, the Americans retaliated by bombing Phu Yen and Gia Lam (officially this latter base was never attacked). The attacks forced the VPAF to abandon these fields and to operate their secondary fields, utilizing the undamaged runway at Phu Yen (this base was finally put out of action on the fifth attempt). With the help of the local population, many air bases could be repaired within 24 to 48 hours. During October the Americans shot down eight MiGs, four of them on the 26th, even though the VPAF lost only one pilot during the month. Due to this loss of aircraft, the VPAF was forced to transfer its MiGs to Chinese bases such as Mingling and Jiangoingxu or face total extinction as a fighting force. Nevertheless, pilots such as Nguyen Van Coc and a handful of others still made successful interceptions, despite facing against odds of 6 to 1 or more, when the opportunity arose.

A notable victory occurred on 26 October when the future Senator John McCain was shot down by a SAM on his twenty-third mission, while he was flying an A-4 Skyhawk from the carrier USS *Oriskany*. The F-4s claimed four victories on 26 October, but the only MiG 21 kill fell to Lt. Robert P. Hickery and Lt. Jeremy G. Morris from VF-143 of the USS *Constellation*. Jeremy Morris recalls, 'Our aircraft fired a Sparrow III from a 6 o'clock position on the MiG …. in which exploded on the left wing of the MIG 21,shooting down the aircraft …. the MiG 21 pilot apparently ejected out of the doomed aircraft.'

In early November Van Coc shot down an F-105 and an F-4: these were his fourth and fifth kills, making him the first VPAF MiG 21 ace.

On 8 November, VPAF radar picked up a formation of American aircraft approaching Ha Noi. To intercept this formation the 921st FR put on standby just two MiG 17s. When Nguyen Hong Nhi and his wingman Nguyen Dang Kinh were ordered to scramble at 0800 hours, they flew out low because of trigger-happy SAM units and in order to avoid American radar. The Americans were flying their escorts in front of the formation:

because of this the MiGs and F-4s made visual contact almost simultaneously. The F-4s began to peel off towards the two MiGs; Hong Hoi then attacked the F-4s head on. He got within range and fired a missile: both missile and F-4 seem to become one for a split second, then the missile detonated inside the F-4, engulfing the American fighter in a ball of flames. Within an instant Hong Hue flew through the debris and looked for the next F-4 to attack. In another part of the sky, Dang Kinh latched on to the tail of an F-4, but the American pulled up into a cloud and contact was lost. In the spirit of a true hunter, Dang Kinh waited for the American to break out of the clouds – a wait of seconds felt like an eternity, knowing that at any moment he himself could become the hunted. The F-4 broke through the clouds and at that very instant Dang Kinh fired his missile, hitting the F-4 and sending it earthbound in flames. With these victories the MiGs were ordered to break off the engagement and run for home. Both pilots were credited with their first kills on their return to Phu Yen. The Americans replied to this MiG activity by attacking Phu Yen airbase on six occasions during November alone.

On 17 November, Kien An airfield was attacked but was made operational within 48 hours. On 19 November a flight of MiG 17s landed there, even though the Americans still believed the airfield to be out of service. A formation of more than twenty F-4s and A-4s were about to make a bombing run on Haiphong's rail targets and in response Ho Van Quy, Le Hai, Nguyen Dinh Phuc, and Nguyen Phi Hung were scrambled in their MiG 17s. They attacked the formation, each selecting a target from above and releasing a barrage of cannon fire. Three of the four pilots saw strikes on their targets and three F-4s crashed in the Haiphong area. With this action Le Hai brought his total to three kills and Dinh Phuc and Phi Hung scored their first kills.

In the second sortie of the day, three MiG 17s flown by Le Hai, Luu Huy Chao and Cuu Van Suu were scrambled to intercept another American formation. They were vectored to make a head on attack and managed to break through the American formation. Van Suu in the lead MiG 17 closed in to within 450 yards of an F-4D and started to score hits with his cannon: after the second burst the F-4 started to go down over Thai Nguyen. The dogfight, which started at such close range, suited the MiGs. Nevertheless, Major Bernard J. Bogoslofski and Captain Richard L. Huskey managed to fire a 20 mm burst on the MiG of Huy Chao, forcing him to break away from the combat area and make an emergency landing at Phu Yen. Le Hai fired at a F-4 from nearly 1,000 yards but scored no hits.

It was a successful day for Ha Van Chuc who opened his scoring account by downing a F-105 over Yen Chau, 80 miles west of Ha Noi near the Laotian border. Vu Ngoc Dinh and Nguyen Dang Kinh each claimed a pilotless EB-66.

Operations by the VPAF were stepped up as American attacks on airfields decreased. On 12 and 14 December, MiGs from the 921st FR shot down one F-105 and an F-8, but the names of victorious pilots have never been traced. However, these two kills were confirmed because wreckage of these aircraft were found in Song Dong and Ninh Giang districts respectively. Americans claimed a MiG 17 shot down on 14 December but this cannot be confirmed through VPAF records.

The month of December 1967 was to be one of the most intense since May. On 17 December three MiG 21s and four MiG 17s of the 921st intercepted thirty F-105s and their F-4 escort, resulting in a 'furball' attack. Even though the North Vietnamese pilots were only given orders for a single pass on the American formations, Vu Ngoc Dinh and Nguyen Hong Nhi both decided to make repeated attacks against the F-105s. They were rewarded for their actions when they shot down three of the F-105s near Viet Tri. In addition, on this day two novice MiG 17 pilots from the 921st FR downed another two F-4s in the same area. (The VPAF lost two MiG 17s to the F-105s on the same day.)

On 19 December more 'furball' attacks were made against F-4s and F-105s. This was when Nguyen Van Coc claimed his sixth kill by downing an F-105 over Tam Dao, 40 miles northwest of Ha Noi, by using his famous tactic – attacking in a lone-wolf style. He would fire from maximum range and continue firing until he had a kill or he had

Nguyen Phi Hung of the 923rd FR downed an F-4 Phantom on the 19 November 1967 over Hai Phong. (Vietnamese News Agency)

to break off his attack. The author has spoken to Vietnamese military historians who credit Van Coc with as many as fourteen kills: he certainly flew the famous MiG 21 with fourteen red stars, which many observers believed to be the aircraft of the mythical Colonel Toon. Nguyen Van Coc achieved the rank of Lieutenant Colonel in 1972.

On the debit side the VPAF lost three MiG 17s, with Nguyen Dinh Phuc and Nguyen Hong Thai both being killed. The first two MiGs were shot down by F-105s, the third by 20 mm cannon fired from an F-4 at close range. The third pilot may have been Nguyen Nhat Chieu, who ejected successfully and landed near his own home! The VPAF was running a kill ratio of nearly 1 to 1 but could not sustain such attrition for long. On average the combat ratios were 8 or 9 to 1 against the VPAF. The MiGs had to stand down again and neither side made any further claims until January 1968.

The USAF alone lost 334 aircraft during 1967, highlighting the necessity for more escorts because of the perceived 'MiG threat'. Even so, 94 of these escort F-4s were themselves lost, three of them to SAMs. The SAMs also accounted for seventeen F-105s, with eleven of these confirmed by both sides. In return for these losses, the Americans flew 878,771 combat sorties and dropped 681,700 tons of munitions (more than all the tonnage used against Germany and Japan during the whole Second World War).

In 1967 the pace of the war had been heightened to a level where there was no such thing as a non-restricted target. According to Vietnamese experiences every major and minor target was attacked. All airfields were systematically attacked in order to prevent any MiGs from taking off. Nevertheless, no matter how many times these airfields were bombed, an army of workers would make them serviceable the next morning. The North Vietnamese became experts at repairing airstrips in record time. For its part, the VPAF shot down hundreds of American aircraft, using every weapon at its disposal, yet the end seemed very far away (for both sides).

In 1967 the MiGs claimed at least 31 air-to-air victories and the SAMs downed another 56 aircraft. The Americans claimed seventy-four MiGs, giving them a 2.3 to 1 success ratio, but if SAM and MiG figures are combined to reflect the team effort they made, then the ratio becomes almost 1 to 1. On the debit side the VPAF lost approximately forty-five MiGs from all causes, with 39 pilots killed.

Dong Van Song downed an A-4 Skyhawk on 11 July 1967 over Hi Duong district. He was credited with five kills. (Vietnamese News Agency)

Dong Van De (2 kills) reads the works of Uncle Ho (Ho Chih Minh) with Nguyen Van Coc (9 kills) (left). A MiG 17F ('Red 2587') is in the background. (Vietnamese News Agency)

7 End of Rolling Thunder

JANUARY 3 1968 would be a busy day for the VPAF, starting at 0733 hours, when American aircraft were being detected heading towards Ha Noi. When they were within range, Bui Duc Nhu and Nguyen Dang Kinh were scrambled in their MiG 21s to intercept the American formation. Each pilot had already shot down an F-105 in the Van Yen area (about 30 miles north of Ha Noi). On their return to Kep, Dang Kinh may have sustained hits from an F-105 and overshot the runway, writing off his MiG.

Later in the afternoon, four MiG 17s were vectored to an American formation between Tam Doa and Thai Nguyen. The pilots of the 923rd FR involved in the attack were Luu Huy Chao, Bui Van Suu, Nguyen Hong Diep, and Le Hai. The escorts spotted the MiGs very early on and the F-4s fired their missiles before the MiG 17s could get into cannon range: almost immediately Hong Diep was hit and had to eject. It is very likely that Hong Diep was downed by an AIM-4 Falcon missile fired by Lieutenant Colonel Clayton K. Squire and Lieutenant Michael D. Muldoon in an F-4D. This was the third confirmed kill in Vietnam by a Falcon missile.

In anticipation of another raid two MiGs took off from Gia Lam and landed at Thong Xuan. Le Hai and Luu Huy Chao refueled, then took off again at 1425 hours and did a 'top cover', a ploy designed to prevent American fighters from attacking MiGs as they were taking off. Both pilots, as usual, flew low until vectored by ground radar to intercept aircraft over the Thanh Chuong area, 45 miles northwest of Thanh Hoa. They then climbed to about 8,000 feet and dived on the American aircraft, which were flying at 3,000 feet. The squadron leader, Le Hai, got to within cannon range and started firing from 700 yards. He pressed the trigger again

and again as he closed and observed the F-4 crash over Thanh Chuong, making this his third kill. Meanwhile Huy Chao downed another F-4 with three cannon bursts for his first outright victory. Dinh Ton claimed further success when he intercepted a flight of four F-4s and downed one of them in a classic hit-and-run maneuver with his wingman, Nguyen Tien Sam. His prey crashed in the Do Long area, west of Vhin. Dinh Ton would end up as one of the most respected pilots of the VPAF (but sadly he was to lose his life because of upper jaw cancer at the age of 44.)

14 January brought further success for Nguyen Danh Kinh when he achieved a hat-trick of successes over EB-66s; this triple kill was shared with Dong Van Song.

The Tet Offensive brought increased B-52 sorties against North Vietnam: the VPAF High Command therefore decided to hit American TACAN installations based in Laos. Such installations were located high up in mountainous areas and were being used as beacons to create staging points for bomber attacks against North Vietnam. The 919th Air Transport Regiment made a reconnaissance of Hill 1688 (about 7 miles from the TACAN site on Pa Thi) in Laos to gather information and prepare the groundwork for an air attack on 12 January. At 1143 hours four Soviet-made An-2s were sent out. (These were single engine biplanes - little more than museum pieces.) Each of these aircraft was fitted with UB-57 unguided rocket pods and three 12.7 mm machine guns. Only three of the An-2s reached their target at about 1230 hours, but they made a series of firing passes using their entire ordnance. On the way back, due to their slow speed, an American UH-1 helicopter attacked them. Two aircraft took direct hits from the UH-1. It was observed that both aircraft then collided at a low altitude, killing all crew members as they hit the side of a hill. The loss of flight leaders such as Tran Si Tieu and Pham Thanh Tam on this operation may not have justified this action. The TACAN site only received superficial damage and was in operation the same day.

The Tet Offensive forced the very small 919th ATR to handle operations beyond its limited capabilities. Some Soviet-made Il-14 transport machines were used to fly night operations to supply friendly units around Hue, Quang Triang Khe Sanh. On 7 February, an Il-14 (no. 514), piloted by Hoang Ngoc Trung, dropped 1.4 tons of supplies and returned without incident. Another Il-14 was not so lucky as it was written off when it overshot the runway. It had successfully attacked six small patrol craft on the Cua Viet River, destroying three of them. However, Il-14 no. 502 took hits during its flight and hit a hill, killing all six crew members on board.

12 February marked the first attempt by the VPAF to bomb American warships at the offshore seaport of Cua Viet near Ha Tinh. The responsibility for this mission fell to the pilots of the 919th ATR. They would fly Ilyushin-14 transports converted into makeshift bombers, each carrying four 500 lb bombs. The relatively slow speed of the Il-14, coupled with its vulnerability to defensive fire, made this mission suicidal in nature.

Nguyen Van Bang was put in charge of this operation because he had more than 1,000 hours flying time and was an experienced night flyer. The other pilots involved in the attack were Nguyen Van Ba, Vo Minh Chung, Pham Thanh Ba, Hoang Lien and Hoang Ngoc Chung. The six-aircraft formation took off at 1835 hours into the dark cloudy sky and after an hour's flying time was on course as it flew over Ha Tinh, which is 40 miles south of Vhin. After 10 years of flying experience Van Bang could not only fly purely by instruments but was a firm believer in his instincts. By 2000 hours, low-level clouds began to appear over the target area, which made it impossible to find and hit their targets unless they resorted to dive-bombing tactics. At this point, ground control gave Van Bang the option to turn back but he continued on, as he wanted to attack the enemy at any cost.

He instructed his formation to fly lower than the cloud cover at a height of 1,000 feet. This would bring his formation below American radar cover and make the lights from the American ships visible at a great distance. Before long he saw a whole string of lights in the distance, like a floating city that was approaching him. He had to destroy the largest ship in the squadron to maximize the damage. By now the six Il-14s were flying just above the waves and when the ships were within range he gave the order to attack. Then in unison all six aircraft pulled up through the clouds to gain height before diving into their prey.

Van Bang in the lead aircraft was seen to target one warship: he dropped a bomb that hit the ship, producing a loud bang which was followed by a large column of smoke. Within seconds this was repeated five more times as each of the Il-14 pilots found their mark.

With the American ships burning below, Van Bay had accomplished his mission at this point, but he had two more bombs and made the decision to attack a second American warship near the centre of the cluster of ships. The ships had by now begun to return a wall of very intense fire, but Van Bang continued in his dive even though his aircraft was now taking more and more hits. When the warship was less than 3,000 yards away he was able to place the entire ship within his target sight, but at that critical moment his aircraft took a hit on the wing, which started to burn away, thus making his aircraft lose

Luu Huy Chao scored three kills as a 923rd FR pilot He downed his first F-4 Phantom on 14 June 1968 in a MiG 17 over the Thanh Chuong area. (Vietnamese News Agency)

The first squadron from the 923rd FR with leading Ace Luu Huy Chao (third from left). He downed an F-4 Phantom in a MiG 17F on 14 June 1968. In the background is a Fresco C 'Red 2315'. (Vietnamese News Agency)

1:72 Scale

MiG 17F, 'Red 3029'. Painted all over dark green with silver wing undersides. Stars on top of wings and fuselage sides only. The 923rd FR used this aircraft in the ground-attack role.

stability. In spite of this, his bomber kept on closing the distance to its target despite taking hits all the time. Van Bang managed to drop his last two bombs dead centre of the American ship, causing two large explosions as his aircraft pulled away. Then, when he looked to have made good his escape, other pilots witnessed the fire spreading into his cockpit as the left wing of the Il-14 broke off, causing the entire aircraft to smash into the sea like a fiery torch, killing all on board.

Three of the Il-14s were shot down, with the loss of 16 crewmembers. The loss of pilots such as Nguyen Van Bang, Vo Minh Chung and Pham Thanh Ba, all with hundreds of flying hours between them, would not be easy to replace. Sadly, their deaths did not do much to alter the general situation on the ground: this prevented the VPAF from launching similar attacks on naval targets until April 1972. Nevertheless, the 919th ATR completed 257 sorties in a ground-support role during the Tet Offensive. The unit managed to airdrop 3,115 crates weighing 631 tonnes in support of North Vietnamese ground units.

From June to the beginning of August 1968, the MiGs claimed three more F-4s. The surviving unofficial diaries of some pilots such as Dang Rang and others reveal a more personal side of the conflict to us. According to Dang Rang one day (1 August 1968) was extremely hot, due to the hot wind from Laos (known as 'Laos wind' in Vietnam) making life even more unbearable for the pilots in their pressure suits, waiting around

their MiGs in the sweltering heat. At 1100 hours twelve A-4s took off from the carrier USS *Enterprise*, escorted by a similar number of F-4s, to attack Thuy Harbour. Nguyen Dang Kinh, Phan Van Nao and Nguyen Hong Nhi, in their MiG 21s, were vectored to Nghe An province to intercept this raid.

Near the intercept point, flying low along Highway 15, Hong Nhi spotted four F-4s (possibly F-8s). In order to make a successful attack he radioed to Dang Kinh and Van Nao to attack the F-4s immediately and keep as many American aircraft busy while he tailed his intended victims. Hong Nhi still had not released his long-range tanks as the Americans had not seen him because he was cruising behind them, slowly inching his way closer.

The diaries of Le Thiet (chief ground controller) continue at this point, 'Nhi could clearly see the enemy aircraft and by now we (ground control) had informed him that the Americans were aware of his presence.' Trying to improve his position, Hong Nhi flew in a wide arc about 45 miles in length to set him up for a head-to-head attack on the Americans. Le Thiet Hung takes up the story from here again: '...suddenly, Nhi discovered the front of the enemy formation ... he attacked the third F-8 with missiles and he saw the missiles hit home but several enemy missiles also exploded around his MiG....' The F-8 crashed in the Do Luong area. However, Nhi's MiG caught fire and he took to his parachute when his control system failed. His MiG crashed along the coastal area of Cua

'Red 4124' and 'Red 4122' were MiG 21PFDs used by the 921st FR in 1966. The PFD carried only two K-13 air-to-air missiles, but was equipped with the improved RP-21 Sappire radar and updated PK-1 gun sight. The PFD could also be used as a ground-attack aircraft and fighter-bomber. (Vietnamese News Agency)

Le Hai (six kills) showing his comrades how a MiG 17 would cut across in a turn with a Phantom and kill it at close range with cannon fire. Le Hai downed one of his Phantoms on 14 June 1968 in a MiG 17. (Vietnamese News Agency)

Sot. However, it is very likely that Lt. Norman K. McCoy in an F-8 had shot him down, using a Sidewinder air-to-air missile.

By the end of 1968 Hong Nhi would claim eight American aircraft downed. His country honored his actions when Ho Chih Minh personally handed him his eighth medal honor (one for each kill) on June 18 1969. Other pilots similarly honored were Pham Thanh and Nguyen Van Coc. When Ho Chih Minh died two and a half months later, Hong Nhi was selected from all the VPAF's pilots to lead the farewell fly-past.

American and North Vietnamese air activity gradually decreased during the August to October period, although there were brief flurries of activity toward the end

The top ace of the Vietnam War was Nguyen Van Coc who scored an impressive nine victories (possibly 14). He downed three Phantoms in a three week period from mid-October to the beginning of November 1967. (Vietnamese News Agency)

MiG 21 PFM, 'Red 4324', belonged to the 921st FR and was flown by Nguyen Van Coc, when he downed a Phantom F-4B on 7 May 1968. Six different pilots scored 14 kills in this MiG. No stars and bars on the wings.

MiG 21 PFM, 'Red 4324', Nguyen Van Coc, 921st FR, May 1968.

of this period. On 26 October, two MiG 21s took off from Thoung Xuan and did a covering flight over the area. As usual the intercept flight flew behind the covering flight. They were vectored towards Yen Chau (about 90 miles west of Ha Noi.) The F-4s were intercepted and the MIG 21s of the 921st FR shot down one of the F-4s less than five miles from the Laotian border. No one pilot could claim this kill, the last one for 13 months, although a number of unmanned drones would be shot down in the interim period.

The VPAF flew further from its defensive circles around Ha Noi and Haiphong when air activity fell to a level that allowed it to take on a more offensive posture. Normally it could not sustain such a high level of highly intensive combat scenarios due to its limited resources. The VPAF took this fall in activity (late 1968 and early 1969) to rebuild its airfields and strengthen its air defense.

During April and May 1969 the Americans attacked 6,000 targets over North Vietnam, targeting all known VPAF airfields, so the task of rebuilding and repairing the damage was immense. To initiate this the Chief of Command mobilized three army divisions (367th, 368th and 377th). As the VPAF had moved further south and extended its operations, it had made preparations to protect the supply networks to those areas. The areas around Ha Noi were divided into three defensive zones, each with its own regional radar units who would liaise with main regional radar units to co-ordinate the air defences of the main cities and supply routes. Zone 1 would cover Ha Noi itself; Zone 2 would cover Gia Lam and Phu Yen; Zone 3 would cover Kep (North), Kien An (East), Hao Lac (West) and Thoung Xuan (South). Other airfields that suffered damage at Vhin, Dong Hoi, Cam Thuy, Ann Son and Gat were made operational, while other bases at Na San, Dien Bien, Thoung Xuan, Vhin, Do Luong, Anh Son and Dong Hoi were given defensive revetments and bunkers for retreat from air strikes, as well as new and extended runways.

By 1 November, President Johnson had declared a unilateral end to the bombing of North Vietnam. With this action the Rolling Thunder campaign came to an end.

In 1968 the Americans admitted to losing 900 aircraft, 257 of these lost to anti-aircraft units alone. They claimed 12 MiGs shot down, nine of them by F-4s (six MiG 17s and three MiG 21s) in 1968, and 119 MiGs in total since 1965. In contrast to these figures, the VPAF claimed 218 American aircraft of 19 different types during 1,600 sorties. The cost of this success was the loss of eight MiG pilots killed and 12 MiGs lost in combat in 1968. The VPAF had lost in total 71 MiG pilots killed and 87 MiGs lost from all operational causes.

The Rolling Thunder campaign was a strategic failure as well as a financial drain on the US taxpayer. The Americans dropped 600,000 tons of ordnance on Vietnam, using 400 aircraft making 300,000 aircraft sorties during the campaign. However, more than one thousand aircrew lost their lives, with a direct cost of $450m.

The VPAF losses of approximately 71 MiGs when compared to the American losses of 56 combat aircraft to MiGs, would favour the Americans by 1.2 to 1. This figure is much lower than the generally accepted 3 to 1 ratio. Even so, the VPAF still had to replace more than 90 per cent of its MiGs and about 80 per cent of its pilots during the 1964 to 1968 period. Moreover, with North Vietnam's limited resources in terms of men and material, such losses could not be sustained indefinitely. In the final analysis, the United States Government may have stopped the Rolling Thunder campaign six months too early by calling 'time out'.

The VPAF would grab this opportunity and see it as victory. Even when the campaign came to an end, North Vietnam had 8,000 anti-aircraft guns, more than at any time previously in the war.

Bui Van Sui of the 923 FR shot down a F-4 Phantom over Van Yen in a MiG 17 on 3 February 1968. He finished the war with 3 kills. (Vietnamese News Agency)

Mai Van Cuong scored all of his eight kills flying a MiG 21 whilst with the 921st FR. (Vietnamese News Agency)

8 The intermission period 1968-1972

THE end of Rolling Thunder came about mainly because of a change in American policy towards North Vietnam. The campaign had inflicted serious damage on all forms of communications in North Vietnam: nearly all transport links and heavy industries were disrupted and put out of action. The 'time-out' gave the VPAF the chance to repair the damage and increase its combat effectiveness. By February 1969, a new fighter regiment, the 925th, was made operational, with Major Nguyen Quang Trung as the first Commanding Officer.

The unit would receive new MiG 19s from China and also used the MiG 17 PF. The unit would use Yen Bai as its main base. Pilot training was also increased and a whole new generation of pilots returned from China and the USSR. It is estimated that between 1969 and 1972 about 280 new fighter pilots were trained for combat, but it is estimated that only 100 of these saw active combat. The pilots started to attend flight theory classes and all pilots increased their flight time as soon as airstrips became operational. Flight training included instrument flights in all weathers under both day and night conditions.

At the 919th Air Training Regiment, instruction included training pilots in ground-attack techniques, as the VPAF realized that such training would be essential when they started to take the offensive against the South. Training also included seaborne exercises against warships and other maritime targets, as plans were afoot to make surprise attacks on American ships. As the new MiG 21MFs began to arrive, all pilots from the 921st FR were converted to the new MiG 21MF model; and MiG 17s from the 921st and 927th Fighter Regiments were upgraded to MiG 21 status. In addition, five hand-picked pilots were given advanced training in all-weather flying and five more pilots were given night-fighter training.

The new generation of VPAF pilots would be better instructed and better prepared to tackle their well-trained American foes. Contrary to popular belief, very few of the VPAF pilots who participated in the air battles of 1972 were veterans of the Rolling Thunder campaign. Most of them were novices with little combat experience, but their better training gave the Americans the impression that they were pitched against experienced adversaries. Very few VPAF pilots who flew during the 1964 to 1969 period could claim any victories after 1971.

The VPAF was also receiving replacement aircraft. It is estimated that the VPAF received forty-odd new MiGs to supplement the twenty operational machines already on hand at the end of 1969. However, pure figures can be misleading as the very humid weather took a serious toll on the MiGs. Many aircraft would simply rust away where they were parked and the lack of spare parts grounded about 60 per cent of all fighters at any one time. The situation was further aggravated by lack of trained technicians to service the growing number of MiGs. By March 1969, the VPAF had about 45 fighters in various stages of repair but only 43 technicians to service these aircraft. In fact, another 60 per cent increase in technical staff was needed to service these MiGs and those

Always a reliable wingman, To Nha Ba contributed to many successes of the 923rd FR. He survived the war with at least two possible kills. (Vietnamese News Agency)

that were being delivered. The usual number needed is between two and three ground crew per MiG. The VPAF had difficulty training these ground crewmen because of the speed of expansion of its air arm and also because the population base of North Vietnam had low educational levels from which to start: this made the pace of training such personnel far too slow. It is during this period that advisors from China, Hungary, Cuba, Poland, the USSR and other Communist countries were warmly welcomed (at least for the duration of the conflict).

Airfield reconstruction was being carried at Tho Xuan, Vhin, Hoa Lac, Anh Son (known as Coconut Airport by VPAF pilots), Dong Hoi and Quang Tri. All these bases underwent complete reconstruction and were brought to combat readiness in a matter of weeks, sometimes days. Responding to meet further attacks and gathering resources in line with the VPAF's more aggressive stance, more airfields further south were constructed; in Cam Thuy, Gat and Phu Quy. The base at Quang Tri was in operation for the main purpose of shooting down a B-52.

The work that had to be carried out bordered on the Herculean, given the resources available to the VPAF. For example, the airfield at Phuc Yen had thirty major craters in it, making it look like a lunar landscape. The airfield at Kep had thirteen craters, making it unsuitable for combat operations. All major support buildings at these airfields were completely destroyed or badly damaged. To make matters worse for the VPAF, each airfield needed about 80 engineers and technical staff to complete the repair work, but there were less than 150 of these personnel in the entire country! Nevertheless, by 1971 all work was completed, but repairs to such bases was an ongoing process until the end of the war.

Defence of such airfields took on a high priority, as they would be very likely targets for the enemy. Airbases such as Phuc Yen, Gia Lam and Kien An were allotted a total of 21 100 mm batteries for airfield defence. Each airfield was also given a standing SAM unit with ground-to-air missiles. Bases prone to heavy attacks were also given 37 mm air defense battalions to upgrade their anti-aircraft capabilities. Airfields such as Kep and Phu Yen, that were situated close to Ha Noi, were always given priority treatment because of their strategic significance for the VPAF (and the Americans!).

By mid-October 1969 a detachment of air force pilots went to Truong Son district to observe B-52 flight patterns and figure out tactics which would increase their chances of shooting one down. The talented flight leader, Tran Manh, led this group. Nguyen Nhat Chieu, who was part of this party, recalls, 'We opened a way through the forest and found a 940 metre-high mountain near the Laotian border. On top of this mountain we set up our observation post. When the B-52s appeared, we observed they had dozens of F-4 escorts. We also observed that the escorts separated from the bombers at certain points. We particularly noticed two specialized RF-4 Phantoms that were used to report their bombing success. The American flight pattern became very clear to us at that time.' Other leading pilots who were there included Pham Ngoc Langley Hai, Dang Ngoc Ngu and Vu Ngoc Dinh.

Tran Hanh became a major tactician and respected ground controller / commander during the Linebacker Raids of 1972. (Vietnamese News Agency)

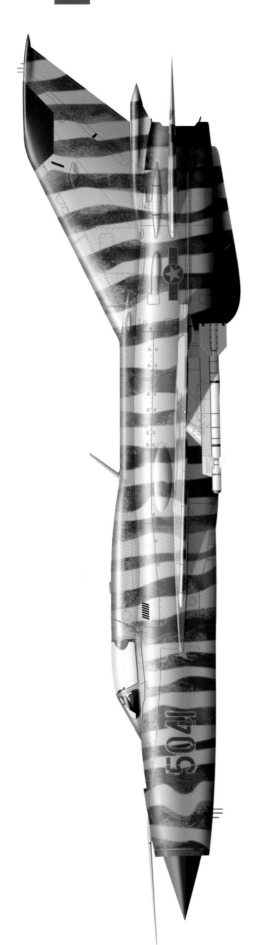

MiG 21 PFMs 'Red 5041' and 'Red 5066' from the 921st FR in 1967. These aircraft had their entire fuselages and wing upper surfaces painted in green zebra stripes with canopy and wing undersides in silver. No stars on wing upper and lower surfaces.

9 Calm before the Storm

BY the beginning of 1970 the VPAF had 81 combat-trained pilots at various levels of experience and between 27 and 45 operational MiGs ready for action. During the period from 1969 to the start of 1970, the VPAF participated in very few combat missions because American air activity had fallen dramatically. However, the MiG pilots still got some shooting practice by destroying three unmanned Firebees out of a total of six that were intercepted.

On 18 January 1970, Pham Dinh Ton made a rare achievement by shooting down two F-4s, the kills being verified by wreckage found by North Vietnamese villagers. These kills would be the first victories of the post-Rolling Thunder period for the VPAF. However, the North Vietnamese fighter pilots would have to wait another two years for their next kills.

In 1971 there were only six combat missions carried out by the VPAF: this lull was used to rebuild and train new pilots, but it reflected a low point as far as the air war was concerned. This brief interlude was merely the calm before the storm, the VPAF's senior command being only too well aware that it only had approximately 45 MiGs and 100 pilots of varied experience.

By this time, American policy had begun to take a less interventionist attitude and President Nixon offered proposals for peace negotiations to start by October 1971. The American public was not very keen on further American involvement and about 71 per cent of the population was against it in principle and wanted less or no involvement at all. The tide was turning and many felt that for a democratic country to bomb another because of political differences seemed rather ironical. However, those selling arms and weapons were not complaining.

The South had to be 'Vietnamised' and fight its own battles (with American arms) to maintain the balance. The South Vietnamese would eventually receive more aircraft than they had pilots to fly them! Eventually, the South Vietnamese Air Force had at least 730 combat aircraft in 30 squadrons. A similar situation could not be said of North Vietnam: despite the supplies from the Soviet Union and China, right up to the end of the war the North never had more than 55 operational MiGs at any one time.

It is interesting to note that the world's aviation industry sold aircraft with a total value of $2,500 million during the war.

On 24 March, four MiG 21s took of from Kien Ann airfield (about 20 miles from Haiphong). It was the first combat mission for two of the pilots but, even so they were thrown in at the deep end by being included in the intercept flight. They had to attack a squadron of F-4 Phantoms launched from the USS *Constellation*. The raw and inexperienced pilots were vectored to the attack positions and told to attack and fire twice. Although the North Vietnamese pilots were told when to attack and the number of times they could fire the timing of such attacks was largely left to the discretion of the pilot.

In this case both North Vietnamese pilots were very inexperienced and fired very early on, then tried to break through the American formation by diving low to break away. On the run home, a F-4 of the 'Ghost Riders', flown by Lt. Jerome E. Beaulier, with Lt. Stephen Barkley in the back seat, turned hard and easily got behind the trailing MiG, shooting it down with a Sidewinder. The MiG blew up in a red cloud, killing Nguyen Van Truang, aged 28 years. This type of combat was to take place many times over the skies of North Vietnam during the course of the great air battles of May 1972. Young Vietnamese pilots only a little better trained than their brothers of the Rolling Thunder campaign would hurl themselves, flying ageing aircraft, against better-trained American pilots flying better and more numerous aircraft. The historian might draw a parallel with the pilots of the Battle of Britain three decades earlier.

One of the curiosities of the air war over North Vietnam was the legend of 'Colonel Toon', who was a kind of Biggles or Red Baron of the Vietnam War. Many American pilots genuinely believed that he existed; in fact Lt. Randall H. Cunningham even believed he had shot him down on 10 May 1972. Unfortunately his victim may have been (as in most cases) only a novice North Vietnamese pilot who was flying for his life and beyond the abilities his American adversary gave him credit for. The existence of Colonel Toon in the mind of an American pilot may have provided a psychological comfort zone if a North Vietnamese pilot should out-fly him or, even worse, shoot him down. Nevertheless, the large majority of American pilots could have held their own against any opponent in the world and were generally held in high esteem by their North Vietnamese foes.

During the dry season of 1971 the North Vietnamese were transporting equipment southwards in preparation for the final attacks against the American-backed Southern government. The ability to make this offensive on land and in the air was largely due to the Soviet Union and Chinese governments, who supplied North Vietnam with an average of 22,000 tons of military equipment a month. The North Vietnamese also received hundreds of SA-2 surface-to-air missiles, which were medium altitude weapons. With this equipment, all American aircraft would be vulnerable to attacks from MiGs at high altitudes and to anti-aircraft gunfire at low level. (This would make places like Ha Noi the most dangerous place to be for an American flyer).

It was this build-up in armaments that eventually led to a renewed American intervention over the skies of North Vietnam. Before long, B-52 activity increased. As yet, the VPAF had failed to shoot down a B-52 so an all-out effort was made to observe their flight patterns. Two radar units were placed about 60 miles apart on the coast, one of them being only a few miles from the 17th

parallel in Vhin Linh and another near Ba Dan in North Vietnam.

On 20 October 1971, four MiGs were stationed in Vhin, an area that formed the crossroads of B-52 routes. Soon afterwards, two MiGs were flown (with great stealth) to a temporary base at Ann Son, about 50 miles northwest of Vhin and 18 miles from the Laotian border. North Vietnamese radar had tracked a group of B-52s over Ban Don, about 70 miles northwest of Vhin. The plan was for a single MiG 21 to make a firing pass at the American heavies and leave the combat area just as quickly. The pilots that were picked for these missions underwent special night and instrument training in the Soviet Union and were under no illusions as to the importance their task represented to North Vietnam, especially in propaganda terms. It would be a good morale-booster to all the other pilots too, even though North Vietnamese pilots usually suffered from over-confidence rather than the reverse.

On 4 October 1971, Dinh Ton flew his MiG 21 from Tho Xuan airbase to Dong Hai (Quang Binh Province) in readiness for his night mission. He flew at very low altitudes over the Pacific to evade the US Seventh Fleet's radar. He was guided at all times by Pham Ngoc Lan at ground control. Dinh Ton landed at Dong Hai at 1640 hours. His aircraft was quickly refueled and weapon systems checked. During this period Pham Ngoc Lan was given the responsibility to oversee anti-B-52 operations south of the 17th parallel.

At 1810 hours Vu Dinh Rang landed his MiG 21 at Dong Hai and it received similar refueling and weapon checks. The 921st FR scrambled one MiG 21 that was piloted by Dinh Ton to intercept a group of B-52s in order to try to shoot one of them down. When he took off he was directed to the bomber stream by ground radar. When he tried to turn on his internal radar, however, it was jammed by the Americans, using a system called 'College Eye' or 'Red Crown'. This system operated over North Vietnam and could track the frequency of the Fansong radar used by the MiG 21. This ECM (Electronic Counter Measures) system was used to track Dinh Ton, so he had to turn his internal radar off and use visual identification, which made it difficult, or well-nigh impossible, to see a bomber in the night sky. Nevertheless, he closed in on the bombers but he was now flying nearly blind without

A four-barrel 14.5 mm machine gun. The Self Defence unit of the Yenphu electricity plant operated this gun. This unit claimed an F-4 Phantom at 1200 hours on 10 July 1972. (Author)

ground or internal radar. Intercepting a group of B-52s with a single interceptor (having to close in to less than one mile) made Dinh Ton's survival chances poor, as the defensive guns of the B-52s would tear him to shreds. With little combat experience Dinh Ton could not locate the B-52s and the mission had to be aborted.

This mission is significant because it was the VPAF's first-ever attempt to shoot down a B-52 with a MiG. Dinh Ton was one of the first of the few North Vietnamese pilots skilled enough to fly a combat mission on his instincts alone without ground control or radar.

At 2000 hours on 20 October, Vu Dinh Rang was given a class one alert, put at cockpit readiness and given his orders. Like Pham Ngoc Lan seven years previously, he was on the brink of making aviation history for his people. It is interesting to note that Dinh Rang had little combat experience and no victories to his name at the time of this mission, but he was still regarded as qualified to fly this kind of mission. However, it must be said that he was far better trained than the previous generation of North Vietnamese pilots and therefore more able to perform such a challenge. The MiG 21 was chosen in preference to the MiG 17 because it had more advanced radar and could track incoming B-52s. It also had an extra 500 mph of speed over the MiG 17 and was therefore better for a quick get-away. The scramble order was given at 2025 hours and by 2045 hours Dinh Rang was closing in rapidly on the bomber. Until four minutes before contact, he kept to a strict flight pattern, flying low and keeping out of American radar range, with his own radar turned off to preserve his security. When he was about two minutes from contact he went into full power and climbed to 16,000 feet, the tension between pilot and ground control increasing all the time. When he reached his attack position he switched on his radar and dropped his tanks almost in one motion: from now on every second could make a difference. He was now tracking the B-52 carefully. On his final approach he applied full power again and as soon as he was within range he fired his ATOLL missile at the tail end of the B-52, holding his breath and hoping for success. He did not see any contact between missile and bomber so he made a hard right and dived for the deck, landing at a small airstrip in Anh Son about an hour after he took off. The B-52 was in fact hit but managed to limp home. This time the North Vietnamese failed but with each successive attack they came closer until the inevitable happened.

A 37 mm AA gun. This gun was operated by the Nguyen Viet Yuan Battalion which shot down 124 US aircraft. (Author)

An aerial reconnaissance photograph of a SAM site. These sites were rarely static and most were deployed around the Ha Noi and Hai Phong areas. (Vietnamese News Agency)

By this stage of the war, the North Vietnamese were receiving about 250,000 tons of supplies per year by sea and this volume was increasing. To try to stop this, the Americans started to attack supply routes, increasing their sortie rate by more than 300 per cent to over 3,150 sorties from June 1971 to June 1972. However, the North Vietnamese viewed this increase as an improved opportunity to shoot down a B-52. This would be regarded as a significant milestone in their history and a great propaganda victory.

However, there was to be no air-to-air success for North Vietnam until April 1972.

The reduction of bombing in late 1971 had brought an unsteady peace over the skies of North Vietnam. There was a temporary agreement between the Americans and North Vietnamese that no American aircraft flying over North Vietnam would be fired upon. On 7 and 8 November 1971 this tranquil period was broken when airfields at Dong Hoi, Vhin and Quang Lang were all attacked because the Vietnamese were accused of locking on to an American aircraft flying over North Vietnam. The locking incident was sufficient reason for renewal of hostilities. The VPAF had set up an advance airstrip just 40 miles from the Southern border for the sole purpose of shooting down a B-52. The Americans were monitoring this development and may have used the lock-on incident to attack this base but within 24 hours it was back in action, ready to be a nuisance to the American bombers throughout the war.

There are reports extant which testify the amount of effort the VPAF put into shooting down a B-52. On 20 November the VPAF decided to lure the B-52s into an ambush by using a decoy in the form of a MiG 21 ('Red

4320') flown by Dinh Ton. He was ordered to fly to an altitude of 19,200 feet, forcing the bombers to change course when they were informed of his presence. He was then ordered to climb to 25,600 feet to make sure all American warships picked him up on their radar. When the Americans were sure that Dinh Ton was out of range, the B-52s returned to their original flight pattern to Quang Binh. At that point another MiG 21 flown by Vu Dinh Rang took off from a small airstrip west of Nghe Ann province. Vu Rang turned off his lights and flew along the Truong Son range. He then tailed a group of six B-52s from a range of 94 miles. When he got to a range of nine miles he switched on his internal radar. From a range of 1,000 yards he fired his missiles and hit a B-52. He saw a fire start which spread to the wing of the bomber as it dropped its load to escape. This went down as a 'possible' kill as it was not seen to crash. This experience shows that the VPAF was on a very steep learning curve in terms of shooting down an American bomber.

The action for the night had just begun as those in the main ground control centre then saw all the blue arrows on their map pointing to Ha Noi! One ground controller recorded, 'They [the Americans] have deployed such a mixed force, even deploying helicopters to pick up any of their downed pilots ... they tried to keep this attack a secret but the size of this force made it impossible.' The Americans were targeting all known MiG bases: they hit Noi Bai at 2010 hours, Kep at 2015 hours, Yen Bai in the north at 2030 hours and Hoa Lac in the west at 2050 hours. In response, Dao Dinh (chief ground controller) ordered Dinh Ton and Dinh Rang to prepare to scramble and ordered Pham Tuan to level three status and await orders.

The attack force then climbed to a higher altitude after hitting the bases. The VPAF radar identified most of them as F-111s. The North Vietnamese respected this aircraft, which was it was hard to detect on radar because it had very sophisticated jamming devices, plus an autopilot system costing more than $15 million each. When Dinh Ton and Dinh Rang took off and returned without results, Pham Tuan was ordered to take off in a MiG 21 ('Red 4342'). He flew over the Red River where he was vectored towards eight F-4s that were escorting the B-52s farther along their route. The bombers were using a 6,000-feet mountain called Pha Luong as a marker - this indicated to the bombers that Ha Noi was only fifteen minutes' flying time away. When Dinh Ton was near his target, ground command then changed his radio frequency to number 4: Dinh Ton complied.

All MiGs in the area were similarly poised, but all had their radars jammed and therefore had to rely on visual recognition to attack. The B-52s were carefully protected because of Dinh Rang's victory on 20 November. Eventually the B-52s came within SAM range and so the MiGs had to return to base. By the time the other MiGs had landed, Pham Tuan had still not found an airstrip. Obviously he had a major problem, as his base was in Noi Bai and all landing lights were turned off because of the attacks. He would have to try to land in total darkness! He was about to eject as his MiG was now flying on empty tanks and the situation was critical. He was less than six miles from the airstrip and just a few seconds from ejecting when a SAM hit a B-52 above him, creating a large ball of yellow flame that lit up most of Ha Noi. Suddenly the airstrip was lit up too, and Pham Tuan was reported to have said, 'I see the airport clear, preparing to land.' The reply, '42 - you can land, check your speed' must have been music to his ears. He landed without incident. Thus ended another typical day of challenge and drama for the VPAF night-fighter pilots.

By the end of 1971 the VPAF would have four full fighter regiments but only about 78 MiGs would be operational, with another 40-plus being in various stages of repair. This would be more than double the number of fighters that the North Vietnamese had at the beginning of the war. Furthermore, 70 per cent of these aircraft would be the more advanced MiG 21 and the latest MiG 21MF was now entering service. The 921st and 927th FR were now fully converted to the new type and MiG 17 fighters would gradually dwindle in numbers after 1972. The Chinese had allowed the North Vietnamese the use of their airbases to convert to the MiG 19 and about 20 per cent of all fighters used by North Vietnam would be of this type. The 923rd Fighter Regiment would fly the MiG 19 until the end of the war.

Facing this little band of 'daring young men in their flying machines' were about 1,200 aircraft from the South Vietnamese Air Force. Many American air units had left or were in the process of leaving, but the USAF and USN still had at least 900 combat aircraft

at their disposal. The New Year (1972) would bring the greatest air battles yet seen over North Vietnam: the Vietnamese would call it their 'Dien Bien Phu of the Air' and the Americans would remember it as 'the Linebacker raids.' In many respects the action seemed like a forlorn hope for the Americans because shooting down more North Vietnamese MiGs would bring them some glory, but not victory.

The North Vietnamese were also now turning to a more offensive posture. As part of this change in tactics, the VPAF started to train its pilots in ground-attack roles using mostly the MiG 17s: this was because it had a slower top speed and was more able to survive taking hits from ground fire, making it more suitable for the task. The days of the MiG 17 as a first-line interceptor were over by the end of 1972. Ten pilots were selected from the 923rd Fighter Regiment and trained by foreign advisors from communist and eastern bloc countries for this ground-attack role. The most prominent of these advisors was a Cuban called 'Ernesto). The Cubans also sent specialist advisors to train North Vietnamese pilots to attack American warships: by the end of February 1972 half a dozen pilots were operational who had qualified in attacking maritime targets. All these pilots came from the 923rd Fighter Regiment which was equipped with MiG 17s. At this time the 403rd Radar Company based in Cua Nhat Le (only a few miles east of the Dong Hoi airbase) was tracking all US warship

All incoming raiders were plotted by hand on glass boards by female auxiliaries. (Vietnamese News Agency)

activity. To reflect the high priority given to this task, Commander Cao Thanh Tinh was stationed at Dong Hoi to take overall control of any attacks made against US ships. This was given such a high priority that Nguyen Phuc Trach, Deputy Commander of the Air Arm, took personal control of all air operations against US warships. He was stationed at Quang Trach in Quanb Binh Province.

The beginning of 1972 was also the beginning of the end of large-scale combat between Vietnamese MiGs and American aircraft. The American withdrawal was going ahead and nothing could change that by then.

The United States government was determined that 'Vietnamisation' was going to happen. This however, merely gave the Communists more confidence to start a land campaign with the objective of ending the war by the end of 1972. The air combats that took place were a direct result of the increasing North Vietnamese activity on the ground. The VPAF also started to increase its air activity by increasing its sorties and training missions: this was not without its price, as two pilots were lost as a result of accidents, one of them being Nguyen Van Tam, an experienced pilot with more than one hundred combat sorties to his credit.

On 18 January 1972, an RA-5 Vigilante reconnaissance aircraft was sent from the carrier USS *Constellation* to take photographs of Quang Lang airfield: there had been reports of growing numbers of MiG 21 MFs stationed there, poised to make intercepts over in Laos. The RA-5C was escorted by twelve F-4s but, as a diversion, a group of thirty-five aircraft comprised of A-6 Intruders, A-7 fighter-bombers and F-4Js flew towards Ha Noi. After making their diversionary flight paths (during which time they were being tracked by North Vietnamese observation units and radar units), they flew over an airfield well equipped with SAMs and anti-aircraft guns. The North Vietnamese opened up with all they could throw at the Americans. One of the F-4Js, flown by Lt. Randall H. Cunningham, evaded eighteen SAMs fired at his aircraft without taking any hits. The North Vietnamese then scrambled their MiGs, not to intercept the Americans but to fly for cover until the attack was over. It was then that Lt. Cunningham spotted two of these MiGs flying at very low level, trying to evade F-4s and SAMs. In response, Lt. Cunningham increased his speed and

closed in on the leading MiG, releasing a Sidewinder. The MiG pilot waited until the last moment then turned hard right, pulling higher and away all the time. Lt. Cunningham then eased off a little power and turned hard right. He thus managed to get inside the turn radius of the last MiG and fired a second Sidewinder: a few seconds later the MiG began to turn left, pulling in front of the F-4, but the missile hit the tail of the MiG before it could complete its turn and blew off its tail section, sending it crashing earthwards to its doom. This was the first fighter shot down in 1972 and the first by Lt. Cunningham. Many more fighters from both sides would be shot down before the end of 1972.

By the beginning of 1972 the VPAF began to regroup its meagre resources north of the 20th parallel in anticipation of the renewed American attacks to counter the North's coming offensive. The 921st FR, equipped with the latest MiG 21 MF fighters, were used in operations wherever they were needed. On 3 February the 927 '*Lam Son*' Fighter Regiment was activated (equipped with MiG 21PFMs): it was to protect areas above the 20th parallel and to support the 921st FR in covering Ha Noi and Haiphong. The east and northeastern parts of the country were to be protected by the 923rd FR's MiG 17s, while the the Chinese-supplied MiG 19s were given the task of covering the western and northwestern parts of the country.

Other arms of the air service continued to develop as well, with the small bomber arm having responsibilities for hitting ground targets and extending its training program. The only bomber squadron in operation in 1972 was the 929th Bomber Squadron which used Soviet-made Il-28s. The only transport squadron was the 919th Air Transport Regiment but it was largely ineffective because of American air superiority, which restricted both the air transport and bomber squadrons in carrying out any operations. The position became so bad that nearly all pilots were transferred to fighter squadrons and the Bomber Squadron was actually put into storage for a short period.

Air activity was steadily picking up in 1972 and on 21 February Major Robert Lodge became the first USAF pilot to down a MiG that year. The importance of this claim to the Americans was that it was also the first night kill of a MiG. Major Lodge was part of the famous 555th Tactical Fighter Squadron or 'Triple Nickel Squadron' and he was given the

MiG's position by 'Red Crown' and summarily shot down the MiG with a Sparrow missile. Lodge claims the MiG went down about 90 miles southwest of Ha Noi. The Vietnamese records do not confirm this kill and no pilots were lost in action on that day.

By the end of March 1972 American forces had declined to 20,000 Air Force personnel in Vietnam, but there were still 85 attack aircraft in South Vietnam and a further 245 in Thailand, of which 163 were F-4s. To back this up, the American Navy had another 170 combat aircraft at its disposal. The VPAF had about 60 MiGs (about 40 operational) and about 119 pilots who were in various stages of combat readiness. The MiG 21 had by now taken over from the MiG 17 as the mainstay of the VPAF's air defence and, contrary to popular belief, most Vietnamese pilots preferred the MiG 21 to the MiG 17 in all situations, except as a ground-attack aircraft. According to pilots such as Nguyen Nhat Chiew and Pham Ngoc Lan, Vietnamese pilots were very much more confident in taking on the American F-4 in a MiG 21.

On 29 March the North Vietnamese launched their long-awaited offensive. The main objective of this campaign was to confront the weak South Vietnamese Army, destroy it in one large offensive and capture a large section of the South. There were three main objectives; one was aimed at the town of Quang Tri, another was to push north over the Laotian border to take the town of Kontum (cutting the Southern army in half) and the third attack came from Cambodia to capture An Loc near Saigon. The North Vietnamese used twelve of their fifteen available army divisions in this daring gamble.

On 30 March Captain Fred Olmsted claimed a MiG 21 destroyed, but Vietnamese records do not show any MiG lost to enemy action that day. The MiG that Captain Olmstead attacked was one of three MiGs trying to shoot down an AC-130 gunship operating just inside North Vietnam. At this time nearly all MiG 21s were pulled to the far north around Ha Noi and Haiphong in anticipation of American retaliation, and only a few MiG 17s from the 923rd FR were used near the border in a ground-attack role.

When the invasion began, the Americans did not have the manpower on the ground to hold back the North Vietnamese over a sustained period. Their only weapon was air power and Nixon and his administration immediately put into operation a strategy

whereby air power would inflict such catastrophic losses on North Vietnam that its commanders would change their strategy: this was supposed to teach the North the folly of its ways. In this respect the Nixon government constantly misjudged the North Vietnamese people. The USAF units in Southeast Asia were eventually reinforced to a level where a major air campaign could be launched against North Vietnam. This reinforcement operation was codenamed 'Constant Guard' and large numbers of aircraft were moved. Within five weeks of 'Constant Guard', 1,200 aircraft of all types were ready for action against North Vietnam, which had about 55 MiGs at operational readiness to meet this threat. The stage was once again set where the few would take on the many (and eventually win).

By 14 April 1972 the North Vietnamese offensive had lost much of its impetus. The push for Saigon began to falter when the North's forces proved unable to take An Loc, since helicopters were supplying this besieged city. As a result, air activity began to escalate: the Americans claimed another MiG 21 destroyed on 16 April but North Vietnamese records do not corroborate this.

The North Vietnamese had been planning to attack the American Seventh Fleet since the early days of the war: by 1972 this was to become a reality. They knew that they could only achieve a 'pinprick' attack, but such an attack, if successful, would have obvious propaganda benefits and also make the Americans use up men and materials in preventing further attacks. A makeshift airfield with a very short runway was established in Quang Binh province: on 18 April, four MiG 17s were flown in to land at the tiny airfield at Gat and put on standby. The attack would consist of one flight of two MiG 17s that were specially modified to take off from short airstrips. The first flight consisted of Nguyen Van Bay (the younger) and Le Xuan Di, both of whom belonged to the 923rd Fighter Regiment. The MiG17s had to use a very short runway, since the VPAF did not want the Americans to spot it from the

Le Xuan Di scored two kills in MiG 17s during the Rolling Thunder campaign and survived the war as a Hero of Vietnam. (Vietnamese News Agency)

air, and therefore, booster rockets had to be attached to the aircraft. Truong Khanh Chau, a graduate of the Soviet Zhukovski Aviation Institute, was given the task of preparing the aircraft for the mission. On 19 April, the 403rd Radar Company tracked a group of American warships about 20 miles from Le Thuy, but bad weather prevented them from taking off immediately at 1500 hours; however, the all-clear was given shortly before 1600 hours.

When the order was eventually given to take off and attack the small group of ships less than 12 miles away, it was Van Bay, the flight leader, who took off first, followed by Xuan Di. They flew at low level towards the hills inland to conceal their intentions from American radar. This route took them along the coast to a rendezvous point: the whole team of four then banked towards Ly Hoa and the American ships came into view about five miles ahead. At this point all four MiGs increased power to full speed, each selecting a target. Van Bay'a aircraft flew over the destroyer USS *Higbee* and dropped a 550 lb bomb on it. Meanwhile, Xuan Did in the second MiG selected the USS *Oklahoma* as his victim. Xuan Di instantly claimed a hit with a 550 lb bomb. This certainly met flight objectives, so the team withdrew. On landing, Xuan Di's MiG was damaged, causing him to overshoot the short runway and he was fortunate to survive the ensuing crash. Nguyen Van Bay (the younger) landed last without incident. Sadly, he would lose his life two months later when he was shot down by an A-6. He is credited with shooting down one A-6 in combat.

The twenty-minute attack was hailed as a great moral victory. The Vietnamese could see columns of smoke coming from the direction of the US warships and this was sufficient proof of their success. The USS *Higbee* had sustained major damage and the USS *Oklahoma* received minor damage when it was hit in the stern. By this attack the North Vietnamese made a point to the Americans that the latter could not let their forces relax or lower their guard. The Vietnamese also realized that only superficial damage had been done but the attack would force the Americans to use up more men and material to prevent a repetition. This was at a point when US forces were already being scaled down in the area. The VPAF did not attempt another attack on the American fleet again as they had made their point.

The American response was to hit Dong Hoi and Vhin on 19 and 20 April. When they located the makeshift airfield at Gat on 22 April, they attacked it with a force of 33 aircraft, completely destroying one MiG 17 and damaging another. Because of this attack the VPAF abandoned Gat as a clandestine airstrip and all three remaining MiGs were withdrawn to Gia Lam.

On 27 April ground control scrambled four MiG 21s from Noi Bai with Hoang Quoc Dung and Cao Son Khao in the intercept flight, (Son Khao was to lose his life in the air battles on 10 May). Both MiGs were vectored to attack an American formation from behind and above. On this occasion all went according to plan, as two F-4s were seen by Quoc Dung and Son Khao flying at six o clock low about four miles away. Almost immediately both pilots were given the order to attack. Quoc Dung, as leading aircraft, got immediate missile lock and from about 1200 yards he fired a single ATOLL heat-seeking missile: it found its target, destroying the F-4 flying to his right. The F-4 blew up, with most of the wreckage being found near the town of Vu Ban about 55 miles southwest of Ha Noi. The rear seat pilot, Commander James B. Souder, ejected and survived to tell the tale. The other F-4 escaped by diving away.

Many Vietnamese pilots believed that the Soviet-made ATOLL was an excellent air-to-air missile and claimed that they rarely missed at range, which is contrary to the American view that it was a failure, scoring only three kills during the whole war.

With the increasing number of sorties flown by American aircraft over North Vietnam, the remaining MiG 21s were positioned around Ha Noi, Kep, Hoa Lac and Noi Bai airfields. A few were stationed at Yen Bai to cover American aircraft coming from Thai airfields. The North Vietnamese constantly moved their MiGs around during 1972 and it was common for more than one fighter regiment to use the same airfield at the same time (Kep and Gia Long being two examples of this).

North Vietnam also boosted its radar cover by activating the 26th Radar Company and expanding the 45th Radar Company.

By the end of April the Vietnamese had claimed another F-4 downed but lost one pilot killed in action in return.

10 Time of the Red Eagle

THE month of May 1972 heralded the beginning of large-scale air activity over North Vietnam. The Americans began the first of two air campaigns known as the 'Linebacker Raids'. The North Vietnamese in response threw everything they had into the skies, including any reserves, in order to inflict as heavy casualties as possible in order to sway US public opinion even more in their favour.

The level of air activity intensified from 8 May, when North Vietnamese radar units picked up four American fighters approaching Yen Bai at 16,000 feet. The VPAF interpreted this to be an attack on the base. Immediately two MiG 21s from the 921st Fighter Regiment were scrambled to draw the American fighters away: they acted as 'bait' by flying towards Tuyen Quang (about 60 miles northwest of Ha Noi). The US aircraft turned towards the two MiGs as hoped and at 0845 hours, four MiG 19s were scrambled to get behind the American fighters and 'bounce' them. At an altitude of 13,000 feet the four F-4s were spotted by the intercept flight, flying about two miles to their left. The American aircraft had been warned of their approach by the long-range radar from the Yankee station known as 'Red Crown'. All four F-4s turned into the MiG 19s and fired a salvo of four missiles, all of which missed. Nguyen Tiem Sam in the leading MiG had ordered his flight into a full dive at the Americans. In response the F-4s broke into two pairs in order to attack the MiGs from two sides. In seconds, the two MiG 19s on the left took on the two nearest F-4s and the other two MiG 19s dived after their two targets which were breaking away to the right.

The sky now witnessed two separate combats. Tiem Sam and his wingman evaded two missiles fired by a F-4 and evaded certain death by a series of erratic and sharp turns. Eventually, Tiem Sam got on the tail of the second F-4 and with height advantage dived on his erstwhile pursuer. The F-4 tried to use its better speed advantage by pulling hard and fast to starboard, but Tiem Sam had built up a great speed momentum in his dive and when he got the F-4 in his sight, he fired all his cannon in a three-second burst.

However, the American pulled up into a cloud as the tracer flashed past the left wing of his F-4. Having only seconds to adjust his position, Tiem Sam pulled his MiG 19 off to his left and dived on the other two F-4s. Closing in to about 800 yards he fired a series of short bursts, closing in all the time while the F-4 tried to escape into the clouds. The damaged aircraft finally plunged into the cloud and spiraled down, later crashing near Yen Bai. However, all this time the second F-4 was closing in on his wingman: Tiem Sam tried desperately to cover his comrade, but his MiG was beginning yaw from side to side, making it useless as a gun platform, and he was ordered to break away and land.

Meanwhile the other dogfight was being fought across the sky at lower levels. Pham Hung Son was chasing an F-4 which escaped by climbing to 6,500 feet, although the MiG continued to fire short bursts at it. In all the intensity of combat, Nguyen Hong Son, a very inexperienced pilot, released his braking parachute (for landing) by accident instead of dropping his tanks. The speed of his MiG caused the parachute to tear away, giving the impression that a pilot had ejected: worse still, the parachutes slowed the MiG down sufficiently for the second F-4 to fire a missile at him. Fortunately, he evaded certain death by weaving his MiG and this, combined with a few erratic turns, enabled him to evade the

Shenyang F6, 'Red 6058', was flown by Nguyen Hong Sno (Son A) credited with one kill, Pham Hung Son (Son B) - one kill, and Nguyen Hung Son (Son C) - three kills, all of the 925th FR. Each scored an F-4 Phantom kill. Vietnamese records show all three pilots survived the war. (Author)

Shenyang F6, 'Red 6058', 925th FR.

missiles. By this time the F-4 had gained sufficient speed to overshoot his MiG, giving Hong Son the chance to fire, but the F-4 flew into a cloud with Hong Son hot on his tail. The F-4 dived low to escape when it came out of the clouds, but Hong Son doggedly stuck to him. When the two fighters were at an altitude of only 1,600 feet the F-4 finally took cannon hits and flames erupted from it. At this point, Hong Son was ordered to break off the attack as he was too near a mountain. He landed only 30 minutes after he had taken off at Yen Bai. All four MiG 19s had returned safely.

The Americans claimed two MiG 21s and a MiG 17 downed that day, including a MiG 21 kill by Lt. Randall Cunningham. The North Vietnamese records show no MiGs or pilots lost on this day.

On 9 May 1972 President Nixon gave orders to start placing mines in Haiphong harbor to prevent any supplies from coming into North Vietnam. He thus started a siege campaign to force a change in North Vietnamese policy towards the South by air power alone.

10 May would usher in one of the most controversial days of the whole air war over North Vietnam. It would also be the first day of the Linebacker campaign, when the USAF would claim its first air ace of the conflict in the shape of Lt. Randall Cunningham.

The North Vietnamese had anticipated a major attack and had placed their MiGs in Yen Bai, Noi Bai, Gia Lam, Kep and Bac Mai to defend the Haiphong and Ha Noi areas. The total North Vietnamese fighter force did not amount to more than 55 serviceable aircraft at this point. By this time the VPAF senior command began to treat its fighter force as a single unit, with fighter regiments sharing airbases and equipment.

The Americans wanted to destroy North Vietnam's means and capacity to sustain the war. In order to accomplish this, the full might of its conventional air forces was to be unleashed upon the North. Part of this objective was the destruction of the MiG forces of the VPAF. All available aircraft from bases in Thailand, South Vietnam, Yankee Station and Guam were to be used in this unfettered offensive. Areas that were targeted were Haiphong, Bac Ninh, Phai Lai, Son Dong and Luc Ngan in Ha Bac province.

On the morning of 10 May, North Vietnamese radar had been tracking large numbers of carrier-based aircraft heading for the Haiphong area. Two MiG 21s from Kep were put on level 1 alert (i.e. pilots sitting on aircraft wings). The pilots were Dang Ngoc Ngu and Nguyen Van Ngai from the 921st FR. The North Vietnamese were aware that the Americans would send low-level fighters that would fly below radar cover and weave through mountains in order to catch any MiG on the ground but the necessity of intercepting the American fighter-bombers overrode any dangers this would pose. There were reports reaching VPAF command headquarters that F-105 fighter-bombers were on their way to bomb the Paul Doumer or Phu Luong Bridge, on Highway 5 which connected Ha Noi to Haiphong. At this point both pilots were put on a level 2 alert (which meant that they climbed into their cockpits).

The two MiG 21s were then given the scramble order at 0830 hours and without hesitation they made their way on to the runway. The weather was fine with a gentle wind, a little mist to the mountainous area to the north of the airbase, and some cloud cover. There was still with no reported enemy activity nearby. When the take-off order was received the two silver MiGs eagerly taxied forward, gradually increasing their speed. They had just lifted off, still with wheels down, when disaster struck. In a flash, four US Navy F-4J Phantoms came screaming up the runway at supersonic speeds. Almost immediately, four missiles were fired at the MiGs, one barely missing Van Ngai and exploding just outside his turn. Both MiGs dropped their tanks and banked to their right. Then another missile (fired by 2nd Lt. Curt Dose) hit Van Ngai's MiG, causing it to explode and killing him instantly. Ngoc Ngu was now on his own, virtually defenceless and being attacked by eight F-4s. To make matters worse, all communication between him and the control room had been knocked out by the American attack. He could only communicate with command HQ and the two other MiGs of Le Than Dao and Vu Duc Hop. As one eye witness recalled, 'We were all very worried for him, even though he was an excellent pilot with six victories to his name. However, he always fought in disad-vantageous situations so we hoped that he could parachute to safety.'

Ngoc Ngu knew in order to survive long enough for his MiG to get enough speed, he had to jinx his aircraft from side to side and fly as low as possible to the ground, making himself a difficult target. He managed to survive the first wave of missiles by weaving desperately as missile after missile tore past him: when he cut inside an F-4 to fire, he was forced to break off because another missile was on its way. He lost the opportunity to fire at least four times in this way. Eventually, by flying close to mountain sides and constantly turning, Ngoc Ngu found himself flying over the airbase and he could see the wreckage of the burning MiG. Ngoc Ngu's heart sank at the loss of his closest friend - Van Ngai's parents would lose a son forever; his young fiancé would lose a future. Such thoughts gave him more determination to survive and take revenge. The trails made by the missiles fired at him all round the airfield made him realize that he had to take the initiative or die. He had been evading certain death for ten minutes (an eternity in such situations). When he felt that he had gained sufficient acceleration, he began to turn defence into attack. With the instincts of a truly great fighter pilot, Ngoc Ngu pulled his MiG into a near vertical climb, darting towards supersonic speed. He directed his MiG into a cloud to conceal his next action. In one bold move, Ngoc Ngu had not only achieved a height and speed advantage but also gained the element of surprise before the F-4s below could make visual contact. He expected the Americans to use their speed advantage, to follow him into the climb, but not all the F-4s could accomplish this manoeuver before he came out of the clouds again. Ngoc Ngu then looped out of his climb, dived through the clouds and found himself, as he had planned, behind the last F-4. He quickly brought his prey into his sights and fired a missile at a range of 1,300 yards. The missile went straight into the exhaust of the F-4, causing it to blow up like a torch in the sky. Most of the wreckage fell on the Kep airbase near Van Ngai's burning MiG. This seemed to stun the American pilots, who then broke up in different directions. To take advantage of this chaos, Ngoc Ngu fired a second missile at another F-4, but unfortunately the missile jammed on its rails and the chance of another kill was lost. He then latched onto another F-4, switched to his 12.7 mm guns, and began firing. The F-4 seemed to take a few hits but still managed to get away with some damage. As the sky had cleared, Ngoc Ngu called it a day, landing at Noi Bai at 0915 hours.

Because of this combat, Dang Ngoc Ngu was awarded the title 'People's Military Forces Hero'. (The description of this combat was summarized from eyewitness accounts and from the combat statements of Dang Ngoc Ngu himself.)

The Americans then switched their attentions to Ha Noi and the surrounding area at 0930 hours, but F-4s kept a 'cap' over the fighter bases at Kep and Noi Bai. Two MiG 21s were scrambled from Noi Bai at 0944 hours to fly towards Tuyen Quang, about 60 miles northwest of Ha Noi. They hoped this would draw American fighters away from the bases. Also from Noi Bai, four MiG 19s of the 925th FR took off: the intercept flight was headed by Pham Hung Son, with Cao Son Khao as his wingman. Both pilots found themselves in combat the moment they took off, both firing their cannon at F-4s flying around them but they scored no hits. They soon found themselves in a turning dogfight with four F-4s from the 432nd Tactical Reconnaissance Wing (based at Udorn). Hung Son soon turned inside a F-4 and fired his cannon at a distance of 750 yards. The F-4 seemed to slow down as Hung Son continued his attack, firing again at 250 yards. This time the F-4 blew up into two halves and crashed outside Kep. Captain J. Harris and Captain D. Wilkins, both of whom are listed as killed in action, may have flown this aircraft. Then Cao Son Khao engaged the other F-4, but Cao Son was himself being followed by an F-4 and he had to break away after firing three two-second bursts. Unfortunately Cao Son's aircraft was hit, possibly by a SAM: he died the same day of his injuries. It is very possible that Captain Lodge, who fired a Sparrow missile at a MiG 21, in fact shot down Cao Son, although this cannot be confirmed from North Vietnamese reports. The remaining MiG pilot managed to land at Noi Bai airfield with sixteen cannon holes in his aircraft. The whole combat lasted for about 25 minutes. The covering flight also had problems, mainly with low fuel levels. Pilot Nguyen Duc Tiem had to attempt a landing at a steep angle from a height of 5,000 feet, making him overshoot the runway in spectacular fashion. He survived but his MiG 17 was completely destroyed.

The second MiG 19 flight took off to take over: this team consisted of Nguyen Ngoc Tam, Nguyen Thanh Long, Phung Van Quang and Le Van Tuong. They immediately found themselves in the thick of the action against four F-4s from 'Oyster Flight' from the 555th TFS based at Udorn. In the midst of the battle,

The self Defence unit of the Yenphu Electricity plant operated this four-barrel 14.5 mm AA gun. It shot down an F-4 Phantom on the 10 May 1972 at 1200 hours. (Author)

The 77th Missile Battalion operated this SAM. This unit was honoured when it shot down three B-52s on 20 December 1972 over Hanoi. (Author)

This UL-269 bulldozer was used by the 28th Field Engineer Battalion. (Author)

Le Duc Oanh was one of the six pilots killed on the 10 May 1972. The American Ace Captain Richard S.Ritchie may have shot him down. (Vietnamese News Agency)

Captain Richard S. Ritchie fired two Sparrow missiles from 2,000 yards, shooting down a MiG 21 flown by Duc Oanh. The MiG was observed to have blown up, instantly killing the pilot. At this point the remaining MiG 19s dived from above, with Le Van Tuong firing at the leading F-4 flown by Captain Lodge. He immediately saw hits and closed in and fired a second burst, by which time the F-4 started to smoke and go into a flat spin. Captain Locher in the back seat ejected and parachuted to the ground, where he was taken captive, but Captain Lodge, with at least three kills to his credit, was sadly killed in this action. (It has been said that Captain Lodge's victor that day was the famous Le Thanh Dao, however Thanh Dao was not flying MiG 19s but MiG 21s during this phase of the war.) Van Quang got behind another F-4 and fired three times but did not register any hits and the F-4 escaped.

The MiGs were in the air for nearly 20 minutes: the pilots knew they were running low on fuel and had to land, even though American fighters were circling the base. All four MiGs had to make emergency landings, coming in at high speeds, otherwise they risked being shot down. The first to land was Nguyen Ngoc Tam who managed to get in without any mishap. Next, Van Quang came in but excess speed meant that he overshot the runway: fortunately both plane and pilot were safe. Then Le Van Tuong tried to land, completely out of fuel: he lost control of the MiG when he tried to land at a 45-degree angle. He hit the runway so hard that the inertia dragged the MiG over the edge of the runway, killing him with the initial impact. The victor over Captain Lodge had himself been killed on the same day. Thanh Long, on his approach to land, was attacked by two F-4s, but he managed to turn inside the American fighters who themselves turned away and left the scene, allowing Thanh Long to land at 1047 hours. The North Vietnamese

had lost six MiGs and four pilots, but only three MiGs were actually shot down through enemy action. In return the North Vietnamese claimed three F-4s shot down. The VPAF had scrambled eight MiG 19s and four MiG 21s to meet the American threat even though as many as 30 MiGs were in the air as covering flights. There was only going to be a few hours' rest for each side before the next attack, as the most controversial episode of the battle began in the early afternoon.

The North Vietnamese expected heavier attacks in the afternoon so all-available fighters, numbering about 30 MiGs of all types, were on standby awaiting the next onslaught. Many pilots were under the greatest of strain, having to cope with a war of nerves. At 1225 hours a strike force of 26 aircraft, comprising A-6s and A-7s with their F-4 escorts (from the 'Fighting Falcons') were tracked by ground radar, trying to attack Hai Dong and the bridges at Lai Vu and Phu Luong. The intercept flight of the 923rd FR scrambled four MiG 17s, flown by Nguyen Van Tho, Ta Dong Trung, Tra Van Kiem and another pilot. The MiGs spotted A-7s trying to bomb the bridges and at once dived to engage them. Dong Trung started to fire at an A-7 but did not get any result and he turned back, flying along the coast using the Thai Binh River as a visual guide and landed back at Kep. Meanwhile Van Tho was attacking an A-7 but did not see any hits as the American fighter-bomber escaped. The other two MiG 17s were attacking a single A-7, which seemed to stray into the combat to admire the scenery after having dropped its bomb. As both MiGs closed in for the kill, two F-4s came from behind and before Van Tho could warn his comrades the leading F-4 fired a Sidewinder and hit Van Kiem s MiG 17, causing it to go into a fatal spin. Amazingly, Van Kiem managed to eject. (Lt. Michael J. Connolly may have achieved this victory.) It was reported that Van Kiem was killed by fire from a F-4 as he came down in his chute. No attacking aircraft were lost and Connolly and his radar operator (Lt. Thomas J. Blonski) were both later awarded the Navy Cross for their bravery in this action. The fourth MiG 17 managed to escape. Van Tho was also attacked by an F-4 but he managed to turn inside its path and fire his cannon until he ran out of ammunition. Immediately he tried to break away to return to Kep but was caught by another F-4 and was shot down by a missile. Van Tho managed to eject and lived to tell the tale.

The MiG 17 was now way past its operational peak. The loss rate of 50 per cent from nearly every combat sortie it participated in forced the VPAF to plan the withdrawal of all MiG 17 fighters as front-line interceptors.

More waves of American aircraft were streaming towards their targets in Ha Noi and Haiphong. All available MiG 21s from the 927th FR were then scrambled, with Le Thanh Dao and Vu Duc Hop leading this intercept flight, and were vectored by ground control to an altitude of 35,000 feet, about 21 miles from Hai Dong.

At 1030 hours, two squadrons were vectored to intercept a formation of 24 A-6 and A-4 fighter-bombers escorted by 12 F-4B Phantoms. One squadron, consisting of two MiG 21s flown by Le Thanh Dao and Vu Duc Hop, were to intercept the American formation from above. The other squadron, made up of MiG 17s, was to intercept the same formation by attacking from below. The MiG 17 squadron claimed an A-4 shot down on its first pass as they reached the American formation ahead of Thanh Dao and Duc Hop. The MiG 17s lost one of their strength when Squadron Commander Le Van Tho was shot down by an F-4, (although he survived without injuries when he ejected). At this point the remaining MiG 17s broke off this engagement, leaving the two MiG 21s to deal with the American formation by themselves. Thanh Dao was vectored to deal with these 'Black Crows' by the legendary flight controller Le Thanh Chon, who ordered him to drop his tanks about 20 miles from the American formation.

Thanh Chon recalled, 'I wanted to make it clear to Thanh Dao that he was going to attack the interceptors as the American bombers had already left the scene. He accepted the situation without hesitation and immediately increased his speed to attack.' At this point four F-4s broke off their combat with the MiG 17s and flew to meet the two incoming MiG 21s, flown by Thanh Dao and Vu Duc. Two F-4s were spotted at a distance and Thanh Dao was able to follow their 'calling card' smoke trails. As both MiGs closed in, four missiles were fired at them by the F-4s but Thanh Dao evaded them with skill that few could match - the Americans knew this was no rookie pilot! The F-4s flew in different directions in order to split the MiG formation. The first F-4 dived under Thanh Dao, giving him no chance to fire. The second F-4 pulled into a steep climb but Thanh Dao followed the F-4 in this climb (a maneouver 2nd Lt. Cunningham claims to have experienced on this same day). Thanh Dao realized that he was facing American pilots of great skill when he was unable to get into any reasonable firing position – they covered each other with uncanny teamwork.

Thanh Dao used all his skill to try to break up the American formation. When the chance came, he fired a missile at 1,600 yards at the leading F-4 , causing it to blow up in mid-air. (The wreckage of this aircraft was found in the Hai Dong area.) Using their height advantage Thanh Dao ordered his wingman Vu Duc to attack four F-4s flying at a lower level who were trying to make a break for home. Vu Duc successfully targeted the second F-4, his missile producing a ball of flame in the sky. The two MiGs then left as quickly as they arrived and were vectored back to home base in Kep, landing with two confirmed kills. These kills were the 927th FR's very first victory claims of the war. (The above combat is taken from the statements Le Than Dao.)

The victories had such an impact on the American pilots that on 15 May Reuters in Bangkok quoted one of them saying that they were attacked by a 'Terrible Red Eagle'. Because of this, many ex-VPAF members still know Le Thanh Dao as the 'Red Eagle'.

The Americans began to attack in earnest again after 1400 hours and the most controversial moments of the battle were about to unfold. The Americans used about 30 aircraft to attack the Bac Mai airbase. In response, the North Vietnamese scrambled eight MiGs to act as an intercept flight. Two other flights covered the airbases of Noi Bai and Hoa Lac. Two more MiG 21s were scrambled from Kep to intercept an American formation (F-105s and F-4 escorts) heading for Ha Noi. Another two MiG 21s were vectored to Ha Noi and ordered to fly at 2,000 feet higher than the F-105s. This pair was ordered to intercept the Americans when they were flying at a distance of eight miles from the fighter-bombers. After a few minutes the pilots noticed four F-4s to their left flying at an altitude of 22,000 feet. When they got within striking range, Ngo Van Phu and Ngo Day Thu turned in to attack the F-105s, dropping their fuel tanks in the process to increase their speed. After closing to within 1,000 yards, Van Phu fired a missile and saw it hit and destroy one F-105. By this time the escorting F-4s had also closed in on the MiGs and Ngo Duy did some very erratic and violent manoeuvers to evade the F-4 that had latched on to him. He knew it was closing in on him continuously and he just evaded a missile that was fired at him. Fortunately, he managed to escape and land at Noi Bai in one piece. Duy Thu may have crossed swords and survived a combat with the American ace, Lt. Cunningham.

The battle dragged on a little longer for Van Phu, who followed a group of F-4s and fired a missile at a range of 1,400 yards: this hit an F-4, which did not seem to take any evasive action and crashed into the sea. This victory may have been exceptional since the victim was possibly Lieutenant Cunningham. The American has claimed a SAM shot him down at this stage of the battle, although he ejected safely. The Americans have asserted that Lt. Cunningham shot down three MiGs in succession during this period of the afternoon, which would give him the status of 'ace', but in the excitement of combat even the best pilots can over-claim. Both Lt. Cunningham and Lt. Steven C. Shoemaker claim to have shot down a MiG 17 at 1401 hours exactly. The possibility that both pilots were shooting at the same aircraft must be high.

Furthermore, Cunningham claims to have shot down another MiG 17 around the Haiphong area after 1401 hours, but no MiG 17s are reported to have intercepted incoming aircraft at that time. Most claims were usually verified by gun camera evidence but as Cunningham's F-4 crashed into the sea it can be assumed that such evidence was not available to confirm his kills. The circumstances surrounding Lt. Cunningham's claims do not throw any questions on this great fighter pilot, but merely show how pilots on both sides may have inadvertently over-claimed or even under-claimed! Perhaps the desire for the Navy to celebrate its first ace of the war was the overwhelming factor.

The whole month of May continued to see a rise in American air activity as their fighters began to hit runways, parked MiGs and any target that might be of use to the North Vietnamese. Many MiGs were also attacked as they took off and the VPAF began to lose pilots in this way. For example, Vo Sy Giap (an 'F-4 killer' himself) was killed when his MiG 21 was bounced by an F-4 when taking off from Kep on 11 May. As the intensity of air strikes took their toll, ground control units began to vector intercept flights to more than one target, thus creating a high degree of confusion between pilots and radar units. To make matters worse, units flying the MiG 17 were seldom in a position to successfully complete any mission due to the age of their aircraft. In addition, many of the older pilots who did so very well in the early battles (1965 to 1969) could not keep pace with the new and faster type of conflict: as their rate of victories slowly began to whittle down, many of these pilots were promoted to non-flying positions and instructor roles.

On 12 May four MiG 19s from the 925th FR shot down an F-4 over Ha Noi but lost one aircraft, although the pilot ejected safely to fight again. 18 May saw the 925th FR achieve further success when its intercept flight of two MiG 19s shot down another F-4 over Noi Bai, but lost two of its aircraft to enemy fire (although the pilots survived). Their victors were most likely Lt. Henry A. Bartholomew and Lt. Patrick (Pat) Arwood, both using AIM 9.

Later in the day a mixed bag of two MiG 17s from the 923rd FR, two MiG 19s from the 925th FR and two MiGs from the 921st FR were scrambled from Kep to intercept American fighters over their airfield. The MiG 17s began fighting in pairs, making the most of their maneuverability by harassing the F-4s from close range. This tactic paid off when the first kill went to a MiG 17 using its cannon at only 300 yards range. When the F-4s pulled away from the slower MiG 17s, another two MiG 21s came in on them and downed another adversary from 200 yards range with a missile.

On 20 May Do Van Lan shot down an F-4 with a missile over Sui Rut just before the American fighter was about to kill his flight leader. 23 May saw Nguyen Hung Son, Pham Hung Son, Nguyen Van Dien and Vu Van Dang take their MiG 19s into the skies to intercept twelve or more F-4s from the 366th TFW (based at Da Nang). The MiG flight entered combat the moment they took off from Yen Bai so they separated into two flights of two aircraft. The first flight, consisting of Hung Son and Pham Hung Son, were vectored to fly along the Red River. Both pilots managed to turn into the unprotected tails of four F-4s and shot down one each over Yen Bai. However, the covering flight (Nguyen Van Dien and Vu Van Dang) was

attacked by four F-4s: before they could take any evasive action both pilots were shot down and killed. The Americans claimed four victories, with Lieutenant Commander Ronald McKeown claiming two MiG 19s that day. On the same day, two MiG 21s from the 921st FR engaged F-4s, shooting down one, but the identity of the victorious pilot in this skirmish was never established. Many North Vietnamese pilots at this stage were very inexperienced and the opportunities for victories were never fully exploited. They were keeping pace with the Americans in terms of victories, but they could not afford to take the losses like their opposition could. On the plus side, American public opinion was slowly turning against the war and every American aircraft shot down would, in some way, affect that opinion even further.

During the latter part of May 1972 the 921st FR, flying MiG 21s, took the brunt of the intercept duties as other units were being held back as reserves or because of mounting losses.

At the end of May a high-level VPAF conference was called, with all squadron leaders, to discuss what change of tactics could be adopted and how such changes could be implemented. Pilots such as Pham

Ngoc Lan were instrumental in advising how the MiG 17 could be used in conjunction with the faster MiG 21s. Furthermore, the number of combat-ready pilots was increased. The senior command decided to allow its pilots more independence to act according to their instincts, but because of the large number of inexperienced pilots this was never universally applied.

In May, the VPAF lost twelve pilots killed and more than twenty MiGs destroyed, which represented 30 per cent of all new pilots supplied for the whole year and about 25 per cent of its MiG strength. On the plus side the North Vietnamese claimed at least seventeen American aircraft destroyed, sixteen of them being F-4s. The Americans claimed twenty-seven MiGs shot down, seventeen of them MiG 17s and ten MiG 21s.

Ground crew assist the pilots of MiG 21 MFs to deplane after an operation. In general, the VPAF left its MiGs in a natural metal finish with camouflage being applied only for specific operations. (Vietnamese News Agency)

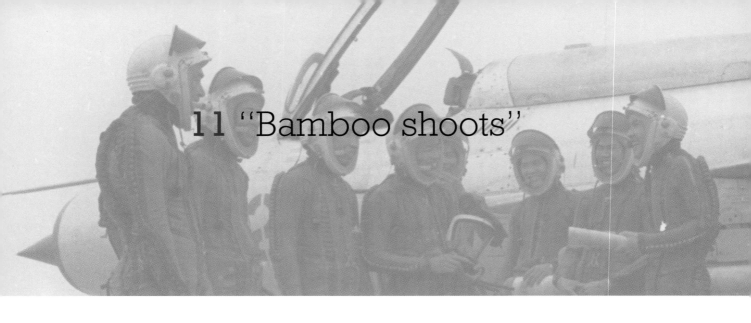

11 "Bamboo shoots"

DURING June 1972 the Americans stepped up their campaign to destroy the industrial heart of North Vietnam. The objective was to bomb vital targets in order to bring the country to a standstill, making the North Vietnamese pay for their offensive in the South.

The Americans constantly watched the North Vietnamese airfields and most fighter units had to be dispersed to smaller airfields. Many MiGs were kept in makeshift huts, disguised as living quarters for farmers when seen from the sky, while others were parked close to mountain sides. MiG 21s would use small dirt runways with small booster rockets attached to them to give extra lift in quick take-offs. In this way the VPAF could put up fighters throughout the campaign. Nevertheless MiG 17s were now slowly being phased out, flying fewer and fewer sorties, and it is not surprising that the 923rd FR, equipped with MiG 17s, had very little success during the last six months of 1972.

On 2 June, more than 250 USAF and USN aircraft were used to hit all strategic targets in North Vietnam. During the day, MiG 19s from the 925th FR and MiG 21s from the 921st FR twisted and turned in dogfights: on a few occasions they prevented the Americans from completing their objectives, but fatigue and the weight of numbers took their toll. Two MiG 17s attacked four American F-4s when they became separated from their main formation. The MiGs attacked from a near-perfect position from behind, opening fire with their cannon from 700 yards. However, the pilots concerned were not very experienced: they stopped firing and pulled away instead of pressing home their advantage. However, flight leader Pham Trong Van carried on the attack alone and became involved in a turning dogfight

with two F-4s. Meanwhile, Trong Van became sandwiched between two other F-4s. When he seemed to be in a firing position on the lead aircraft, the second F-4 (flown by Major W. Handley) fired a 300-round burst from a range of only 100 yards. Trong Van's MiG 19 took cannon hits along the wing root, causing it to go into a dive with its left wing breaking off before it crashed into the ground. Trong Van was killed instantly. It was the only MiG lost that day to enemy action.

On 8 June the Americans attacked targets in the southern part of North Vietnam with B-52s, destroying communications and storage facilities. Surprisingly, the VPAF did not scramble any intercept missions that day, even though B-52 flight patterns were carefully observed.

10 July brought some success for a pair of MiG 21s from the 921st FR. They attacked and destroyed an F-4, first with a missile hit and then with cannon fire from close range as it was attacking Lang Chi hydro-electric plant. The F-4 may have belonged to the 8th Tactical Fighter Wing.

At this point, the Americans began to hit dams and dykes in order to cause extensive destruction to rice fields and to increase the dislocation of the human population: this tactic caused thousands of deaths downstream of such raids. The policy has never been affirmed officially by the Americans, but such attacks continued to happen with regularity.

North Vietnamese fighters continued to intercept American attacks with even more ferocity. It must be noted that extensive damage was never inflicted on the major dams even though the Americans had the ability to do so. On July 11 the older MiG 17s were again pressed into action when two of their number from the 923rd FR intercepted

Using models, Nguyen Doc Soat shows to pilots and groundcrew how he would make an approach on an enemy aircraft. He is credited with six kills. (Vietnamese News Agency)

The Van Dien Phosphate Fertilizer factory used this twin barrel 14.5 mm A.A. gun. This gun shot down a F-4 Phantom on 12 June 1972. (Author)

As a pilot of the elite 921st FR, Do Van Lanh scored four kills .His first was scored against an F-4 Phantom on 20 May 1972 over Phu Ly in a MiG 21. (Vietnamese News Agency)

A well respected pilot to all that flew with him, Dong Van De was the son of Major General Dong Bay Cong. Van De was born in the south and moved North in 1954. he was the first Vietnam trained MiG 21 pilot. (Vietnamese News Agency)

33 American aircraft along the Red River. One F-4 was shot down by Nguyen Van Phuc (as seen by his wingman). In the ensuing combat, his MiG took a hit from a F-4 flown by Commander Foster S. Teague (from the USS *Coral Sea*), resulting in both pilot and aircraft being lost. In trying to escape, the other MiG 17 was destroyed by another F-4, flown by Lieutenant Winston W. Copeland. The Warrant Officer pilot ejected and was saved.

The dismal combat record of the MiG 17s did not improve when they took part in intercept missions without the co-operation of MiG 21s, as they either failed to make contact or were shot down. Only the most talented and experienced pilots such as Nguyen Van Bay were able to return from missions unscathed.

13 July proved more fortunate for the MiG 21s of the 921st FR when Do Van Lanh and Phan Phu Thai intercepted an American force of 33 aircraft from the USS *Saratoga*, who were attacking the Phu Ly bridges and transport staging areas. The Americans were also targeting rail and road bridges around the area. The MiGs were given the scramble order and were climbing into the American formation only five minutes after take-off as the weather was clear that day. When the MiGs closed in, Van Lanh fired an ATOLL at the last of four F-4s. He saw the missile shoot up and curve into the target, followed by a flash of light, but not wanting to hang around amongst a swarm of angry F-4s to confirm his kill, he dived for low level and escaped. No visual confirmation of this kill was made but the wreckage of an F-4 was found in the area of Vhin Phu so the kill was credited to Van Lanh.

This was not the end of Vanh Lanh's scoring streak as, on 21 June, four MiG 21s from the 921st FR attacked a flight of F-4s from VF-31 based on the USS *Saratoga*. The formation broke up before it could reach its target, unnerved by Do Van Lanh's attack from the covering clouds, and his shooting down of an F-4 with cannon fire (this is known as a cobra kill by the VPAF). This was

the second kill to his credit. He then attacked another F-4 and saw it breaking to his left. He fired both his missiles in quick succession but could not confirm any hits. (Colonel Vojvodich may have flown this aircraft.) The Americans claimed two MiGs downed and another damaged. The North Vietnamese have no records of any MiGs lost to enemy action that day.

On 24 June some 35 US aircraft attacked industrial targets in the Thai Nguyen district and targets along Route package 1. Two MiG 21s from the 921st FR were scrambled to attack this formation with Nguyen Duc Nhu and Ha Vhin Thanh at the controls. The ground control unit directed them over Thanh Son to lure the escorting F-4s away from the main American formation. This enticed an F-4 to attack the MiGs: in unison both MiGs broke away and the F-4 started a deadly chase of 'catch me if you can' over the skies of Vietnam. The covering flight, with Ngo Duy Thu and Nguyen Doc Soat, was ordered by ground control to increase the pressure on the Americans by closing in on the main formation. For some reason, none of the F-4s seemed to react to this second attack so Doc Soat, not needing any second invitation, calmly lined up his MiG and killed the tail end F-4 with a missile. When Doc Soat tried to fire again, he found that his closing speed had brought him too close for a missile kill so he broke left and fired his cannon but he had lost his momentum and did not see any hits. The rest of the US formation dived for safety and this gave Doc Soat the chance to turn and head for Noi Bai where he landed to fight another day.

Meanwhile the lone F-4, which was chasing the two MiGs in another part of the sky, was caught in a pincer movement. The MiG 21s of Vhin Thanh and Duc Nhu broke in two opposite directions and began to attack their isolated prey from two sides. Before long, Duc Nhu got behind the F-4 and shot it down with a missile as it was about to take evasive action from an attack by Vhin Thanh. After this kill, Duc Thu dived on another F-4 coming to help his stricken comrade. The area was becoming a target-rich environment for any daring MiG pilot: he fired again at a second F-4 but did not score any hits as his target seemed to pull into a power dive and as the ATOLL missile missed its mark and hit the ground.

Later in the afternoon, at about 1540 hours, Nguyen Van Nghia and Nguyen Van

Tranh Hanh (far right) briefs pilots before take-off. The pilots are wearing full G-suits and Soviet supplied GS-1 helmets. 'Red 4320' was a MiG-21 PF which was finished in natural metal. (Vietnamese News Agency)

Toan attacked a small formation of F-4s that strayed from the main body. Although they were detected, the speed of their attack brought them into the midst of the American formation and both pilots fired their missiles. Van Toan scored a direct hit on the F-4 flying on the extreme right, causing the aircraft to go into a spin and crash a few moments later. The North Vietnamese claimed three F-4s downed that day without loss to themselves.

By the end of June the new commander of the American forces, General F. C. Weyand, was given the responsibility by President Nixon of defeating the latest Communist offensive in the South. This was to make sure that the American withdrawal from Vietnam progressed smoothly. The military situation on the ground for North Vietnam began to worsen: supply levels became ever smaller as the constant attacks from the air began to take their effect. The North Vietnamese had begun to win the political war, but it would take nearly three more years before it could win the military war. During May and June that year the Americans had dropped 3,000 tons of ordnance on North Vietnamese targets and 90 per cent of it had hit its mark.

It has been calculated that North Vietnamese imports had fallen to 30,000 tons a month in June from a pre-bombing level of 160,000 tons. President Nixon was even quoted as saying, 'The situation has been completely turned around'. Because of American attacks the Vietnamese leadership decided to shift its air force headquarters from Gia Lam to Ngoc Dong. The airbase at Gia Lam was relegated to the role of a fighter-cum-transport base. It was primarily used by the 921st FR but other units used this base to concentrate their defensive response when Ha Noi was attacked. The blockade of Hai Phong harbour meant that jet fuel was kept hidden in underground storage facilities at Gia Lam. However, this did not amount to more than 200,000 tons.

One of the ironies of the American bombing was that petrol and oil levels actually rose during this period by 35% than before the bombing! In contrast, the operational level of all MiGs had fallen to only 20 per cent of available fighters because of a serious lack of spare parts and because of the pitiful numbers of trained technicians (less than 40 per cent of the number that were needed). This resulted in the increasing

An APA-46 (QK-41-69) electric starter truck operated by the 12th Company of the 927st Fighter Regiment. This truck was used on 11,800 occasions. (Author)

numbers of advisors from China, the USSR and all Warsaw Pact countries. Chinese-trained technicians were preferred as there was still an element of mistrust of Russian technicians working on MiG 21s. (Most of the Russians were stationed in Noi Bai and Kep.)

The end of June saw the arrival of the last MiG 17-trained pilots. From July all pilots would be trained on the MiG 21 and conversion training would proceed with current MiG 17 pilots. All told, the VPAF received about 35 new fighter pilots during the course of the year, but lost 32 killed in action in 1972 alone! In addition, plans were drawn up to shoot down that elusive B-52 and 18 hand-picked pilots were selected to undergo instrument and all-weather training in Russia for that purpose. The radar units and ground control units were further integrated for this aim.

The month of June accounted for twenty-one American aircraft over North Vietnam, MiGs claiming thirteen of these but losing eight of their own, with three pilots being killed in the process. The Americans admit to these losses but state only two aircraft lost to MiGs. Whatever the true figures, pilots from both sides were being killed with unwelcome regularity. It is no wonder that morale was low among pilots from both sides as losses mounted. Lt. Fred Knee, who flew A-7s from the USS *Kittyhawk* in 1972, recalled, 'Guys were getting killed and the morale of the ship and our squadron plummeted.' Nguyen Nhat Chieu of the 921st FR commented that '...pilots died like green bamboo shoots in a storm.' Even so, pilots from both sides did their duty until they died or the war ended.

MiG 17F, 'Red 2047', was
flown by Nguyen Van Bay,
the younger, (KIA 6.5.72) to
bomb the US destroyer
'Higbee' on 19 April 1972.
This MiG still carries the type
of 500 lb bomb that was
used in that raid. (Author)

1:72 Scale

MiG 17F, 'Red 2047', flown by Nguyen Van Bay, 923rd FR, May 1972

12 The tide changes

BY the beginning of July the Americans began to lose the initiative in the air war and this trend continued until the end of the conflict.

On 5 July Nguyen Tiem Sam and Ha Vhin Thanh took off in their MiG 21s and were vectored to intercept F-4E Phantoms carrying bombs to hit the airfield at Kep. The Tiem Sam and Thanh both arrived just as the F-4s were turning for home base over the Ha Bac area. The MiG pilots flew lower than the American formation and both Vietnamese pilots could see the F-4s as inviting targets 'hanging like lemons' waiting to be shot. When Tiem Sam guided his MiG to about 2,200 yards, he let fly a missile, which looked like a sure kill even though the ATOLL exploded before hitting its target. Strangely, the Americans did not seem to react to this as Tiem Sam closed in to about 1,100 yards, firing at the second F-4 in the group. The missile seemed to hit the F-4 dead centre in its exhausts and it blew up in a ball of flame. Miraculously both US pilots managed to eject. Meanwhile, Vhin Thanh had his own ambitions and went directly for the leading F-4, which sensed danger and broke right. However, before it could complete its getaway, Ha Vhin fired both his missiles and saw hits on its wing. Captain Don Logan, who was flying this F-4, recalled, 'As we rolled I felt a violent jar, and looked out to see the outboard portion of the left wing, past the wing fold, badly damaged … I looked over my shoulder and saw a North Vietnamese MiG 21 … both his rails were empty.' Captain Logan and his back-seat radar operator ejected into safety, but eventually found themselves as residents at the Ha Noi Hilton!

The Americans came back for revenge on 8 July when three MiG 21s from the 927th FR were shot down. The opening kill of the day

was claimed by Captain Richard F. Hardy flying an F-4E from the 4th Tactical Fighter Squadron. It began when two MiG 21s attacked from above, making a cannon-armed 'cobra' attack and closing on Captain Hardy with each second. He responded by reducing his speed, making the MiG 21 overshoot him: before it could react Captain Hardy fired two Sparrow missiles, destroying the North Vietnamese aircraft. The pilot, Vu Van Hop, was killed.

The other two MiG 21s were destroyed by the future American ace, Captain Steve Ritchie, flying an F-4E from the 555th TFS. Both MiGs were vectored to what was known as Banana Valley, 30 miles south-west of Ha Noi. Captain Ritchie recalls, 'I maneuvered to a 5 o'clock position on the number two MiG [Nguyen Ngoc Hung], obtained an auto-acquisition bore sight radar lock and fired two AIM–7 Sparrow missiles. The first missile impacted the number two, causing a large fireball as the MiG broke into parts.' The pilot (Ngoc Hung) was killed.

Ritchie further recalls, 'I then unloaded again for energy and turned hard right in pursuit of the lead MiG 21, who was now in a rear quarter, threatening our aircraft… Another radar auto-acquisition lock was obtained and one AIM–7 missile fired… resulting in a large yellow fireball.' The pilot, Dang Ngoc Ngu, was killed.

These two kills gave Ritchie his third and fourth victories of the war. This action proved the value of the 'Top Gun' training given to selected US pilots who were instructed how to deal with the MiG in air-to-air combat.

11 July saw more action for the VPAF when, at 0535 hours, two MiG 17s flown by Hoang The Thing and Hoang Cao Thang from the 923rd FR took off on a training flight. A few minutes after take-off they spotted a

Nguyen Tiem Sam
finished the war as
joint top-scoring pilot
of the 923rd FR with
six kills. (Vietnamese
News Agency)

formation of F-4s flying over Phai Lai. Immediately, the two MiGs were given the option to land but, as North Vietnamese pilots were now allowed more freedom to act, both pilots decided to attack. The F-4s were on a direct course for Noi Bai airbase (their intended destination). Hoang The Thing banked to his right and observed two F-4s starting to attack the base. He began to trail them at about 5,500 yards distance. Both MiG17s then dropped their long-range tanks and dived in for the kill. The Thang held his nerve and closed in on the F-4 at a speed in excess of 700 mph. As his MiG 17 picked up momentum in the dive and closing in to less than 550 yards, he fired several three-second cannon bursts (the last from less then 100 yards) and saw shells ripping into the stricken F-4, causing it to nose-dive and crash. His wingman, Cao Thang, fired on the second F-4 but missed, and it managed to escape over Hiep Hoa in Ha Bac province.

Later that afternoon, Le Thanh Dao and Nguyen Truong Ton of the 927th FR, flying MiG 21s, latched onto an F-4 each; Thanh Dao followed his prey towards the sea and shot it down with a missile, the wreckage falling south of Ha Noi. (Sadly, Thanh, a 23-year-old

novice pilot, was later killed by an AIM–7 Sparrow fired from an F-4.)

On 18 July a MiG 21 from the 921st FR, flown by Nguyen The Duc (another novice pilot), was preparing to land after a successful sortie when he was ordered to land at Kep because of American activity over the base. He tried to do as ordered, but his lack of experience made him by-pass Kep and he was then diverted to Gia Lam as an emergency measure. However, before he could make his final approach, he was spotted by Lieutenant Colonel Carl G. Bailey, who fired four Sparrow missiles at him. Not seeing any hits, Bailey closed in and fired a Sidewinder missile that tore off the MiG's right wing, killing The Duc. According to North Vietnamese reports his MiG was hit six times before he received the '*coup de grâce*'. The following day another MiG 21 was lost: the pilot Nguyen Ngoc Thien ejected safely, but he died on 18 August 1972 because of the internal injuries he sustained when he baled out too low and hit a tree.

July 24 brought some revenge for the North Vietnamese when Nguyen Tien Sam and Ha Vhin Thanh, both from the 927th FR, intercepted a formation of four F-4s over Ha Bac province. Both pilots shared a F-4 kill

Pilots such as Tran Van Phuong formed the backbone of the VPAF. He scored one kill in a MiG 17. (Vietnamese News Agency)

when they dived from above and fired from a range of 1,800 yards: the F-4 was seen to crash southwest of Ha Noi. This was Tiem Sam's second kill. Trong Ton was also an 'F-4 killer' for his regiment when he downed the enemy aircraft with a missile near Ha Noi.

The month of June did not bring any kills for the 925th FR but emotions within North Vietnamese ranks ran very high, as the war had turned to one of complete hatred. Many commanders had problems keeping their younger pilots in line. They were over-anxious to do battle with the Americans and on many occasions abandoned prepared tactical plans, thus producing losses that could have been avoided. The North Vietnamese, however, still managed to down at least seven US aircraft, losing five pilots and eight MiGs in air combat. They had fewer than 35 operational MiGs at their disposal and when we consider that they faced the might of seven US carriers carrying 550 combat aircraft (the most powerful force ever assembled) from just the Navy, their results were exceptional. These figures have never been verified by the US military. Nevertheless, the USAF and US Navy still continued to lose aircraft over the skies of North Vietnam, showing that the North's air defense system had improved beyond recognition since 1964. It was based on the Soviet model of interlocking ground radar units which fed information from which the MiGs could intercept incoming American aircraft.

During the month of August 1972, North Vietnamese air activity declined compared to earlier in the year. This was mainly attributable to constant air combat and attrition taking its toll on men and machines. The VPAF had lost 34 aircrew killed since February and this represented more than 50 per cent of its total training programme for the year. As if the Gods had intervened, bad weather arrived during early August and persisted throughout the month. This restricted the Americans to just sixteen missions over North Vietnam and gave the VPAF time to recover.

For the rest of the month only MiG 21s from the 921st FR and elements of the 927th FR remained on standby. They flew intercept missions only in small numbers - twos or fours. The entire operational fighter force at this time could not have amounted to more than 25 combat-ready MiG 21s, although it had as many as three times this number in various stages of serviceability. Most combats therefore took place between SAM units and US aircraft.

On 10 August, the Americans tried to intercept a MiG 21 flown by Nguyen Ngoc Thien from the 921st FR when he was on a training mission in the Vhin area. The USS *Saratoga* launched Lieutenant Commander Gene Tucker in an F-4 who flew skillfully behind Ngoc Thien as he made his way towards Than Hoa. Lieutenant Tucker then positioned his F-4 about two miles behind the MiG and fired two radar-guided Sparrow missiles and within seconds Ngoc Thien's MiG, blew up killing him instantly. This was credited as the first night kill by a Navy aviator using a Sparrow missile.

Two days later, a flight of three F-4s from the 921st FR was directed by ground radar to intercept a pair of F-4s. The 'Red Crown' alerted Captain Richard in the leading F-4. He turned in towards the MiGs, who in turn then spotted their adversaries at about three miles' distance. The MiGs were then ordered by ground control to break away, but as they broke to their left, they were chased by the F-4s, which used their superior speed to close in. The second MiG was hit by a Sparrow missile as it was diving away and it crashed but the pilot was saved. Captain Richard claimed a MiG shot down. It is interesting to note that his wingman was flying an unarmed RF-4C Phantom!

15 August brought a contact between two MiG 21s from the 927th FR when eight F-4s were intercepted over Viet Tri, northwest of Ha Noi. One MiG 21 returned from the combat damaged but another MiG claimed a F-4 destroyed using cannon fire.

On 19 August four MiG 21s were scrambled from Phuc Yen to intercept American bombers flying above the port of Hon Gai. The MiGs were alerted that four F-4s were closing in on them but the pilots pressed on, regardless of the danger. Before the intercept could be made the F-4s positioned themselves behind the MiGs. At this point the MiG 21s dived for the deck but Nguyen Thang Duoc (a 22-year-old novice pilot) did not

follow his squadron into the dive, deciding to meet his foe head-on. He then changed his mind and this gave the F-4s enough time to close in and fire AIM–7 missiles at his MiG, destroying it. Thang Duoc managed to eject safely, but he died the following day due to injuries he sustained from this action.

The Americans did not have it all their own way. On 26 August, for example, a F-4 from the USS *Midway* was downed by a SAM, with both crewmembers becoming prisoners of war. The North Vietnamese were obviously learning from their experiences as on the same day (26 August), two MiG 21s from the 921st FR intercepted a USMC fighter and shot it down with an ATOLL missile, killing the pilot, Lt. Sam Cordova. Also, one of the USS *Midway*'s F-4s was shot down by a SAM, both crewmembers ending up as prisoners of war.

On 28 August, Captain Steve Ritchie became the first US Air Force ace when he claimed a MiG shot down. However, North Vietnamese records show no pilots or MiGs lost on this day from enemy action.

On the ground, things began to go badly wrong for North Vietnam as only one division was left out of a total of fifteen committed to the offensive in the south: more than 100,000 fighters had been killed. To compound the situation, many tanks were destroyed and power stations were put out of action. The North's ability to supply its forces was being stretched to its limits because of the limited number of trucks available. Diesel generators produced limited amounts of electricity, but any ideas for an

offensive had to be abandoned for the time being.

However, the Communists had time on their side, as American presence was dwindling by the day. By the beginning of September there would be less then 40,000 American military personnel in Vietnam.

During August 1972, the Americans flew about 4,800 sorties: the VPAF flew less than 300. Seven American aircraft were shot down while the North Vietnamese lost two pilots killed and four MiGs. The situation in the air did alert the highest levels of the Communist Party to initiate a system where all pilots would report any combat failings to an intelligence officer who then collated them and analyzed them in the light of the circumstances. This seemed to suggest that even when inexperience was to blame for many shortcomings, the over-emphasis of ideology in pilot recruitment meant that many men were not thinking as fighter pilots in a rational way. Research has found that pilots lacked any element of fear of the Americans and this made them reckless, resulting in unnecessary losses. The VPAF implemented new measures, deciding not to send pilots back into action too soon after being shot down if they showed signs of shock or combat fatigue. Pilots were also encouraged to analyze their individual tactics within the squadron and to develop their approaches to combat with the emphasis on learning and then applying their experiences.

Some MiGs carried booster rockets to reduce take-off distances by as much as 70 per cent. On the left is an improved ATOLL with infrared guidance system. The photograph shows that it was impossible for a MiG pilot to use his centre line air brakes when the 130 gallon drop tank was attached. (Author)

MiG 21PFM, 'Red 5020', was attached to the 927th FR. On 5 July 1972, Nguyen Tiem Sam (six kills) shot down two F-4 Phantoms in this aircraft. Others who flew this MiG were Le Thanh Dao flew it (six kills), Nguyen Van Nghia (five kills) and Nguyen Doc Soat (six kills). (Author)

MiG 21PFM, 'Red 5020', Nguyen Tiem Sam (and others), 927th FR, July 1972

MiG 21 PFM, 'Red 5015', was camouflaged in light green with a dark green mottle. The canopy retained its natural metal finish. 'Red 5020' was a MiG 21 PFM and Red 4526 was a MiG 21F with a forward-hinged canopy and narrow fin chord. (Vietnamese News Agency)

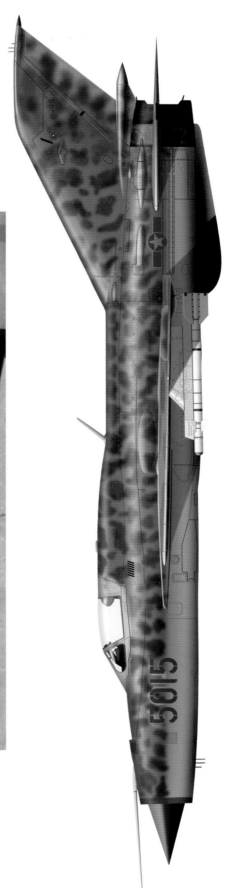

MiG 21PFM, 'Red 5015'

13 No quarter given

NORTH Vietnamese air activity was still very low during September as the result of the accumulation of losses and of the change in tactics: now only a few MiGs would be committed during selected encounters.

On 2 September four MiG 19s from the 925th FR were scrambled to intercept a 'wild weasel' formation consisting of two F-4Es and two F-105s that were used to attack missile sites using specialized air-to-ground missiles. As the MiGs were vectored behind the American aircraft, they separated into two pairs in order to attack from two directions at once. When the MiGs approached the airfield at Phuc Yen it was already under attack. The two jets, piloted by Pham Hung Son and Nguyen Van Thuan, each attacked an F-105. At that point, the F-105s broke in opposite directions but Van Thuan latched on to the leading aircraft. He fired an ATOLL missile, which just flew past the American aircraft by a mere 15 to 20 feet. The F-105 turned hard to its right as Van Thuan dived past. By this time Hung Son had made a cannon attack on this second aircraft but he dived for home when he saw no hits. The other MiG 19, flown by Van Thuan, followed his leader towards the sea. However, below, unseen by the attackers, an F-4E (flown by Major Jon I. Lucas) turned behind Van Thuan, obtained radar lock and fired a missile which hit Van Thuan's MiG. He was forced to eject and died of his injuries a few hours later. This was to be the only casualty for the VPAF during September 1972.

The Americans lost an A-4 Skyhawk to anti-aircraft fire on 6 September and its pilot (Lt. W. F. Pear) was captured. An F-4J was shot down on 8 September, this time by gunfire: both crewmembers were rescued. The Americans were achieving a respectable degree of success against the North Vietnamese but US aircraft were still being shot down with regularity over North Vietnam and any aircraft lost at this time was one too many for the American public.

The following day MiG 21s from the 921st FR intercepted four F-4s. They were vectored behind the four F-4s, the two leading MiG 21s being flown by Do Van Lanh and Bui Thanh Liem. Both of them closed in on the rearmost of the four F-4s and Van Lanh fired both his missiles at his prey (known by this time as 'BlackCrows'). He saw the impacts turn the F-4 on its side and plunge it earthwards, and it crashed in the outskirts of Ha Noi. On seeing this success, both MiGs broke off the combat and dived for the deck and home base.

North Vietnamese targets were hit on 10 September but the Americans lost an A-7 shot down. Its pilot, Lt. S. O. Musselman, was killed as he tried to attack the Paul Doumer Bridge.

On 11 September, the US Marines opened their scoring account but not without price. The Marine F-4J Phantoms took off from the USS *America* and headed for Haiphong. The MiG 21s from the 921st FR were kept on standby as the American formation was tracked. When the F-4s were about 100 miles away, two MiG 21s were ordered to scramble from Phuc Yen. After taking off, the MiGs flew below 1,000 feet to keep out of the American radar and slowly flew closer towards the F-4s, waiting for the right moment to climb and attack from behind. The F-4s seemed to abandon any idea of escorting the A-7s to their target and turned towards the MiGs. This caught the North Vietnamese pilots by surprise and within minutes the leading USMC F-4, flown by Major Lassiter, turned in towards the second MiG and fired a barrage of missiles (possibly

This MiG 21MF ('Red 5151'?) of the 921st FR could be using American made 500 lb bombs. The MF was a multi-role fighter capable of ground-attack and interceptor roles. The VPAF captured large amounts of equipment after the fall of Da Nang. (Vietnamese News Agency)

five or six). The MiG pilot banked hard right, seconds from death, as the missiles flew past him: he then turned hard left to wrong-foot the F-4 but this slowed the MiG sufficiently to take a hit from a Sidewinder. The stricken MiG managed to pull away, giving the pilot time to eject safely and fight another day. Meanwhile the second MiG had latched onto Major Lassiter's F-4 and fired a missile: this hit the F-4, which crashed into the sea. Luckily for the American pilots, they were later rescued.

The Vietnamese also claimed that a SAM shot down a second F-4, which was seen to crash into the Gulf. The American pilots reported that they had to ditch the aircraft because it suddenly ran out of fuel on the way home. North Vietnamese records currently available do not reveal the names of the pilots of this combat: the chaotic nature of the times prevented detailed notes being taken at all times. This lack of information is compounded even further by the fact that North Vietnamese pilots, in general, did not keep logbooks as their counterparts in Western air forces did.

The MiGs did draw further blood on 12 September as two MiG 21s from the 921st FR attacked four bombers which were targeting the La Danh storage caves. The MiGs managed to climb above the bombers and the lead jet then aimed at the last of the bombers. Before they could react, the MiG 21 fired a missile at a range of 1,000 yards and scored a direct hit, then dived away. On

landing at Phuc Yen, the VPAF pilots were delighted to hear that the US pilots had been captured when they parachuted down to earth. The victorious pilot may have been Hoang Tam Hung (who would be killed in action during the Linebacker raids of December 1972.) The North Vietnamese records show that no MiGs or pilots were lost to enemy action on this day.

The Americans continued their attacks throughout the month but North Vietnamese air activity was muted: many targets were not worth risking pilots and aircraft for, while other targets were already hit and not worth defending. However, SAM units and anti-aircraft units still made life hard for the Americans wherever they went in North Vietnamese skies.

On 15 September 1972 the Vietnamese knew that Nixon would win the election and they began to conserve their resources because they anticipated a long, hard war with Nixon in charge. The weather improved in September so the Americans increased their ground attacks against any 'legitimate' North Vietnamese target. No quarter was given or taken.

The USAF claimed seven MiGs as shot down. The North Vietnamese claimed three American aircraft shot down, losing one pilot and two MiG 21s in return.

14 A false dawn

THE Americans believed that North Vietnam was almost defeated and began to attack major airfields such as Phuc Yen, Yen Bai, Vhin and Quang Lang, claiming as many as nine MiGs destroyed. This proved to be another 'false dawn', because the damage inflicted was grossly overstated by the Americans.

in fact, the North Vietnamese tended to keep their MiGs away from such areas by hiding them in undergrowth and jungle, which made them virtually undetectable. Jet fighters were often relocated, to be hidden in nearby villages and many of those that were 'destroyed' were, in reality, bamboo mock-ups.

Due to the blockade of Haiphong harbour, the North Vietnamese were running low on anti-aircraft ammunition and SAMs. Nevertheless, they were not totally beaten as American aircraft were still being intercepted by MiGs and were still being shot down by ground fire.

The month also brought about more air-to-air success when, on 5 October, two MiG 21s from the 921st FR intercepted and shot down an F-4 flown by Lt. James Latham, who was attempting to attack a truck storage area. He made the cardinal mistake of loitering to see if any trucks were indeed parked there. This allowed the MiG to fire a missile at the F-4: anti-aircraft units also fired at the enemy aircraft, so both claimed this victory since the F-4 crashed near the sea, both crewmembers ending up as 'guests' of the Vietnamese people.

6 October brought even more success for the MiGs when the ground control unit tracked four American aircraft flying towards the iron works at Thai Nguyen as a hunter-killer team, two F-4s flying as killers and two F-105Gs flying as hunters in a fighter-bomber

role. The idea behind this was to give the MiGs a surprise should they try to intercept the slower F-105Gs with their bomb-loads. Even so, the VPAF was aware of this tactic and the F-4 did not instill any undue fear in North Vietnamese pilots, especially when they were flying the MiG 21MF which they considered more than a match for the American F-4.

The MiGs were given the scramble order and only a few minutes after take-off they were trailing the F-4s: by now both F-105s had quickly departed the scene when the MiGs closed in. Both MiGs were given the order to fire only once as the mission was already deemed a success by ground control once the F-105s left. Both F-4s dived for the deck when the MiGs got into firing range. The first F-4 pulled out at the last moment and used its superior speed to break away before the MiG could open fire, but the second MiG fired a missile at the following F-4 (both flying at an altitude of less than 300 feet), hitting it just before it could escape through the valley. Both MiGs then departed at high speed as ordered by ground control.

The VPAF also decided to do some bombing of its own. On October 9 two Il-28s – light Russian-made bombers – were taken out of storage (only two days after they were stored!) to bomb the American base at Ban Luong in Laos. The idea was similar to the attack on the US fleet in April 1972, by using a single surprise raid on a so-called 'safe target' that would make the Americans use up valuable resources on preventing similar attacks. (In 1968, the VPAF had created the 929th Bomber Battalion but this unit was converted to the 923rd FR.) Two pilots from the original batch of pilots sent to China for bomber training were recalled from their units for this mission. The first bomber would be piloted by Bui Trong Hoan, with Nguyen

Dinh Nhan as gunner and Nguyen Van Ta as navigator. The second bomber was crewed by Nguyen Van Tru as pilot, Thanh Xuan Hanh as gunner and Ngo Van Trung as navigator. The bombers were each fitted with eight cluster bombs containing 1,500 smaller bombs, which would explode like lethal grapeshot when released. Four MiG 21s from the 921st FR would act as escorts, two for each bomber.

The crew had to fly purely by instruments, as there was a risk of being picked up by American radar if they had contact with ground control. The American base was on a hill about 3,900 feet high, so crews had to practice the attack approach to avoid flying into the target instead of bombing it!

The weather on 9 October was near perfect as the bombers approached the target undetected. When they reached Moc Chau (100 miles west of Ha Noi and five miles from the Laotian border), they vectored towards Ban Loung (60 miles inside Laos) for their attack run. The pressure and excitement within the small bomber force was intense as it slowly edged its way towards the target. All crews were aware that F-5As fighters of the VNAF (South Vietnamese Air Force) were stationed along the route. They could be intercepted at any moment and their only insurance was the sight of the green and silver MiGs flying nearby like guardian angels.

Eventually the target could be seen below and the bombers approached it without any reaction from the forces on the ground so the surprise was complete! They released their bomb load, causing utter chaos and confusion below. The pilots could see pillars of black smoke coming from the base, indicating major destruction. The bombers did not need any invitation to return to Noi Bai as they expected the fighters based nearby to react like angry hornets.

The escorting MiGs were now low on fuel and even at this stage, total success was not guaranteed. The F-5s stationed at Xam Nua were scrambled but before they could get close enough to make contact with the bombers, they turned away at the North Vietnamese border. There were also four MiG21 from the 921st FR, which were loitering at the border to cover the bombers' retreat, should the F-5s chase them over into North Vietnam. It transpired that the anticipated combat between a MiG 21and a F-5 did not happen.

Upon the crews return, they were given a hero's welcome and the pilots were made

'Heroes of Vietnam', one of the highest awards that Vietnamese military personnel could receive. The attack did not change the overall situation but it did have the sobering effect of driving home to the Americans that there was no such thing as a safe target. As this incident happened in Laos, where American involvement was never made public at the time, the bombing officially 'did not happen'.

The VPAF now limited its activity because once again lack of spare parts and low maintenance levels grounded many MiGs, (at least 50 per cent of the available MiGs were not airworthy.)

On 13 October, one MiG 21 was destroyed by an F-4 flown by Lieutenant Colonel Curtis D. Westphalia. The MiG had taken off from Kep with another MiG, hoping to intercept an American formation but because of inexperience, pilot Nguyen Van Tue did not react quickly enough to his squadron leader when ordered to break away.

Another F-4 closed in on a lone MiG and downed it with a Sparrow missile. This victory made Captain Jeffrey S.Feinstein the third American ace of the war.

Behind the lines of action much quiet negotiation had been going on with the help of intermediaries. Both sides decided to engage in 'political stocktaking' and on 17 October a peace treaty was signed in Paris. The direct consequence of this was that President Nixon produced the olive branch and stopped the bombing of North Vietnam north of the 20th parallel, bringing to an end the first of the 'Linebacker raids'.

Nevertheless, American military aid increased to South Vietnam and the distrust continued as American reconnaissance aircraft (some were unmanned Firebees) continued to fly over North Vietnamese airspace. Some of the Firebees were shot down by the VPAF.

The North Vietnamese, for their part, continued their study of B-52 flight patterns, hoping to shoot down another of the prized bombers.

The total tonnage of bombs dropped on North Vietnam during the campaign was

Nguyen Phuc Ninh was a very competent pilot who scored two victories in MiG 17s. (Vietnamese News Agency)

Nguyen Van Nghia flew MiG 21s for the 921st FR scoring five kills. (Vietnamese News Agency)

155,548 tons, much of this because of the heavy payload of the B-52. The USAF admits to 44 aircraft lost and 27 downed by MiGs. The Navy admits to losing 45 aircraft but, surprisingly, only one to a MiG. The Americans justify these losses by claiming 62 MiGs shot down. The North Vietnamese MiGs in their turn shot down more than 60 aircraft, with 43 of these being verified by wreckage or gun camera evidence. It is also interesting to note that anti-aircraft units and SAMs claimed at least another 300 aircraft downed. The author has traced a total of 24 North Vietnamese pilots killed in action, with about 40 MiGs lost in combat from May to October 1972.

An uneasy truce
During November the air war quietened: both sides held back their fighters during an uneasy truce, but this was only to last a month. The Americans viewed the first Linebacker campaign as a success because its primary objective was to destroy the military capabilities of North Vietnam. Furthermore, the Nixon administration believed that a

psychological blow had been inflicted on the communist leadership and that this would undermine the latter's popularity with the North Vietnamese people.

In fact, any physical damage done had little consequence to North Vietnam. The country manufactured very little of its own military equipment and was obtaining even more military aid from its allies as a result of the bombing! The Nixon administration underestimated the Vietnamese people, who supported their leadership even more as the bombings fuelled nationalistic feelings to fever pitch. The North Vietnamese viewed their leadership as representative of their expression and thoughts, so they became even more stubborn. Just as the Blitz of London hardened the resolve of the British people against the Nazis, similar treatment did the same for the Vietnamese.

The psychological war even turned in favour of the North Vietnamese when the Americans admitted to losing a first B-52 to a SAM missile on 22 November. The bomber belonged to the 307th Strategic Wing based at U-Tapao in Thailand.

The turning of American military attention on the cities of Ha Noi and Haiphong proved to be a major mistake, as it began to increase public and international hostility against them. This mistake would be repeated in the Second Linebacker raids of 18 to 29 December 1972. Many Vietnamese believe that the 'Christ-mas bombings' only lasted for twelve days because the Americans had come to terms with the fact that they had lost the war of wills with the Vietnamese people.

Pilots being briefed on dogfighting tactics in front of Chinese made MiG 19s, known as a Shenyang J6. These aircraft were supplied to the 925th FR in 1971, the only unit to operate the MiG 19. China delivered 50-plus of these jets but it was quickly superceded by the MiG 21. (Vietnamese News Agency)

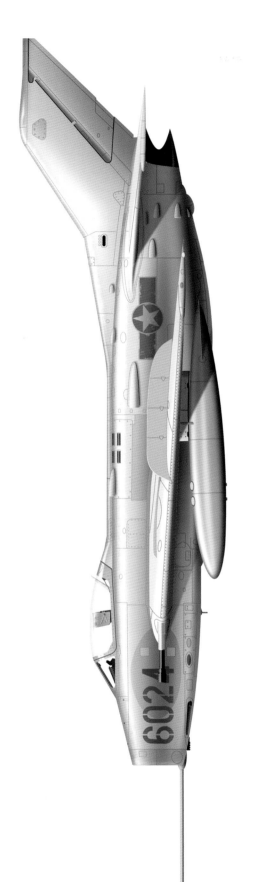

'Red 6024' is a Chinese made Shenyang J6 (MiG 19). These J6's were soley used by the 925FR because of its short range it was quickly replaced by the MiG 21. This aircraft was in natural metal and the stars were in the usual six positions.

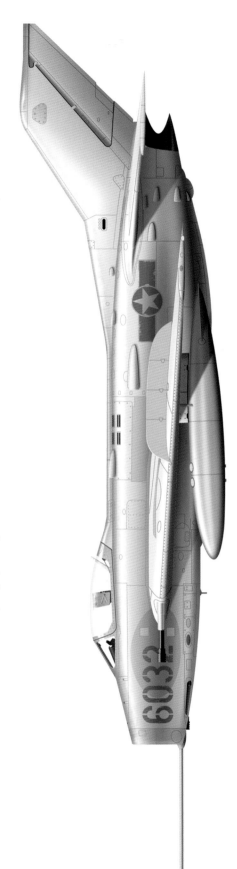

'Red 6032' was one of fifty J6's (MiG 19) delivered from China in 1971. This aircraft would have most certainly have participated in the May 1972 battles (the Dien Bien Phu of the skies) because of its limited combat exposure less than four kills have been J6 action.

15 The Christmas bombings and the war with the B-52s

INFORMATION concerning the period covering the Christmas bombings has always been very thin on the ground. The author has had the fortune to speak to pilots and ground crew who witnessed and experienced these bombings, and has been fortunate enough to be able to draw upon the diaries of Le Thanh Chon. A series of contemporaneous accounts have been collated for this part of the story, giving the reader a first-hand account of the emotions and thoughts of those concerned as never before revealed (outside a small circle of people in Vietnam). Many of the accounts do not distinguish between the individual or the group and all events were recorded as a collective experience, so the words 'we' or 'I' mean the same thing. In the West this would be unthinkable in most circumstances but the culture of the people has to be taken into account when the histories of this period are read.

Most of the accounts were written anonymously and even though they cannot be authenticated by cross-checking with their originators, many of the details are supported by events found in the official history of the Vietnamese People's Air Force, Volumes 1, 2 and 3.

On 18 December 1972, comrade Le Duc Tho, a special government envoy, returned from negotiations with the Americans. When the Russian-made IL–18 (numbered BH-195) landed at Gia Lam in Ha Noi without bringing home any agreement with the Americans, the instincts of the Vietnamese leaders told them the worst was yet to come.

The newspaper of the provisional government of South Vietnam, the *Nhan Dan*, and the Ha Noi paper called the *Quan Doi Nhan Dan* bore editorials showing how the Americans had cheated the Vietnamese

people in Paris. The Vietnamese knew that the bombings were inevitable but the people became unified in the belief that surrender would not be an option. The Vietnamese were of the opinion that the Americans were going to use the Apollo moon landings to deflect world attention away from any bombings that they were planning for North Vietnam. It was known that the Americans were definitely planning some major activity, as reports had been coming in of the largest number of B-52s ever assembled - about 50 per cent of all such aircraft available worldwide. To support such a campaign the American Navy had six carriers in the area: the USS *America, Hancock, Kittyhawk, Midway, Oriskany* and *Saratoga*.

On 18 December, Nguyen Van Bay recalled, 'We had just had dinner and were about to watch a movie (like we did every week) when there was an emergency alarm! Following this, all the pilots returned to base and reported to the base commander as usual. We were then shown a map which showed us the American air movements and awaited our orders.' During this alarm many airmen busily noted down the latest developments in the sky. The information would then be given to two female officers who then would plot the movements for all to see. Even at 800 km distance it could be seen that the American aircraft were shaping up for an approach on Ha Noi.

The pilots then received their orders from the supreme commander to stand by and get ready for an alarm start scramble. Dang Rang recalled, 'Although we had been given this order many times over the last few days, we did not expect the attack this soon'.

It was reported that in Ha Noi itself many people were walking about, looking up at the sky while others huddled in their homes, listening to the cultural radio station for news about the coming raid. Many people longed for peace, their only crime being that they would not give in. The blue-black smoke trails made by the American aircraft became longer as they worked their way towards their targets. Everyone in Ha Noi knew by this time that the heavily laden B-52s were streaming towards the capital, coming nearer by the minute.

The pilots on the airbases shared this tense feeling. They looked out of the windows and saw '... the whole sky brightly lighted like dozens of lamps'. This was because the anti-aircraft guns had begun to fire at the incoming aircraft as they came into range. Le Thanh, the famous Vietnamese painter, wrote at the time, 'For the last eight years under this sky we have seen all kinds of attempts by the Americans to bomb us, but still they continue to fail.' On this day his entire house was burned to the ground when the wreckage of a B-52 fell on it after it was shot down. The author had the honour of confirming the story, as the wreckage is still in the garden today!

A radar unit in Quang Binh province tracked the bombers from the direction of Guam towards Ha Noi until the Americans jammed it. Later in the day, the 18th and 45th Radar Companies reported a group of B-52s heading towards Haiphong at 1830 hours. The 16th Radar Company followed the bombers' steady course north towards Haiphong. The course was plotted and an intercept was ordered. Pham Tuan, one of the most experienced night fighter pilots in the VPAF, was ordered to take off in his MiG 21MF. He took off alone, flying by instruments in the dark and deadly sky, to play a game of cat and mouse. When in flight, he noticed that the F-4s were illuminated by all the anti-aircraft fire and he could just make out their black trails. Coming over Hoa Binh he became a target for the SAMs and had to increase power to stay alive as two SAMs barely missed him. Nevertheless, he still had to keep up with the formation of American aircraft ahead of him. He soon lost track of the formation because he had to turn off his internal radar to avoid being jammed by the American ECM.

When he spotted another group of American bombers he felt he was near enough to turn on his radar again, but it was quickly jammed. Pham Tuan felt that the bombers had been notified of his presence

and had increased their speed. Before long he lost contact and was ordered to return to Noi Bai as his fuel was running low. When he carried out his final approach, the airbase was under attack by B-52s, but he was already fully committed to landing because all his fuel gauges were at zero. In the final few seconds of his blind approach, there was an immense explosion as a B-52 was hit by anti-aircraft fire. It lit up the whole runway making it possible for Pham Tuan to land without incident.

This photograph of Duong Ba Khang was taken after 1975. He was one of the most experienced of all VAPF pilots and claimed a B-52 kill. (Vietnamese News Agency)

The VPAF has always claimed a greater degree of success against the B-52 than the Americans ever admitted too. According to ex-fighter pilot Vu Dinh Rang, 'I knew even by December 17 1972 we had shot down a total of twenty-seven B-52s, most of these bombers crashing in Vhin Linh (15), Nghe An (5), Quang Binh (3), Thanh Hoa (2), Ha Tinh (1) and Haiphong (1). Sadly most of the wreckage was not easy to trace as they fell in the jungles and others crashed in Thailand. When we finally got some evidence we brought it to the Headquarters and showed it to our commanding officer (with the help of the air force museum staff). Eventually, of course, such pieces of wreckage were shown to foreign journalists, much to the displeasure of the Americans.'

On 19 December the American raids began in earnest: a radar unit operator wrote, 'We were ordered to deploy more forces with the task of attacking the American tactical air force and protecting our "fire dragons" [SAM sites]. The air force commander briefed the pilots about the situation the night before them, ending with "all men in all units will have to do their duty" ...At 0800 hours when we were all at our stations ready for battle in the control room, we heard a commotion outside. Some officers called us to the window where we saw the wreckage of a B-52 crashing near Noi Bai. On a scrap of metal was a painted badge showing a fist with three lightning bolts and an olive branch with the words STRATEGIC AIR COMMAND.' An American air force official was quoted in November

This MiG 21 PFM belonged to the 921st FR. 'Red 5121' was one of 22 MiG 21's to claim a total of 137 US aircraft downed. It was flown by Pham Tuan when he downed a B-52 on 27 December 1972. (Vietnamese News Agency)

MiG 21, 'Red 5121', Pham Tuan, 921st FR, December 1972

as saying that the loss of an $8,000,000 dollar B-52 was equal to a sinking of a US warship!

A little after 0810 hours on that day, all MiG pilots from the 921st and 927th FRs were at full alert, sitting in their cockpits awaiting the scramble order. The Americans were using large numbers of aircraft to attack Haiphong and seek out and destroy any SAM sites. In the west the VPAF noticed that Americans were attacking in groups of eight aircraft. During daylight hours the Americans usually had three times the number of escorts to bombers in case of MiG attacks.

At 0840 four flights, consisting of eight MiG 21s from the 927th FR took off to intercept an American raid. Four of the MiGs made contact with the attackers but were not able to confirm any victories.

At 1300 hours eight F-4D fighter-bombers, escorted by twelve F-4E fighters, took off from their base at Ubon. The formation was being tracked by North Vietnamese radar as it flew over the Laotian border, going along Highway 6 to attack the SAM site in the Thanh Dai district of Ha Tay. This site had been previously bombed by B-52s without much success and with the loss of at least two bombers. The radar scanned the formation at different levels to make sure an ambush could be executed. The question was whether the lowest level of the formation could be attacked with success: if this could be answered in the positive, then MiGs would be scrambled to intercept. On this occasion the high command decided to attack. The official war diaries take up the account from here:

'Nguyen Duc Soat and Van Quy took off at Noi Bai and headed in the direction of Phu Ly where we "adjusted" the flying direction of our squadron [a VPAF squadron being two or more aircraft] to create a horizontal distance between us and the enemy. This would make the F-4s' radar useless even though they were moving up and down to broaden their search scales. We then turned right and approached from behind. The ground control ordered the MiG 21s to speed up to full power (about 1,400 mph). As they closed in, both pilots fired a missile each at a F-4. The Americans knew of our presence so four F-4s turned in to attack our squadron, leaving only four as escorts. Then Soat and Quy saw the black traces of smoke made by the F-4s, suddenly two of them flew right, two flew left, two flew up and two flew down. They were trying to create a situation of "fish in a basket"...'(an ambush).

The North Vietnamese pilots reacted by splitting up, with Duc Soat ordering his wingman to keep an eye on the F-4s on the right whilst he feigned an attack on the F-4s on the left. These turned and dived. The other F-4s turned to the left to support their colleagues on the left. It was then that Duc Soat, in the flash of an eye, reversed his turn and headed for the fighter-bombers. Soon he could see the black trails of the bomb-carrying F-4s and by this time the escorts were wrong-footed and too far away to defend their charges. The F-4s decided that discretion was the better part of valour, dropped their bomb loads and, using their superior speed, swung into in a dive to escape. The MiG pilots were then ordered to break away and head for home.

During the course of the night the missile units were also active, firing an estimated 180 SAMs at the attackers. The North Vietnamese were using huge supplies of SAMs because they could be fired as unguided missiles to explode at the height of the bombers, which proved very effective. This was done in order to prevent the Americans tracking the radar transmissions given out by guided missiles and destroying their launching sites.

The above-mentioned mission shows how a few MiG pilots could succeed against very unfavorable odds, even without shooting down any of the enemy. The RAF in the Battle of Britain practiced this simple principle: it is not the number of fighters shot down that count but victory is achieved when the attacker cannot complete his objective. However, President Nixon saw things very differently, choosing the next day to extend the Linebacker campaign indefinitely.

After another nine days of similar actions the North Vietnamese MiGs fared well on 23 December, with an F-4 kill over the Hoa Binh province, bringing down an aircraft which was trying to destroy a SAM site.

According to North Vietnamese records, 18 B-52s had been shot down by 24 December. The fighter pilots of any nation have pride in their skill and the North Vietnamese were no exception, as they still desired to have a B-52 kill which they could categorically prove. This position is clearly expressed by Dang Rang when he recalled, 'We became impatient as we had not shot down any B-52 that we could prove. Our MiGs took off every evening and whenever we approached the bombers, we had our radar jammed. To make matters worse, the

A rarely seen and dramatic sequence of photographs taken around 1967, showing a US aircraft (possibly a B-52) falling to earth and breaking up after being hit by a SAM Missile. (Vietnamese News Agency)

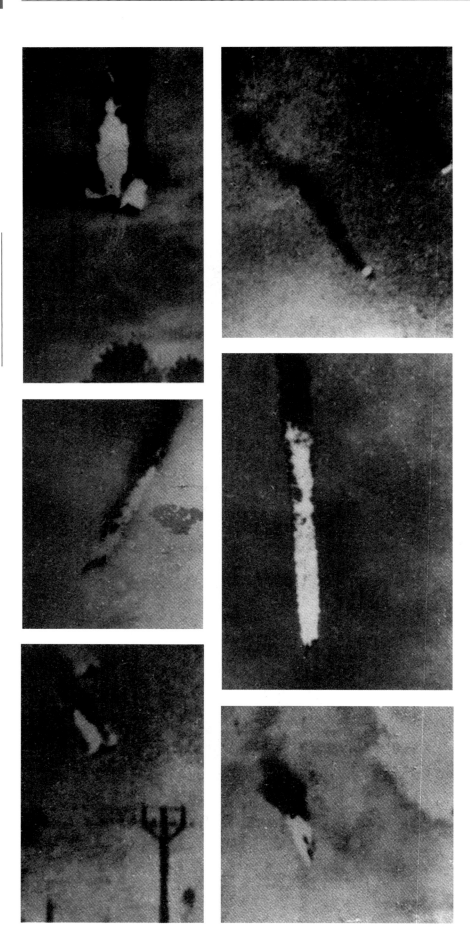

Though of slightly poor quality, this rare photograph shows a heavily camouflaged painted MiG 17 parked near a SAM Missile. The relative size of the missile is apparent and it is easy to see why US aircrew called them 'flying telegraph poles.' (Vietnamese News Agency)

A propaganda photograph taken at Gia Lam airfield around 1967 showing pilots discussing their aerial successes as they walk away from their very clean MiG 21s - they may have been newly delivered. (Vietnamese News Agency)

A group of pilots in high altitude pressure suits, training to be night fighter pilots with a MiG 21 PF, 'Red 4321', behind. From left to right: Le Tron Huyen, uknown, unknown, Tranh Hanh, unknown, Dong Van Song, unknown and Nguyen Dang Kinh (Vietnamese News Agency)

SAMs were modified in Vietnam to increase their altitude to 90,000 feet. On 19 December 1972 SAMs downed six B-52s. The psychological impact on American crews was such that numbers of aircrew reporting sick increased dramatically. (Vietnamese News Agency)

It had been realized that all B-52s had eight jamming devices to thwart MiG radar sets whenever they were turned on. The VPAF was also aware that each bomber carried six rockets that could be used against any attacking MiG. This basic problem was discussed during this meeting.

Below is an extract from a diary written by one who was present and taken from the Vietnamese chronicle *Nine Layers of Clouds*):

'We had all managed to study different drawings and plans to look for the "light". Many ideas were given out, with many counter-ideas. "Let us now summarize our plan," Commander Dao Dinh Luyen (who chaired this meeting) said. "We must assume that our radars must be turned off in the attack and attack on visual. This will eliminate the jamming equipment, this we are agreed upon. However, two questions remain: firstly, how do we judge the distance between MiG and B-52; and secondly, how does the pilot find his way to the bomber without radar? The pilots have already stated that they can see an object as far as 200 meters at night as all American aircraft are lighted to avoid collision. We have also gathered from our intelligence reports that American pilots have confirmed the existence of seven standard lights and two yellow ones on the B-52's tail. There are two red lights on the left wing and two blue ones on the right wing. We have heard from Nguyen Dang Rang that, based on the lights, we can calculate the distance between MiG and B-52..."

'The meeting went on at length exchanging ideas but eventually agreed that further attacks could be done without radar.'

All squadron leaders returned to their units to consider how best to apply this at unit level. This was the first ever study made on how to intercept bombers at such a level yet the above events were not even recorded in the official records because of their high secrecy level.

The night of 26 December witnessed the greatest number of aircraft to date used by the Americans to bomb Ha Noi. During the night, MiGs from the 921st FR flew six missions to intercept B-52s. The next morning at 1000 hours, F-4s started to raid SAM sites around Ha Noi. The VPAF scrambled two MiG 21s, flown by Nguyen Van Sang and Bui Thanh Liem, to act as 'bait'. The pilots climbed to a high altitude, hoping to draw the F-4s away from their bombers. Meanwhile, another MiG, flown by Tran Viet,

bombers were even more heavily es-corted than on previous occasions. We viewed the escorts like many layers of "fences" that a interceptor had to overcome and they became like "flying mine sites" that could explode if you got too near.'

On Christmas Day 1972, the Americans showed their festive spirit by not bombing North Vietnam. The VPAF used this kind gesture to organize a high-level meeting of the Air Command to plan how to shoot down a B-52. The main focus of this meeting was to look into the causes of their lack of success. All the experienced pilots were present, the most notable being Nguyen Van Coc, Nguyen Nhat Chieu, Pham Ngoc Lan and Pham Tuan. The North Vietnamese were, in reality, fighting a poor man's war against the richest country in the world and any plan had to take into account their limited resources. The people of Ha Noi also wished success for their fighter pilots because so much prestige and pride was at stake.

took off and flew at a low altitude along Highway 1 heading towards Phu Ly. This ploy worked, as nearly all of the 24 escorting F-4s dived for the two MiGs at the higher altitude, leaving the 12 fighter- bombers to fend for themselves.

The desire for a MiG kill, or even to become an ace, was too much to control for some American pilots. The description of the following combat is taken from the statements of Van Sang, who recorded, 'We let the interceptors go for a while. Then the ground control instructed Tran Viet to climb from his low altitude (and go for the bombers) but even before he could complete his turning pattern he saw the F-4 bombers at an angle of 140 degrees'. The ground control report adds at this point, 'We [ground control] decided to advise Tran Viet to shoot at the bombers as he was climbing towards them. At this point we knew that Tran Viet had applied full speed.' This approach seemed to bring the MiG on the blind side of the F-4s, closing to about two and a half miles from them. Tran Viet then did the unexpected by flying behind the F-4s at the same altitude. Aiming at the tail-end F-4, he then launched his missiles; a yellow ball of flame was seen then a black trail of smoke seemed to burst out of it before it went straight into the

ground, crashing in Hoa Binh province. (The two crew were saved.) The remaining bombers, however, continued on the flight path and released their bombs. The interceptors who were following Van Song and Thanh Liem then turned around and went for Tran Viet, who was by then flying at a very low altitude: he managed to escape along the Red River and landed without incident.

Later that same afternoon the VPAF shot down another F-4 under interesting circumstances. At 1400 hours two MiG 21s, flown by Do Van Lanh and Duong Ba Khang, were returning to base from an intercept mission over Viet Tri when they were followed by four F-4s. The ground radar warned the MiGs, who then swept up into the layers of cloud above. At this point the F-4s split into two pairs to try and sandwich the MiGs. Ground control observed the actions of all six aircraft and ordered Van Lanh to fly as 'bait' - orders were orders! The commander instructed Duong Ba Khang to cut speed and drop behind the attackers and 'nail' them just before they could kill Van Lanh. In order to execute this move, Ba Khang did a ninety-degree turn which made the F-4s completely lose contact with him. Time was now of the essence as the F-4s were

The 77th Missile Battalion operated this SAM. This unit was honoured when it shot down three B-52s over Hanoi on 20 December 1972. (Author)

closing in on Van Lanh and coming perilously close to missile kill range.

Within a few moments Ba Khang was flying dead level behind the F-4s. He then targeted the second enemy aircraft while both American pilots were transfixed on Van Lanh's MiG, possibly thinking about the next red star they were going to paint on their F-4s, little realizing the danger that one of them could himself become a star! As Ba Khang closed the distance between himself and his target, he realized with some fear that the distance between the F-4s and Van Lanh was also very similar, making it impossible to save his friend as one F-4 would still get the chance of a shot at his wingman. It was then that Ba Khang whispered to himself, 'He who successfully shoots first will live', just as he heard Van Lanh on the radio calling, '70, shoot or I will die' (Ba Khang was flying Red 5170). Then Ba Khang shouted, 'BREAK!', simultaneously firing his missile, which hit the right wing of the F-4, sending it spinning fatally earthwards, eventually hitting a hill. Two parachutes hung in the sky like a testament to the victory. The lead F-4 then flew into a cloud and disappeared.

As darkness was approaching, the commander ordered that Pham Tuan take off and fly to Yen Bai in his MiG 21 and await orders. Yen Bai airbase had recently been attacked and, according to intelligence reports, the Americans still believed it to be out of action. North Vietnamese intelligence had reported that the American high command estimated that it would take two days to repair Yen Bai, an assessment based on aerial photographs. However, the air base was in fact ready for operation, as local people and air force personnel had been able to repair it in less than 18 hours. They had skilfully perpetuated the American belief by making the base look 'abandoned'. Three other MIG 21s, flown by Vu Xuan Thieu, Dinh Ton and Tran Cung, would join Pham Tuan a few hours later. These pilots would be stationed in small satellite runways around Yen Bai, making detection of their positions virtually impossible.

At 2030 hours the VPAF received intelligence reports that a large raid was imminent: lights were turned up higher in the cities to brighten the skies, giving the MiG pilots more chance of spotting the B-52 bombers through the darkness. The commanding HQ was even busier than normal, with staff racing to position at the double and telephones ringing constantly. All SAM and anti-aircraft units were put on full readiness: MiG pilots sat in their cockpits wondering if they would be able to shoot down a B-52 or even pondering if this would be their last day on earth. The air command then made a final call to the instruction unit in Moc Chau which, in turn, instructed intelligence officers to go over the night's tactics with each pilot: nothing could be left to chance. A Warrant Officer intelligence officer was quoted as saying 'We were trying to check and leave no space for mistakes.'

The commander, Dao Dinh Luyen, scanned the 'sky' (the large map of North Vietnam) in the command HQ, seeing the American aircraft approaching like little black dots from the corner of the map. Soon these little dots were joined by more, then even more dots. (Black dots showed B-52s and blue dots represented F-4 Phantoms.) He could see that American aircraft were coming from Thailand to co-ordinate their attacks with the B-52s. They were being joined by Navy aircraft from Yankee Station and all were heading for Ha Noi or Haiphong. The senior VPAF officers knew that they had less then twenty night-fighters to combat this marauding horde. The commanders were also very aware that many of these formations were taking 'dummy' patterns to try to provoke the North's air command commit its MiGs too early and also to disguise its primary intention. The VPAF tracked a formation of over twenty B-52s heading for Haiphong.

There were also many groups of aircraft appearing over the southwest and east of Ha Hoa. The chief radar operator, Le Thiet Hung, sat tensely with his assistant, watching the situation slowly unfold before their eyes and still not knowing the enemy's exact target - a game of cat and mouse was afoot! It has been documented in the unofficial diaries that Le Thiet was heard saying, 'They are changing their tactics, there are numerous escorts all over Ha Noi but no sight of the B-52s!' The F-4s were flying in pairs doing a 'MIG cap', hoping to prevent any night-fighters from taking off. At this moment the radar operators saw the tell-tale signs of a bombing run (that is, bombers forming into a straight line and being joined by other bombers). The bombers were, in fact, not looking for MiGs, but their radar station! It has been recorded that Thiet Hung screamed, 'Watch the fourth group of bombers', then two large explosions could be heard nearby,

Pham Tuan gained
fame by joining the
elite group of pilots
who managed to down
a B-52.
(Vietnamese News
Agency)

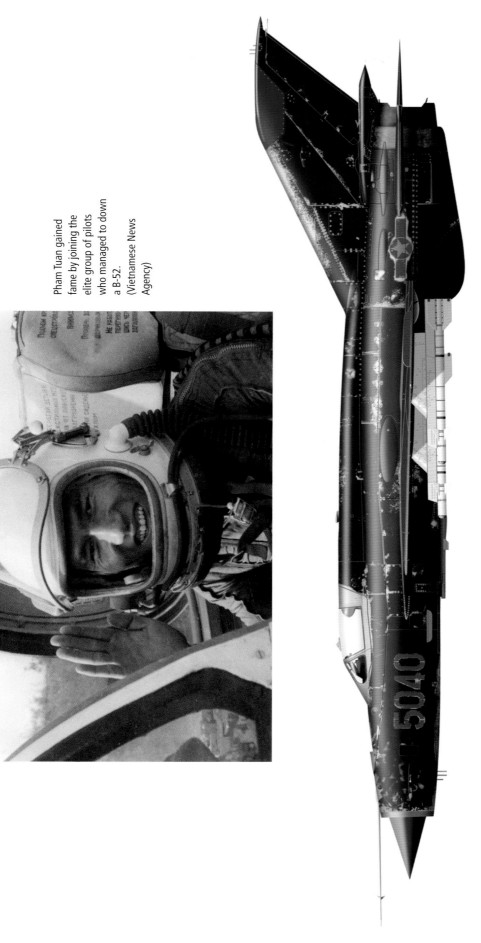

MiG 21 MF, 'Red 5040'. Painted in very dark green with a silver canopy, it may have been flown by Pham Tuan as a night fighter. The MiG 21 MF was used by the VPAF as a multi-role fighter up to the end of 1974.

An interesting assortment of ten to fifteen MiG 21s. The fourth MiG 21 MF is in Dark Green camouflage with no tactical numbers. Such a MiG may have been used in night operations. (Courtesy of Toperczer)

only just missing the radar station. The radar also picked up sings of a squadron of B-52s flying over to the Laotian border.

The commander then said, 'Have Pham Tuan scramble and instruct the station at Moc Chau to direct him to his intercept point'. Pham Tuan took off from Yen Bai and headed far west instead of southwards to conceal his approach until the last moments. He was to execute an 'outer edged attack'; this meant that he had to fly a 180-degree arc compared to the flight path of the B-52s. The main disadvantage of this tactic was that it would take him more time to complete. The diaries explain, '...We figured out that by going far to the west he could avoid the attention of the Americans and get beyond their jamming range of their equipment...'

As Pham Tuan flew with just instruments in order to limit ground control contact, he followed the previously agreed route religiously. The high command in Ha Noi were notified of the possibility of shooting down a B-52, so they had been given a copy of this flight plan and could follow his position closely.

When some of the B-52s turned and followed Highway 6 to Ha Noi, another MiG took off, flown by Vu Xuan Thieu. He encountered at least six F-4s over Hoa Binh but managed to successfully draw them away from Pham Tuan. This increased the latter's chances of obtaining a clean shot at a B-52.

Flying over thick layers of cloud 'Red 5040', Pham Tuan found that the sky was getting darker as he headed westwards. He then headed south and turned on the automatic pilot. He calculated that he was between the areas of Na San and Son La, about 120 miles west of Ha Noi. He then received reports from the ground station at Moc Chau saying, '40, fly to heading 220 degrees at altitude 6,000 metres.' A few minutes later he heard, '40, fly to heading 20 degrees, target is on your left 60 km away.' As he was closing in on his victim, the B-52s were receiving a barrage of SAMs. (The North's ground forces later claimed two bombers shot down, one of them crashing onto the village of Ngoc Ha.) In the midst of all this, three MiGs were scrambled into this inferno, having to dodge unguided SAMs and F-4s alike.

Meanwhile, back at command HQ, Dinh Luyen could see all the red markers that showed him the positions of his MiGs. He could see Pham Tuan was slowly approaching his B-52. At this point, Dinh Luyen instructed his deputy Tran Manh to order Pham Tuan to join in the attack on the

third group of bombers, as this was the smallest group. The four MiGs that were in charge of the Hoa Binh area were still covering them.

The control centre at Moc Chau then ordered Pham Tuan to drop his tanks and proceed south. He was vectored to a heading of 030 degrees and was told that the target was only 18 miles ahead. Very stealthily, he then closed in on the giant bomber undetected. He then broke radio silence and informed his commanding officer, '40, report have seen the target on the left, 020 degrees.' Le Thiet Hung replied, '40, attention, target on your right, black crows [F-4 Phantoms] on the left.' To Pham Tuan, the whole squadron of B-52s seemed to stand still, with large numbers of F-4s flying in pattern on all sides of the bombers (at least twenty in number.) The commander then instructed Pham Tuan 'go over the fence': that meant 'fly past the F-4s and go for the kill.' By then the target was less than 12 miles ahead. He could now see the different light patterns of the bombers and their escorts. Then he spotted two red lights of a B-52 ahead and followed them.

Ground control confirmed the distance as 12 miles as he homed in on the bomber. He then shifted the MiG to his right and saw the blue lights of the bomber. At a height of 26,000 feet, the MiG's cruising speed was not much faster then the B-52's, so Pham Tuan had to use greater acceleration; the problem was that this would light up his exhausts in the dark, warning the Americans of his presence. He then decided to cruise along and creep up on the bomber. Without warning, two blue streaks flew past his MiG. These were missiles and he had been spotted! He knew any idea of creeping up on the bomber had to be abandoned, so he speeded up, not caring about detection, and zoomed in on his target. He felt the sky was suddenly full of F-4s all gunning for him. He was now only two miles from the bomber, knowing any second could be his last as he continued closing the gap. He estimated the bomber was traveling at about 600 miles per hour and his MiG was doing 750 miles per hour (as he had slowed down to save fuel). 'In two minutes' time I can fire', he thought.

When he was close enough to attack, he turned on his acceleration again, lighting up the entire sky around him in the process. He knew that the Americans now feared to shoot missiles at him for fear of hitting their own bomber, and it would take too long for them to close in for a cannon attack on him. He closed in to 1,800 yards … 1,650 yards … 1,450 yards (he wanted to get closer to make

Two MiG 21s taking off from Yen Bai during the Linebacker raids of December 1972. (Vietnamese News Agency)

'Red 4023' was an early MiG 21 PF that arrived in Vietnam in late 1965.This example carries 2 k-13 heat seeking Atoll missiles. The radar tracking system is installed within the nose cone. It had a radar range of 12.4 miles. (Vietnamese News Agency)

From 1965 to 1972 the North Vietnamese fired nearly 9,000 SAMs. Because of American electronic counter measures many SAMs were fired 'blind'. They were deployed like conventional artillery. (Vietnamese News Agency)

Left and below: These SAM -2s belonged to the 7 Battalion of the 257 Regiment.
This unit downed a B-52 on 17 December 1972, which crashed in Hoang Hoa Tham Street in Ha Noi. (Author)

A memorial in Ha Noi depicting the downing of the B-52 by the 257th Regiment in December 1972. (Author)

sure) … 1,250 yards … then 1,100 yards and he could actually see the B-52 in the darkness. Tense with excitement, he fired two missiles, then another two, then dropped his MiG by 9,000 feet. Looking up, he saw 'a burning black block in the sky'. Jubilantly, he reported to base '40, mission over, big burning, big burning.' He then landed without further incident. The VPAF museum in Hanoi claims that Pham Tuan flew Red 5121 and scored this kill on the 27 December 1973.

The above combat is recounted at length to portray to the reader how important the shooting down of a B-52 was to the North Vietnamese, but it also provides an interesting inside view on how this type of mission was repeated thousands of times from 1964 to 1975.

The battle against the B-52s continued, with the VPAF trying to build on their success of the previous day. But B-52s were not the only type of aircraft flying over Ha Noi. Another danger was posed by RA-5C spy aircraft that were used to take photographs of missile sites. The US pilots flying these aircraft were highly skilled and knew how to evade any MiG sent up to get them. At 1200 hours on 28 December, at least three squadrons of F-4s flying above cloud level were being tracked by ground radar. The 921st FR decided to scramble two very young pilots, Le Kien and Hoang Tam Hung. They took off at 1220 hours and flew low along the Red River. They were instructed to commence their attack run against the F-4s when they reached Nam Dinh city outside Ha Noi. As the pilots flew, they looked for targets to their south. Soon they spotted two RA-5Cs at 030 degrees to their right. Forgetting about their primary objective, the two young pilots dived at the F-4s, with Tam Hung leading the way. The F-4s were aware of the MiGs, so they dropped their long-range fuel tanks and started to escape at very low level, twisting and winding along the contours of the Vietnamese countryside: the VPAF pilots registered the F-4s flying little more than 80 feet from the ground at times. Both the inexperienced pilots did a good job just keeping up with the Americans but they knew that their heat-seeking missiles were not very accurate against targets that were constantly moving and sliding from side to side. As this deadly chase continued, Le Kien noticed that even with such violent movements there was still a two- or three-second time gap between each move and

decided to shoot when this opportunity arose again - he knew it would be soon, very soon. He concentrated his attention on the nearest F-4 which, as expected, started to turn. This slowed the aircraft just enough for him to fire his missile – it was as if the target pulled the missile in by magnetism. The F-4 exploded in mid-air with the wreckage hitting the foot of Tan Vien hill. The elation of this victory was dampened when it was later learned that his wingman, Hoang Tam Hung crashed in unknown circumstances, possibly flying into the ground when he was chasing the F-4s.

Later that same afternoon, with the temperature rising to mild, Vu Xuan Thieu and Pham Tuan took off from Tho Xuan base and flew to a newly built secret base in the mountains in Hanam province. Their job was to try and destroy another B-52, but it would be even more difficult now, as the Americans would be alert to the tactic used by Pham Tuan.

To understand the actions of a pilot like Xuan Thieu, a little should be known of his military background. Although a thoroughly team-minded man, he always secretly admired those with air victories such as Nguyen Hong Nhi, Nguyen Duc Soat and Nguyen Van Nghia, who had studied with him in the Soviet Union. His other friends included Le Thanh Dao and Nguyen Tiem Sam, who claimed multiple victories, with Thanh Dao claiming at least six. However, as fate would have it, he had still not registered a kill.

A little before 2300 hours the phone rang, commanding Xuan Thieu to prepare to scramble - a level one alert had been put into effect because B-52s were on their way. Command Headquarters was now buzzing with excitement because of Pham Tuan's victory the day before. When Xuan Thieu went into the briefing room he could see female officers preparing both the long-range and short-range maps for the night's coming action. The commanding officer gave him the co-ordinates to an altitude of 9,500 feet and awaited further orders. This was a big day – the night fighters had become celebrities, with messages of congratulations from all members of the Command Division, the Deputy commander of all military forces, and from the hero Tran Hanh who shot his first American aircraft on 4 April 1965.

The Americans varied their tactics on the 28th by having the bombers and escorts appear at the same time; they started to jam radar equipment at the earliest opportunity, taking no chances of having another B-52 shot down by a MiG. (Officially the Americans have never admitted to losing a bomber to a MiG).

North Vietnamese radar had been tracking large numbers of low-flying aircraft heading for Haiphong, while others broke into smaller formations, heading for the air base at Kep.

The North Vietnamese radar units also identified some 'wild weasel' F-4s that were used to destroy SAM and anti-aircraft positions. The long-range chart showed B-52s flying over the Paracel Islands, then along the west side of Hainan Island. In addition, more aircraft came from the Laotian border, identified as those specializing in destroying radar sites. In response to this raid, all lights were turned off in Ha Noi and air raid sirens warned the people to go to their air-raid shelters.

By now Xuan Thieu was on his way, in 'Red 5024', to the intercept point as two MiG 21s took off from Noi Bai to act as a diversion. When Xuan Thieu reached the Hoi Xuan area, he could see the lights of the F-4s above him, flying in the opposite direction, towards Ha Noi. Using great skill and instinct as a pilot, he managed to fly past two waves of F-4s without being detected, by changing his direction and altitude to disguise his MiG

from the American radar. Xuan Thieu knew, like most VPAF pilots, that to beat the sophisticated American equipment required more art then science. The frustrating thing for him on this day was his inability to get a hard fix on any bomber; he felt he was flying in a dark, black void with no end.

Then he heard the voice of Le Thiet Hung, who called over the radio, 'Calling 24, escorts are on your left…'. He then received the co-ordinates of his position and those of the F-4s all around him. He knew by now that the Americans had spotted his MiG. He was also informed by ground control that the Americans were reporting that he was now approaching the distance where they could fire a missile at him. Yet he flew the MiG

The self defence unit of the Luong Yen Engineering factory used this single-barrel AA machine gun. On the 22 December 1972 this unit shot down an F-111 at night using only 19 14.5 mm shells. (Author)

The SA-7 (Strela) was a shoulder-mounted ground-to-air-missile. It was an infrared guided missile with a range of 2.2 miles. As it appeared without warning, few pilots were trained to counter its threat. The SA-7 was especially a threat to helicopters and slow flying aircraft such as the A-1 skyraider and AC-130 gunship. This example was used by the Xung Kich regiment. (Vietnamese News Agency)

This photograph is one that represents a thousand words. Three Vietnamese women trying to make a living – a right that did not come cheap, as the twisted remnants of an aircraft of the greatest economy in the world lies in the water behind as testimony to that. The wreckage is that of a B-52.

onwards almost as if it were a dream, still keeping to his course and speed.

Incredibly, as if fate had something in store for Xuan Thieu this night, the Americans managed to lose him from their radar screens! It was then that the prospect of downing a B-52 started to become a reality. He had breached the last of the 'fences' and was less then 40 miles from the nearest B-52. However, the ground control unit still had to get a fix on a B-52 without the Americans knowing that the bomber was being tracked, otherwise they would jam that tracking and the whereabouts of the bomber would be lost. After that, there would be the small problem of getting past the close escort of F-4s buzzing around the bombers.

The chief radar operator, Thiet Hung, had to calculate the attack route in a few minutes or the moment would be lost. The radar images given out by the bombers and their escorts resembled a large spider's web in the sky: any MiG coming within range and 'touching' the web would set off an indication of a intruder. By this time Xuan Thieu was at the mercy of what he was told by ground control, who initially told him to fly straight, keeping the enemy above him. He could see two F-4s flying just above him, but they still had not noticed him. After twelve minutes of flight he was told, '24, turn right to heading 030 degrees, altitude 8,000 metres.' Later the commander added, '24, drop your long-range fuel tanks, target 15 kilometres ahead.' Then it was, '24, beware twelve F-4s on your right and eight more on the left, over.' Xuan's heart rate must have jumped as he was now very close to a kill, or would he be killed? He then put all faith in his ground control and increased speed as instructed, until he heard Thiet Hung saying, '24, enemy ahead 030 degrees, 10

kilometres ahead, 090 degrees 5 kilometres ahead, four F-4s 10 kilometres behind.' This approach meant that he was closing in on the bomber from a diagonal angle, which would give him a little more time to get inside the escort ring. The danger for any night fighter was the fear that the net would soon close more tightly should his existence become known to the F-4s.

The situation now faced by the Americans was not supposed to happen! According to American radar experts, the MiG should have been picked up: this was of grave concern to the American crews who frantically started to search the sky for their 'lost MiG'. It was then that Xuan Thieu reported, 'Thang Long [ground control], please lead me to a B-52, I can already see the F-4s.' According to known reports, ground control interpreted this as 'I can avoid the F-4s, just direct me to the B-52s.' The deputy commander Tran Hanh then gave the order to lead Xuan Thieu to the bomber at all cost. He was then ordered to adjust to 020 degrees and attack the bomber on the right at an altitude of 28,800 feet.

Xuan Thieu then speeded up his MiG again. In a few seconds he saw a few red tracers zooming towards him: instinctively he pulled his aircraft to the right at the very last second and saw the missiles fly past his MiG. Then two more missiles were fired at him from his right, and he repeated the maneuver and they also flew past.

The situation was now desperate for him as he reported to ground control, 'Cobras [air-to-air missiles] are coming, lead me to the B-52s quickly.' He then evaded four more missiles. He knew that if his target did not appear soon, his luck would soon run out and he would pay for it with his life.

A few moments later ground control ordered, 'Keep up acceleration and keep to heading 030 degrees, target six kilometres ahead, look out for the lights.' By now his MiG was now being attacked by every F-4 in the area, with the sky full of American tracer. In many ways Xuan Thieu resembled a lone horseman in a charge, the only difference being that he was almost oblivious to the danger around him, as he became transfixed on his target.

Many of the missiles exploded near his MiG, the turbulence throwing it from side to side. He could also see 20mm cannon shells flying past his aircraft. He reported, 'Give me instructions on my attack before the

Americans have me for candy': the reply was '24, shoot in series, pay attention to distance.'

Finally a B-52 appeared on his left with all its red, yellow and blue lights twinkling invitingly at him. He targeted a B-52 on the right; he was now little more than 1,700 yards from his target. Then eight missiles were fired at him from an altitude of 25,600 feet, aimed ahead of his MiG, their marksmen hoping he would fly into them. He managed to survive this attack and then prepared to fire his missiles.

In its defense the B-52 dropped its 'yellow apricot' (a device that would trick his missiles into hitting them instead of the bomber). His MiG began to become unstable as it entered the slipstream of the big bomber; he then adjusted to his left and noticed that the chasing F-4s had stopped shooting at him for fear of hitting the bomber. When his MiG stabilized he fired his heat-seeking missiles at the bomber. His heart leapt as the missiles hit the bomber but, unbelievably, it kept on flying, even though he saw a flash on the wing. Because Xuan Thieu believed that he was going to be denied another victory, he broke with accepted practice and flew closer to wipe out the bomber with his cannon, his last words being, 'Let me kill it.' By now he was perilously close to the bomber, with six F-4s closing in on him. He fired his cannon at very close range (less than 800 yards) and must have intended to eject at the last moment, but he flew into the B-52.

The B-52 broke into two halves with huge flashes and explosions in the sky making eyewitnesses look up in amazement. The diaries of Le Thiet Hung continue with the account, 'All those in the air command became silent, only being broken by the official report from the speaker system "Xuan has flown his MiG with great courage, crashing it into the B-52 at an altitude of ... crashing in Son La province." We looked at each other in silence and with tears in our eyes.'

The last combat of Vu Xuan Thieu became shrouded in mystery, as his body and MiG were never officially recovered: rumours persisted that he defected to a neighboring country under American control. In reality he was classified with thirteen other pilots as Missing in Action until after 1975 when he was reclassified as Killed in Action.

By 30 December 1972 there was another bombing halt north of the 20th parallel. This enabled both sides to take advantage of the peace talks in Paris. By the time this final halt was called, the Americans had dropped 900,000 tons of ordnance in just one year and had flown 115,298 attack sorties.

The VPAF claimed a total of 81 American aircraft downed, with five of them being F-4s, but at a price of at least six MiGs, with four pilots killed. The Americans claimed to have shot down seven MiGs, but lost fifteen B-52s, three F-4s, two F-111s, two A-7s, two A-6As, one RA-5C Phantom and one SH-3A rescue helicopter.

On the night of 28 December 1971, Vu Xuan Thieu was killed when he rammed and destroyed a B-52 bomber. (Vietnamese News Agency)

The Linebacker campaign of December 1972 has been acclaimed as a textbook example of how air power can cripple the enemy by selective bombing, and it can be seen as a precursor of the Kosovo bombings of 1999. The Americans flew 714 B-52 sorties, 830 USAF tactical sorties and 386 US Navy and marine sorties. In reply the VPAF launched 1,293 SAMs.

These bare bones may be generally correct, but the fact remained that American aircraft were being continuously intercepted and shot down by MiGs and other ground-to-air defenses. Total air supremacy was never achieved and this is fundamental if any bombing campaign is to be completely successful.

The frustrating aspect of the bombing campaigns for the Nixon administration was that North Vietnam had few targets of any worth to bomb! In reality, North Vietnam 'benefited' by receiving more aid than it would have done without the war. This would mean that such attacks, although tactically successful in the short term, constituted a long-term strategic failure. The political repercussions were also negative for Nixon's administration: his popularity fell by 39 per cent when the scale and impact of the bombing became known. The end result of the bombing was political failure for the United States in Indochina because it strengthened anti-Western feelings in the area for the next twenty years.

16 The beginning of the end

THE beginning of 1973 would herald the last aerial victories for both sides in the air war. However the VPAF would still be involved in a ground-support role until the last day of the war.

On January, Nguyen Vinh Tuong was vectored to intercept a single unmanned reconnaissance aircraft flying over Ha Son Binh Province. He had no difficulty getting behind the unmanned aircraft and shot it down with cannon fire from his MiG 21 from 100 yards. The aircraft was reported to have disintegrated in mid-air. This was the 319th air kill for the VPAF.

At 1115 hours on 8 January 1973, VPAF radar picked up an incoming aircraft flying towards Haiphong. This was soon identified as a reconnaissance aircraft on a spying mission, although the exact identity of the aircraft remained unknown. The North Vietnamese had intercepted many of unmanned aircraft over their territory and this type pf aircraft was the most likely suspect. The Americans used such unmanned aircraft (called 'Firebees') to limit loss of human life and the VPAF used them as ideal targets to train pilots in air-to-air shooting accuracy. These Firebees would fly over the North Vietnamese terrain and 'memorize' data that could be used for the next raid. Therefore, whenever one was shot down, a potential raid would be averted.

At 1205 hours, Nguyen Van Vuong and his wingman Nguyen Van Quay were vectored to such a Firebee. The pilots could see it at 6,000 feet, slightly to their left. They were then given the order to attack so they both peeled to their right. Van Vuong found himself behind the Firebee and began to fire short bursts from his MiG 17F at a range of 300 yards. After the second burst the Firebee began to nosedive and crashed near a small village in Thuy Nguyen district near Haiphong. Its demise was timed at 1207 hours and was the last air-to-air kill for the VPAF.

The Americans also recorded their last kills of the war when Captain Paul D. Howman in a F-4D Phantom downed a MiG 21 with a Sparrow missile on 8 January. His victim was Hoang Coang, who failed to eject and was killed. This was the last air-to-air loss for the VPAF. The final victory and loss for both sides occurred on 12 January when the US claimed a MiG 17. Luu Kim Ngo was listed as KIA on that date.

The final analysis concerning the VPAF cannot be merely viewed with just kill ratios in mind. From the very beginning, the VPAF, main tactic was to force the Americans to abort their missions rather than to shoot down their opponents in large numbers. Nevertheless, the North Vietnamese pilots did stand up to the best air force in the world, taking on the best pilots the United States could offer.

From 4 April 1965 to 8 January 1973, the VPAF scored 319 kills, but lost 146 MiGs and 132 pilots killed. This gives the VPAF a 2 to 1 ratio advantage over the American pilots. This would be at total odds with US claims. The American pilots claimed 196 MiGs were shot down while losing only 76 of their own aircraft to MiGs. They do admit to losing 1,852 aircraft to SAMs. It is believed by the author that many American airmen who claim to have been shot down by SAMs were actually downed by MiGs using air-to-air missiles.

The author has researched official VPAF documents and studied the names of killed aircrew on war memorials in North Vietnam: such records fail to corroborate at least 30 per cent of all American claims.

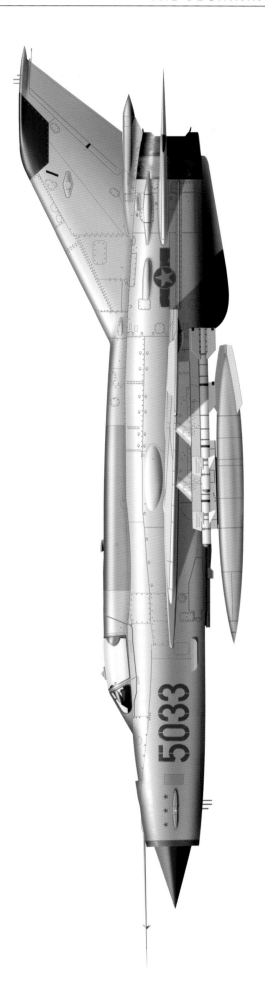

MiG 21 MF, 'Red 5133', was flown by Tran Viet of the 921st FR. He downed three Phantoms with this aircraft, one of them on 28 December 1972. No stars on upper and lower wings.

Le Thanh Dao (right) standing in front of some very rare aircraft. The second MiG from the left is dark green with sky blue undersides. The canopy is in silver with some overspray. The fourth MiG is in air superiority grey. All are MiG 21 PFM Fishbed Fs. (Vietnamese News Agency)

Pilots of the 925th FR at Yen Bai receiving last minute instructions from Nguyen Quang Trung. This unit flew the Shenyang J6/MiG 19 from Chinese bases. (Vietnamese News Agency)

This advanced L-29 Trainer, 'Red 743' was based at Nha Trang. (Author)

The SAM-2 had a range of 19 nautical miles and could reach 85,000 feet. They were fired mobile launchers. The 'flying telegraph pole' as the SAM was called, weighed 2.5 tons and could reach speeds of Mach 2.5. (Vietnamese News Agency)

This F-4 Phantom was flown by Joe Kittinger, Fred Olmstead and Steve Ritchie (serial 66-7463). It became the most successful fighter as no other jet scored more than three kills.

17 The final Victory

ON 27 January 1973, the United States of America signed a treaty that recognized the territorial integrity and independence of Vietnam. This meant that the United States would not intervene in the domestic affairs of the Vietnamese people. For North Vietnam it meant that the southern regime would receive no military aid from the Americans and they could now begin their offensive. From this time onwards the final victory would be guaranteed as the government in the South was weak and lacked the support of the people.

On 29 March 1973, the last American soldier left Vietnamese soil, never to return.

The armed forces of North Vietnam braced themselves for one more campaign, and the VPAF was no exception.

In July 1973 the Communist Party passed down the following order, 'Maintain combat readiness and prepare to defend North Vietnamese airspace…'

The war with the Americans had left a legacy of destruction all over North Vietnam so there was a concerted campaign to rebuild all the damaged airfields and infrastructure. Nearly all maintenance facilities and administrative buildings had been bombed, so one of the first priorities was making the airfields operational. The work started with the rebuilding of runways at 13 airfields, including Tho Xuan, Vhin, Dong Hoi and Phu Tuo. By January 1974 all airfields were fully operational and ready for the campaign against South Vietnam.

There was also a reorganization of the VPAF when the civilian and military aviation departments were merged into a single branch of the military. This incorporated the 919th Air Transport Regiment with the civilian aviation authority. All bomber and fighter regiments were then placed under the direct command of the 371st Thang Long Air Division. However, the bases at Kep, Yen Bai, Kien An, Tho Xuan, Vhin, Anh Son and Dong Hoi were primarily reserved as fighter bases. The result of this change meant that each fighter regiment would use a designated base. The system where fighter regiments shared bases was abandoned after December 1973. The 927th FR was relocated to Kep and the 923th FR was relocated to its new base at Tho Xuan. The 921st FR was based at Noi Bai and the 923rd would operate from Yen Bai. The 921st FR and 925th FR would use the main airbase at Kien An as their command headquarters.

The numbers of technicians and pilots were also increased, with new training programmes being started in January 1973. A group of 40 selected pilots were sent to the Soviet Union for all-weather flying and night-flying training.

The VPAF had very few operational combat aircraft because of the excessive losses incurred during the war. By the end of 1974 it had 40 MiGs ready for combat but nearly 130 pilots to fly them! At one stage the ratio of pilots to MiGs reached an embarrassing 10 to 1 ratio. New aircraft began to arrive at front line units by January 1975 and were made up of 40 MiG 21MFs from the Soviet Union and 20 MiG 19s from China.

The high losses of experienced pilots after eight years of fighting meant that most fighter pilots were very inexperienced and in need of more flying time. By 1974 pilot-flying time could be increased with the arrival of the new aircraft and this helped to raise pilot quality and decrease flying accidents. Nevertheless, as much as 50 per cent of all pilots on active service had participated in less than three combat missions.

This P3 radar unit belonged to the 45th Radar Company. The Long Talk radar (right) was used for air surveillance and air detection of incoming aircraft. The Two Spot radar (left) was used to track height and distances of aircraft. They were carried by a solitary ZIL-157 truck. (Author)

An old control station belonging to a radar unit now serves as a recreational club for local Army personnel. (Author)

The Soviet Union supplied the SA-2 surface-to-air missile, which was used extensively throughout the war. These SAMs shot down 196 or 11 per cent of all US aircraft lost until January 1973. (Vietnamese News Agency)

Not all MiG 21s carried national markings on the wings. There is evidence to suggest that 'Red 5033' was once sprayed flat green. This MiG 21 MF had a top speed of 1,351 mph and a range of 1,118 miles. It carried one 23 mm cannon and 4 K-13 ATOLL heat-seeking missiles. (Author)

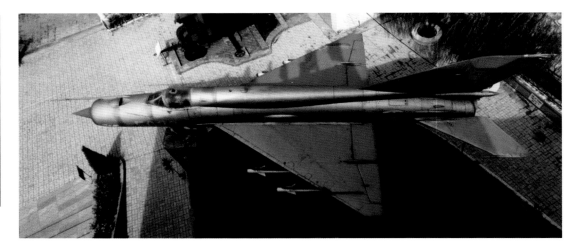

Two MiG 21s overfly two others which are between operations. 'Red 5252' was operated by the 923rd FR. The MiG 21 MF's were armed with 4 Atolls and 1x 23 mm cannon and had a range of 1,118 miles. (Vietnamese News Agency)

The VPAF now had to take a more active role in ground support, so new training programmes and zones of control had to be created in both the North and the South. The 921st FR had to give ground support for Routes 1 and 3 near Ha Noi. The 927th FR covered the areas north and northeast of Ha Noi. The 925th FR had the responsibility to cover North Vietnam west of Ha Noi. The port of Haiphong was to be the responsibility of the 923rd FR and a reserve of one squadron of MiG 21s was to be based at Noi Bai to fill any gaps if any one area was overstretched. Reserve squadrons were also stationed at Tho Xuan and Yen Bai. All units were also instructed to move to airbases further south to support the army in the coming offensive.

The VPAF's obsession of guarding its northern cities comes from the mistrust its leaders and members had of the United States government of the day. The bombing halts that existed throughout the war made

the VPAF view the Paris Treaty of 27 January as probably only another bombing halt! This view only changed after April 1975 when any further US involvement seemed unlikely because of the deteriorating position in the South.

On 22 February 1974 an agreement was signed with China to provide assistance and advice in creating an Air Force Academy where basic flight training could be provided for thirty fighter pilots per year. The academy would also train about 300 technical personnel and start a training maintenance unit, starting with MiG 17 airframes and engines.

With this backdrop the final campaign was planned in Ha Noi to enable the South to be liberated by the end of 1975. The stage was set for the 'fat lady to sing' for the Vietnam War.

On 6 January 1975, Phuc Binh (a major city in the South) had fallen to North Vietnamese regulars. This defeat was the beginning of the end for the South because at the same time the American Congress had also withheld a $300 million aid package. This was a hammer blow from which the Southern Government would never recover. It was now on its own.

The campaign began in earnest on 4 March 1975. Soon the Central Highlands were under Northern control, together with the airfields at Buon Ma Thout and Play Cu. By 26 March the ancient capital of Hue had fallen to the communists, with South Vietnamese troops leaving behind more than $1 billion dollars worth of equipment. On 31 March, a C-130 Hercules transport had to carry nuclear fuel away from the atomic reactor at Da Lam. On 29 March the strategic city of Da Nang fell to Northern forces and the large airfield was quickly put into operation against southern targets. From this point on, nearly all of South Vietnam was within reach of VPAF aircraft. To compound matters for the South, many of their pilots were in fact Northern agents who had infiltrated the selection process years before.

On 8 April, Nguyen Thanh Trung (one such Northern agent) took off in his F-5 fighter and by 0830 hours, he had dropped two 500 lb bombs on the Saigon presidential palace. The attack could have been said to be merely symbolic of the Southern collapse, but news of this bombing had a devastating effect on the morale of Southern forces. Even though neither bomb detonated and damage to the palace was very superficial, President Thieu was forced to make a hasty retreat from Saigon. He resigned two weeks later, alleging that the US was an untrustworthy ally.

On his return Thanh Trung was made a Hero of Vietnam and given a triple promotion to the rank of Captain in the VPAF.

On 21 April, two pilots were sent to Da Nang with a team of technicians to bring a few American aircraft to working order and repeat the success of Thanh Trung. Upn arrival, they selected an A-37 Dragonfly and soon got it ready for a combat mission. The indefatigable Pham Ngoc Lan tested the Dragonflies before handing them over to two MiG 17 pilots. The pilots selected for conversion training were Tu De, Nguyen Van Luc, Mai Xuan Vuong, Han Van Quang, TrangCaoThang and Nguyen Thanh Trung.

By 26 April, four Dragonflies were airworthy and were named the 'Invincible Flight'. The flight took off from Phu Cat at 0930 on 28 April, with Nguyen Van Luc acting as flight leader. The Dragonflies were refuelled at Than Son Airbase and loaded with two 500 lb bombs and two 200 lb bombs. The pilots were briefed and put on a stage one alert and by 1625 hours they took off. Their target was the airbase at Tan Son Nhat, where large numbers of US troops (including the US Ambassador) were grouped for their final embarkation. They had to reduce their flying speed to 250mph in order to avoid a mid-air collision. On the way to the target they flew past two South Vietnamese aircraft without incident and when the target was in sight, the flight leader instructed his flight to climb to 5,000 feet and dive at the crowded airbase in classic fashion.

When the Dragonflies were in line about a mile apart, Thanh Trung started his attack run. They were spotted by the air tower at Tan Son Nhat and were asked to identify themselves. Thanh Trung replied, 'We are flying American-made aircraft' and a few seconds later he dropped two bombs among the American aircraft parked in neat rows. Then Tu De made sure the Americans knew who they were by dropping another four bombs: the third and fourth Dragonfly dropped similar bombs in quick succession. Thanh Trung and Van Luc even managed a second bombing run, causing even more devastation. A C-130 transport succeeded in taking off when a bomb exploded just behind it. Sadly, a second C-130 loaded with passengers was shot down by anti-aircraft fire after it took off. All four aircraft departed for home base in the midst of heavy anti-aircraft fire – amazingly none of them had been hit. A squadron of F-5 fighters was scrambled to intercept them but, in true South Vietnamese fashion, contact was not made.

All Dragonflies reached home base by 1815 hours although Tu De and Thanh Trung landed on near-empty tanks. The attack caused a further drop in morale among the South Vietnamese. Six bombs had exploded on the ramp, destroying several C-47 transport aircraft and three AC-119s.

On 30 April 1975, the war effectively came to an end when T-54 tanks of the People's Army of Vietnam entered the presidential palace. By 1130 hours the North Vietnamese flag was flying over it, marking the end of the Ho Chih Minh Campaign and the Vietnam War for the VPAF.

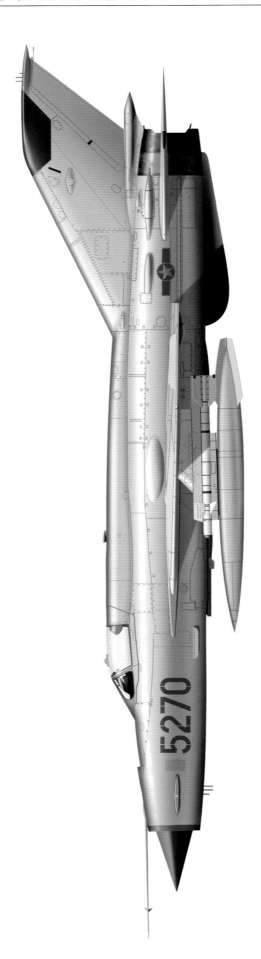

MiG 21MF, 'Red 5270', supplied by the Soviet Union after 1971. Painted in air superiority grey, the 921st FR operated this MiG as a night fighter. It was flown by Pham Tuan and Dinh Ton in 1972.

18 Some conclusions about air victories

IT has been an accepted proposition that the Vietnam air war was won by the United States even though the war as a whole was lost. As one US official said, 'The only thing we haven't done is to fly B-52s over their heads around the clock.' When this book was in its early stages it was assumed by the author that such a proposition would be vindicated.

After going to Vietnam and talking to those who experienced the war, I expected to hear a somewhat contrary view – after all nationalism and propaganda must play their part. However, after looking at things from the Vietnamese perspective and from some new evidence, the VPAF may have been more successful than previously recognised.

The kills of pilots from the VPAF have always been regarded with some skepticism by the outside world as being on the high side. There some American sources who claim that no North Vietnamese pilot achieved ace status (5 kills or more). A similar position arose after World War II when the large number of kills claimed by German and Japanese pilots were made known. Over the years, these kills by the Axis pilots have largely been vindicated by more subjective scrutiny and the author hopes this book will start a similar scrutiny of all air-to-air kills over Vietnam.

The VPAF admits to have lost about 146 MiGs on operations from 1965 to 1973 and their pilots have claimed a total of 320 kills. This would give the VPAF a kill to loss ratio of 2.2 to 1. This ratio is not unrealistic, as MiG pilots faced odds of more than 6 to 1 in nearly every combat. Therefore, throughout the war, all VPAF pilots were presented with a very rich target environment in which to shoot down American aircraft.

Colonel Robin Olds, a man who fought two wars and is a very highly respected fighter pilot, has stated, 'MiG pilots were better than the German pilots towards the end of the war'. This can be accepted on the basis that German pilots, towards the end of World War II (1944-45) claimed a total of about 5,600 aircraft shot down, while losing 9,500 of their own. This would give the Allies a kill ratio advantage of 1.6 to 1. Similarly, if the 138 MiGs lost in combat is compared to the 76 aircraft admitted as shot down by the Americans, the Americans would come out winners at about 1.8 to 1. Remarkably, this is very similar to the Luftwaffe ratios and in accordance with Colonel Old's general observation. The combined US fighter force claimed 196 MiGs in air combat. That would give the Americans a kill ratio of about 2.6 to 1.

However, if this is broken down further, the USAF had a kill ratio of 2 to 1 against the antiquated MiG 17 and only a 1 to 1 ratio against the MiG 21, the main interceptor of the VPAF. The USN claims a kill rate of 5.6 to 1.

The US has admitted to the loss of 76 aircraft to MiG activity. However, the Americans admit to losing a further 146 to unknown causes (over North Vietnam). It is submitted that such 'book-keeping' has failed to consider that these aircraft may have actually been shot down by MiGs and not through 'unknown circumstances'.

The possible figure of MiG victims could be as high as 225. If this is then compared with the 319 MiGs that the VPAF admit to losing, this brings the American overall kill ratio to about 1.4 to 1. In times of air combat, pilots tend to overclaim their victories and the VPAF can not be an exception. The great Japanese World War II ace, Saburo Sakai,

Anti-aircraft artillery and ground fire poised the greatest threat to aircraft. They accounted for 1,580 US aircraft downed. Vietnamese claims are in the 2,500 mark. (Vietnamese News Agency)

Lan (three kills), Nguyen Nhat Chieu (six), Nguyen Van Bay (seven) and Nguyen Van Coc (thirteen) all flew in excess of 550 missions. Therefore it took a great pilot like Van Bay to fly at least 79 missions for every kill he made and Van Coc, the most successful of them all, 42 missions to accomplish every kill. This was very modest if compared to American misssion to kill ratios.

Most American fighter pilots never even saw a MiG during their tours of Vietnam, yet VPAF pilots were nearly guaranteed contact every two to three sorties. It would seem that this would support the view that total VPAF claims must be taken seriously together with all the implications.

The quality of VPAF pilots was higher than many believed, mainly due to a quirk of fate. During the 1940s and 1950s, the Vietnamese had had a much lower level of education than the United States and therefore lower literacy rates. When new pilots were needed, it became evident that academic ability alone would not fill the numbers required for a new air force. The criteria for pilot selection were therefore changed to the following:

stated that a third of all claims can be discounted owing to the heat and confusion of air combat. If a third is deducted from the VPAF claim of 319 then a figure of 213 is achieved. This figure is very close to the 225 US aircraft that failed to return from sorties, almost vindicating the one third rule.

It is thought that the United States lost 2,257 aircraft over Vietnam and the MiG pilots claimed 319 of these. This would mean that only 14 per cent of all aircraft fell to the MiGs. The Americans have long claimed to have shot down some 196 VPAF aircraft. The North Vietnamese received 360 MiGs (unofficial figures) from 1965 to 1973, giving the Americans a staggering 54 per cent kill rate, making the VPAF claims very modest indeed.

Another point to consider is the number of missions flown by VPAF pilots. Like the *Luftwaffe's* pilots, VPAF pilots did not have a tour system so they flew until they were killed or the war ended. Pilots such as Pham Nook

1. All recruits to show track record of nationalism (anti-French activities).
2. All recruits to be extremely fit and healthy.
3. All recruits to have flying aptitude.
4. All recruits to have a killer instinct.

These requirements had to exist before military training started, not afterwards, as one would find in most modern training programmes.

The Vietnamese also found out that academic ability had little to do with

A line-up of eleven MiGs lined up in a neat row at Kep. These aircraft have been previously identified as MiG 21PFMs but some are actually MiG 21 MFs. (Toperczer)

becoming a fighter pilot. Only in the 1980s did the Soviet Union follow their example by starting to apply a more human factor to the criteria in their selection programmes.

Colonel Michael C. Press, a fighter pilot with 480 combat missions over Vietnam, recently expressed an opinion by writing, 'The USAF pilot selection is based on a relatively antiquated system of undergraduate academic grades, officer qualification test scores and 20/20 vision. The pilot selection process does not differentiate between skills necessary for fighter pilots and other pilots ... such a distinction is made later in the training cycle.'

Therefore Vietnamese pilots were possibly more suited to their roles than the better-trained American flyers. This difference may well have been even greater if one considers that 65 per cent of fighter pilots in the USAF were from Tactical Commands and were bomber pilots flying fighters. This would further point to the fact that the 319 kills claimed by the VPAF may be closer to the truth than previously recognized. Many of the 352 kills of *Luftwaffe* ace Gerhard Barkhorn (scored between 1941 and 1945) are said to be genuine because of the opportunities he had. However, the 300-odd kills scored by the entire VPAF over an eight-year period are viewed with suspicion.

The VPAF had a strict system of kill verification, as in most air forces. The vast majority of kills were confirmed by gun camera evidence, but the VPAF realized that two or more pilots could be firing at the same victim, so this had to be counter-checked by eye-witness confirmation and wreckage near the kill site.

It should also be remembered that the VPAF did not put a high priority on individual scores but tended to kill in packs, so a number of VPAF kills may be claimed by two or more pilots. This was one of the reasons that made all VPAF kills seem on the high side. However, this scoring method was only popular with the 923rd FR from June 1966 to November 1967. This was not universally recognized and did not account for more than 15 per cent of the VPAF kills. The Americans, for their part, credited even back-seat radar operators with kills. This resulted in Captain Charles B. DeBellevue having six kills and ending up as the highest scoring American pilot even though he never actively fired a shot or launched a missile. This would seem very strange to VPAF pilots.

It is the author's view (and the view of many others) that flyers such as Charles DeBellevue more than deserved their status as aces and MiG killers: shooting down an aircraft is a team effort. Some American units would recognize air-to-ground kills as kills even though such parked aircraft were stationary and pilot-less. The VPAF in its turn recognized the shooting down of an unmanned aircraft to as a kill, but this conforms more closely to an air kill than destroying parked aircraft. It must be realized that such definitions of a kill are not universal, so American and VPAF kill claims must be viewed with the rules applied by the respective countries.

The war cost the United States more than 3,000 aircraft lost, of which 1,852 were lost in combat over the North. A total of 2,435 aircrew lost their lives, costing $3.1 billion: a straight handout of this amount would have been enough to give every family in North Vietnam one of the highest standards of living in Asia.

The North Vietnamese lost about 400 aircraft and 160 aircrew and countless millions of others suffered when an increased tonnage of bombs was dropped on them than fell on Germany and Japan combined during World War II.

In many ways it is not important who won the Vietnam War or who lost but to realize that the war was a sum total of events that we must try and appreciate from both sides' point of view. Only then can we learn from the sacrifices made by both parties.

MiG 21 MF, 'Red 5142', was finished in natural metal with a very worn appearence, seen here circa 1972. (Vietnamese News Agency)

Squadron Leader Nguyen Van Minh of the 921st FR is shows how he shot down a Phantom. He shot down two Phantoms on 9 October 1966 and was eventually credited with at least three kills. (Vietnamese News Agency)

Ha Van Chue climbs into the cockpit of 'Red 4320'. He scored his only kill in a MiG 21PF. (Vietnamese News Agency)

Right: Ho Chih Minh leader of North Vietnam.

Here, Le Duan, who was only second in comand to Ho Chih Minh, meets VPAF pilots in 1972. The muted expressions of the pilots shows the strains they were under, unlike the Party officials behind Le Duan. (Vietnamese News Agency)

This A -37 Dragonfly ('Red 0475') was liberated from the South in 1975. It was operated by the Quyet Thang Squadron and flown by Tu De on 24 April 1975 to bomb Tan Son Nhat. (Author)

This 100 mm AA gun had a range of 24 miles. The self-defence of the BA Dinh district used it during the Linebacker raids of December 1972. (Author)

This Mi-24 Helicopter Gunship took part in 149 combat sorties and was based near the south-west border of Laos. (Author)

This F-5 Freedom fighter was liberated in 1975 and put into action by the VPAF. Le Khuong and Nguyen Van Khong who attacked Khmer Rouge positions along the Da Ha stream on 6 July 1978 flew this F-5. It was also used to bomb Pol Pot's Headquarters in the spring of 1979. (Author)

19 Three of a kind

Major General Pham Ngoc Lan

WHEN I was given permission to speak to ex-VPAF pilots it was with some excitement and anticipation that I was driven in an official car to meet General Pham Ngoc Lan (retired). This was an opportunity hardly ever given to outsiders and the first by General Pham, who can be regarded as the 'Werner Mölders' of the VPAF.

When I was introduced to the General, he greeted me like an old friend and his warmth was a great surprise to me. I was to learn that this attitude was common to all North Vietnamese pilots of the period and to Vietnamese people in general.

Pham Ngoc Lan was born in 1934; his father was a pharmacist and his mother a midwife. He spent his formative years in the Diet Bien region of southern Vietnam during the last decades of French occupation. As it happened, Diet Bien was one of the first areas in Indochina where the revolutionary struggle for independence began. In this atmosphere of growing nationalism, Ngoc Lan was caught up in the struggle and by the time he was thirteen years-old he had played an active part in the Vietnamese underground. Ngoc Lan admits that, like many of boys from his generation, his family played an influential role in the shaping of his ideology and he admits that his uncle was a leading influence on him in the 1940s and 1950s.

When the French finally withdrew from Indochina in 1954, Ngoc Lan had his heart set on joining the Navy and by early 1955 he obtained his commission. At this time there was a call for volunteers to join the fledgling air arm of the Army. During this period only officers who had the necessary 'ideological' background would be considered for pilot

recruitment. Pham Ngoc Lan immediately volunteered, not because of any desire to be a pilot, but because he felt that he had to contribute to the cause of Ho Chih Minh and Vietnamese Nationalism. All recruits were thoroughly screened to make sure of their loyalty and because Ngoc Lan had fought against the French since childhood, he easily passed the initial test.

The second stage of his training involved a very vigorous physical selection procedure where only the very fittest survived. Pham Ngoc Lan remembered this period as one of the most testing of his early manhood as he recalled, 'Many hundreds volunteered but because of the ideological criteria and physical demands, less than 1% of them were selected for pilot training.'

He was then sent to Ha Noi to complete a further year's academic study, which included physics, mathematics and flight theory. He completed this preliminary course in 1957. In the same year he was one of the very first batch of students who were sent to China for pilot training. He recalled, 'My group was the largest of the first four batches and all sixty

Major General Pham Ngoc Lan sitting in a newly delivered SU-27 Flanker 'Red 6004'. (Author)

Pham Ngoc Lan is seen here with the author in the courtyard of his home in Ha Noi. (Author)

Pham Ngoc Lan showing his flying diversity by testing this captured American made Bell UH helicopter. (Courtesy of Pham Ngoc Lan)

of us would spend the next six years in China. The training was tough and by the end of my course only 50% had graduated.'

Ngoc Lan would spend a total of ten years in China before all his training was complete. He explained, 'We had to spend so much time outside Vietnam because in the early days we were not able to improve on our basic training as there was always a serious shortage of training aircraft … this was a problem that persisted throughout the Vietnam War.'

By the early months of 1965, the 921st FR 'Sao Dao' (Red Star) had a total of 40 MiG 17s on hand and he was given the honour of being its senior pilot. Ngoc Lan recalled, 'From this early stage I was given the authority to formulate and plan all fighter tactics and strategies, not only for my unit but also for the entire VPAF.' He recounted with a little pride, 'I was the one who formulated the attack patterns to get our first kills on 3 April 1965.'

When asked what he remembered most clearly of that day, he said, 'My wing man that day was Phan Van Tuc and it was he that spotted the American aircraft first and he closed in on the F-8 and he began to fire very early. Obviously he missed, and I remember telling him, "Stop firing … stop firing, go in closer." Before long I had closed in on the same aircraft and fired a few short bursts,

we must have been shooting at it simultaneously! What is not generally known about that action was that the first kill was actually shared between Van Tuc and myself. I managed to claim another F-8 a few moments later.' Pham Ngoc Lan realizes that these kills have been questioned by some outside Vietnam but in reply to this he stated, 'The South Vietnamese regime confirmed the loss of these two kills the very next day and gun camera evidence further confirms our claims.'

When asked about his opinion of the MiG 17F he said with much conviction, 'The MiG 17 had no match in close-quarter fighting but I, like most VPAF pilots, preferred the MiG 21.' He added, 'When flying the MiG 17 the best killing range for me was 300 to 400 yards – any closer and bits of flying debris would almost certainly cause damage to your aircraft … but there were pilots who scored kills at ranges in excess of 600 yards but that was rare and not ideal.'

Pham Ngoc Lan always preferred the MiG 21 because, as he put it, 'The MiG 21 was much faster, and it had two ATOLL missiles which were very accurate and reliable when fired between 1,000 and 1,200 yards.' The view that most VPAF pilots preferred the MiG 17 is still prevalent outside Vietnam and may stem from the fact that most kills by the VPAF were actually achieved in the MiG 17 as it was by far the most numerous fighter used by the Air Force.

It was only with much persuasion that that General Pham revealed that he had flown in excess of 700 missions and had three kills to his name. He ended the war as a full colonel and until 1999 was the deputy commander of advanced training. He retired in 1999 as a major-general, but is still actively involved in giving lectures and is always called upon to give advice on to officers who were once under his command. He said, "Although I am retired, it is my duty to assist when I can.'

He runs a little café on Truong Chinh Street in Ha Noi where all his old friends come to talk about days gone by. He feels no hatred against the Americans and says, 'The war is now over and it is time to live in peace and try to forget the past. The Americans were doing their duty just like we were doing to defend our country … I would accept any American as my friend if he extended the same feelings to me.'

The significance of the contribution that this man has made to his country is beyond

doubt. The completion of this book would not have been possible without his comments and advice on events that may have never been told outside Vietnam.

Major General Nguyen Nhat Chieu

NGUYEN NHAT CHIEU now lives on his farm in Tinh Hai Phong about 45 minutes' drive from Ha Noi. The official driver had great difficulty locating Nhat Chieu's farm and he was forced to ask directions some distance from our destination: to my amazement all five people we asked seemed to know exactly who we were looking for and gave us directions until we arrived. When we arrived, Nhat Chieu was waiting for us under a very hot Vietnamese sun about 300 yards from his home.

He is a very private man who now spends his retirement running the local table tennis team, although he devotes most of his time to his grandson and ageing mother. He had cancelled his table tennis session so as not to disappoint me, which did create a tinge of guilt for me.

Prior to my interview he had never spoken to anyone outside Vietnam about his career as a fighter pilot. Like all ex-VPAF pilots he

was actually amazed that I or anyone else would be interested in his life. 'After all,' Nhat Chieu reminded me, 'I only flew the MiGs.' I found out that Nhat Chieu was fluent in Mandarin and Russian, but was very proud of the fact that his grandson had passed his second language examinations in English.

Nguyen Nhat Chieu was born in 1934 in the same house where I interviewed him. He played an active part in the fight for freedom and after the French had left he joined the Marines in the Red River Lantern Regiment as a Warrant Officer in 1954. When he heard that men were wanted to be trained as pilots, Nhat Chieu was captivated by the idea and put his name forward at the first opportunity. He had all the right aptitudes for a pilot and he was one of the first to be selected for pilot training. Like all would-be pilots of the time, he had to complete his high school education up to a grade 10 level (equivalent to high school) before he started his pilot training proper in 1956. Along with 12 other hopefuls, he was sent to an aviation training school in the Beijing area. Nhat Chieu recalled, 'I was the senior officer in charge and I was given the honour to lead one of the first groups of officers to train with other pilots from all over the Communist world … but the numbers slowly increased as the Vietnam War began.'

Nguyen Nhat Chieu sitting in a MiG 21 at a fighter pilots reunion on 5 November 1998. He retired from the VPAF with the rank of Major General. (Courtesy of Nguyen Nhat Chieu)

A very relaxed Nguyen Nhat Chieu with his grandson in front of his home. The shrine in the background is dedicated to his ancestors. (Author)

At that time Nhat Chieu was promoted to 1st Lieutenant, as all pilots in the VPAF were automatically promoted to an officer rank. Many outside Vietnam have only vaguely understood the combat structure of a fighter regiment in the VPAF so I asked Nhat Chieu to explain. He said, 'A squadron could consist of any number of aircraft between two and eight, under the command of a senior lieutenant or captain. A "unit" could consist of between one to four squadrons under the command of a major, and between one and four units would make a fighter regiment. A whole fighter regiment would usually come under the command of a major or lieutenant colonel. In the VPAF at that time the highest rank of an "active" pilot who flew missions was lieutenant colonel. A full colonel would be in charge of all the fighters, which could be from one to four regiments.'

Because the loss rate in some units during the Vietnam War was high (75-100 per cent), the structure varied considerably depending on availability. When quizzed about exact loss rates for his unit, Nhat Chieu admitted that there were times when entire units would be annihilated. The loss rates did fall gradually as pilot training improved but, as Nhat Chieu admitted, 'At times our pilots had no option but to defend their country against opponents who had longer training and more modern equipment. Casualties were suffered when young pilots bravely attempted to face situations that required more experienced hands.' Furthermore, pilots were killed when outnumbered by large numbers of American pilots. Odds of 6 to 1 were common, but all the pilots in my squadron claimed at least one kill each.' The old warrior then explained the situation in a wonderfully graphic way, when he commented, 'Young pilots were like green bamboo shoots that were facing a hurricane - as the war dragged on, the hurricane

progressively increased in intensity ... many could not survive...' When asked about the quality of the American pilots he faced, he replied, after some thought, 'The quality of the American flyer was always very good, he was very well trained and generally had excellent discipline. The Americans always used very sound tactics and were never opponents you could take lightly.' He concluded after some thought.

What was slightly surprising was that he did not notice a discernible difference in the quality of American pilots in the pre-Top Gun period (1965-1970) and those that were Top-Gun trained. He added, 'The Americans had gradually acquired more modern fighters, especially the later versions of the F-4 Phantoms, and this made the main difference. In the early years we had to contend with F-100s and F-105s, which were of a similar generation to our MiG 17s.' He was another of the Vietnamese pilots who had a preference for the MiG 21 over the MiG 17. He added, 'In the early days [1965-66], we flew the MiG 17 because that is all we had and being a poor country we flew what we had available. The MiG 17 was a good fighter that was dangerous at close quarters, could accept very severe punishment and still bring the pilot back to base. I myself was hit on two occasions and survived because of this toughness. On one mission I received eight cannon hits and still flew back to base. On another I was badly hit but my MiG 17 kept on flying for a safe distance, giving me the opportunity to bail out near Ha Noi.'

When asked about the firing range of the MiG 17, he spoke with some hesitation, 'This differed from pilot to pilot; some pilots would fire and score kills from 600 yards or more, but I believe the best killing range was less than 200 yards. This was the distance I began to fire at, then I would close in with two more bursts.' When I told him that some in the West believed that VPAF pilots preferred the MiG 17 to the MiG 21, he replied with surprise, 'I think most pilots did not share this view but for me personally I preferred the MiG 21 because it was superior in all specifications in climb, speed and armament. The ATOLL missile was very accurate and I scored four kills with the ATOLL. The best range for the missile was 1,000 yards, roughly twice the distance of the MiG 17 cannon. When I was a MiG 17 pilot I hoped for the day the MiG 21s would arrive. In general combat conditions, I was always confident of a kill over a F-4 Phantom when flying a MiG 21.'

When Nhat Chieu was asked about general attack strategies and tactics, he revealed that this varied from unit to unit and would change periodically, but most intercepts involved between one and four aircraft. He admitted that he cannot remember more than 30 MiGs used on any one day throughout the war. When I asked about the legendary Colonel Toon, he replied, 'Many pilots shared the same aircraft and kills were attached to an aircraft rather than individual pilots ...' The name of Colonel Toon did not register with him in any way.

From 1970-1973 most of the victories scored were by newly trained VPAF pilots and not by the veteran pilots of the early war years. I asked Nhat Chieu to explain this. He replied, 'It is true that that most victories were done by the new generation of pilots ... we older pilots still flew combat missions but many of us had been promoted to strategic and tactical duties.' Nhat Chieu was quick to add that, during the Rolling Thunder campaign, he flew more than four missions per day and in August 1967 he made contact with the enemy on 21 occasions.

When asked to talk about his most memorable victory he feels his first kill still sticks in his mind. Nhat Chieu recalled, 'It was on 20 September 1965. The day began with bad weather so we were all told to stand down and return to our quarters. Usually this would mean no flying for the rest of the day. However, on this day in particular the weather changed very dramatically. We were told to return to base immediately just when we were relaxing and having a meal. When we returned to the base, a large American formation was heading towards the Nha Nam region so we scrambled and received orders whilst in the air! I was leading a squadron of MiG 17s, consisting of Pham Ngoc Lan, Nguyen Ngoc Do and Tran Van Triem. Everything was so rushed that most of our orders were given when we had already taken off. When we spotted the American formation I latched onto an F-4 and fired a short burst but missed. I then closed in to 200 yards or thereabouts and fired again and observed hits so I closed in even further and fired until I ran out of ammunition. The F-4 began to burn and crashed, I remember that well.'

Nhat Chieu further explained that all kills had to be confirmed by gun camera evidence or eyewitness account. He added, 'It did not serve us to falsify kills. In the MiG 17, for example, every time a round is fired the gun camera would take eight pictures and kills could easily be confirmed. Furthermore, all downed aircraft fell in very localized areas and could be counted with great accuracy.'

When I asked him to explain why MiG 17s were called 'snakes' he said, 'Actually, they were sometimes called snakes because their performance was very good at low level, just like most snakes – it was not about their camouflage patterns. Most MiGs arrived in silver but were soon painted to conform to the terrain: for example, many MiG 17s were painted like sea waves to resemble the sea. Many MiGs were painted very frequently because of changes in the terrain and regularly re-painted also because of low paint quality. Of course painting was not always possible to do in combat conditions.'

Like most VPAF pilots, Nhat Chieu did not keep a log book in the traditional sense, but when I asked him about the number of combat missions he flew he revealed, after some persuasion, 'I personally flew more than 600 missions and scored six kills from 1965 to 1974.'

He retired in 1998; his crowning moment was being introduced to Ho Chih Minh, who made him a Hero of Vietnam in 1966. He took out a photograph depicting this occasion from its place of honour in an ancient cabinet and with great pride confessed, 'This was an important moment for me.' He then unexpectedly left the house and returned with a very large water melon that he had gathered from his field and presented this to me as a gift.

The simplicity and humility of the man and his beliefs had a great effect on me. In a time of globalization and a world dominated by balance sheets and profit and loss accounts, Major General Nguyen Nhat Chieu is without doubt a rare bird. Anyone who has had the pleasure to know this special man would be happy to call him a friend.

Colonel Nguyen Van Bay

NGUYEN VAN BAY is a man of few words and has hardly ever spoken about his military past. When he granted me an opportunity to talk to him I knew my luck was in. He is a soft-spoken man who gives very careful thought to what he

Nguyen Van Bay waves to ground crew upon his return from a victorious sortie.

says. He gives the impression that he is very proud of what he has done and from an early age he had decided to make his career in the military world.

He was born in 1936 and lived his early years in the very south of the country in Dong Thiap province. Like many of his generation, he joined in the fight against the French and by 1952 was very involved in anti-French activities.

In 1953 he was made an officer in the new Vietnamese Army. When Van Bay heard that volunteers were needed to create an even newer Air Force, he could not conceal his delight at the prospect of becoming a pilot and put his name down at the first opportunity. He recalled, 'When I was chosen for pilot training, I was so very happy that I still consider that moment one of the highlights of my life. I think the main reasons I was selected over other more qualified men was my patriotism and my good health.'

Van Bay was sent to China for basic flight training in 1960. In addition to flying duties, he received the necessary broad education up to grade 10 (high school) that is required of all pilots. When he returned in 1964 as a fully trained pilot in 1964, he was immediately assigned to the 921st FR, although when he

became famous as a leading pilot he had transferred to the 923rd FR.

When initially asked about his combat experiences Van Bay was humbly reluctant to talk about it, but he did admit that numbers always played an important part in his life as he is a great believer in coincidences. He explained, 'There were a few other Nguyen Van Bays in the VPAF, but I was always known as Van Bay number 7 because of my kills - the numbers 7 and 4 always played a role in my life.'

When I enquired about his preferences between the MiG 21 and the MiG 17, he replied, 'I cannot say much about the MiG 21 because I never flew it in combat. All my experiences and kills came in the MiG 17. It had few advantages over more modern aircraft like the F-4 Phantom, so most of our kills were made because of careful tactical planning and teamwork. I am a very big believer in teamwork.'

Van Bay further elaborated that because the MiG 17 was so much slower than the F-4, one of the ways to gain advantage over the F-4 was to manouevre into a turning contest, where the US machine's faster speed would be of little use to it. 'Once we got the F-4s into a circular fight, a MiG 17 pilot had to aim at the centre of the imaginary circle and then cut across the circle to fire. Only in this way could we get our kills. Alternatively, a MiG 17 pilot could bring this turning battle to lower altitudes where the MiG 17's performance was slightly better.'

Van Bay explained to me that it was, of course, not easy to get the American fighters to commit themselves to such a battle, so certain tactics had to be formulated to force such combats on them. He added, 'We had to scour every known book and study all fighter tactics since World War Two to solve this problem. Eventually we developed the idea of attacking the F-4s head-to-head. We soon realized that when we did this the American fighters had to turn in order to meet us. It was then much easier to induce a turning fight from this situation. All MiG 17 combats were formulated with this in mind and the traditional attack from behind was generally abandoned.'

Like all fighter pilots, Van Bay had his own system when shooting down aircraft and, like many aces of the past such as the famous German *Experte*, Erich Hartmann, preferred to go in close to get a kill. He said, 'I preferred to go in as close as possible and hardly ever

Nguyen Van Bay's recorded kills:

No.	Date	Type	Place	Status
1	24.4.66	F-4	Pha Lai	
2	25.4.66	A-4	Pha Lai	Shared kill
3	26.4.66	F-4	Unknown	
4	21.6.66	F-4	Pha Lai	
5	21.6.66	F-8	Shared kill	
6	29.6.66	F-105	Tam Dao	Shared kill
7	5.9.66	F-105	Tam Dao	
8	29.6.66	F-105	Tam Dao	
9	24.4.67	F-4	Ha Noi	Shared kill
10	25.4.67	A-4	Haiphong	Shared kill

needed the gun sight to hit the enemy. However, I would always shoot a preliminary short burst to gauge distances before I went in for the kill.' Although Van Bay is credited with seven kills, he admits that he could have claimed others.

The VPAF had a policy where all pilots could claim a kill if they played an active involvement in a kill, similar to a back-seat pilot being credited with a kill in the USAF and USN. This policy seemed to be more rigidly applied by the 923rd FR from June 1966 to August 1967, when a successful pilot like Van Bay could increase the kill rate of pilots who flew with him.

It is generally known that Cuba played a role in training VPAF pilots and was a supporter of the North Vietnamese during the Vietnam War. However, what is not generally known is that the exploits of Nguyen Van Bay so impressed the Cubans that in 1970 General Castro awarded Cuba's highest military honour to him for his bravery and achievements.

The success of Van Bay can be even better appreciated when we look at the Middle East conflict of 1967 where similar aircraft were also in combat half a world away over the same period. During the Six Day War in 1967, the Israelis claimed 469 MiGs destroyed but lost only 46 aircraft in return, a 10 to 1 kill ratio. Many of the victories were scored with the French-made Mirage C, which some regard as slightly inferior to the F-4 Phantom. When Van Bay's kills in a MiG 17 are viewed in context it truly becomes quite a remarkable feat. It took Nguyen Van Bay only a single year's combat to achieve his 7 kills.

Colonel Nguyen Van Bay retired in April 1991 and now lives with his wife in the area where he spent his boyhood years. He spends most of his time looking after his farm and spending time with his family. When I asked him how many missions he had completed, he answered with a smile, 'I cannot remember exactly but it was in excess of 500 missions.'

When aviation historians and enthusiasts talk about the great 'jet-killers' of the age like Heinz Bär of Germany, Joseph McConnell of the USA, Nikolay Sutiagin of Russia and Colonel G. Epstein of Israel, the name of Nguyen Van Bay should be added to this list.

A monument outside Hanoi dedicated to all airmen who died during active service. (Author)

This memorial was built close to where the first American fighter was shot down in Ham Rong. An inscription on the left of the memorial reads: 'Extreme Fidelity, Resolute Attack, Unity and Coordination of Collective Successes.' (Author)

A monument inside the VPAF museum in Ha Noi depicting the communal effort that was needed to acheive victory in the war. (Author)

This MiG 21 PFM was one of the few examples that carried a rear view mirror mounted on the hinged canopy. The aircraft does not have the gun pod attached, carrying only air-to-air missiles.

The basic tactical structure of the Vietnamese People's Air Force

The basic fighting component of the VPAF was the Fighter Regiment, which would come under the command of a Major, sometimes a Captain. During the majority of the war there were three Air Regiments that made up an Air Division. An Air Division would usually be placed under the command of a Colonel or a Major General.

Each Regiment was made of two to three squadrons of two to eight aircraft per squadron. A squadron would usually be placed under the command of a Captain or Lieutenant although, in actual operations, command in the air would pass to the most experienced flyer.

The squadron would be divided into two or more flights. The intercept flight would then have the duty of breaking up the American formation or ideally shooting one of the enemy down. The covering flight consisted of less experienced pilots who would act as long-distance wingmen, creating a kind of 'Phantom-cap'. At times, these covering flights would act as decoys, depending on the tactics employed by ground control.

The VPAF would usually attack in the traditional finger-four patterns with the formation sub-divided into two sub-formations. Each pilot would be given an air number of 1, 2, 3 or 4 (not always according to seniority). The VPAF realized that because of the heavy odds they had to face, this strict numbering could never be rigidly adhered to and this could change during the course of the combat.

Sometimes the VPAF also used a three-ship formation flying in a V pattern with the no.2 and 3 flying behind in support. When this pattern was used, the leading pilot in the no. 1 position would be the most experienced pilot and would undertake the 'killing'. The pilots in the second and third flight positions would fly at similar height from the lead pilot. It was this system that lead many American pilots to believe that VPAF pilots practiced lone-wolf attacks. On some occasions American pilots taking on a single attacker found themselves taking on three instead of one.

The two-ship formation used by the VPAF would ideally consist of pilots with similar experience because there would be no strict wingman or flight leader positions as in the USAF and the USN. In a two-ship formation the pilot with the best chance of a victory would take over as wingman because this made it easier to respond to an opportunity and execute a kill.

A single-ship formation was rarely used in day operations except where a decoy was required. A combat initiated by a single pilot was usually avoided and was rarely sanctioned by ground control leaders. Most single-ship formations were used in night operations because of the lack of trained night-fighter pilots and because single aircraft are harder to detect by night.

The foregoing was gathered after talking to VPAF pilots and tacticians of the time and it must be remembered that tactics differed from unit to unit according to the availability of pilots and aircraft.

APPENDIX 2 # Vietnamese People's Air Force Regiments and Air Divisions

921st Fighter Regiment – the Sao Dao (Red Star)

923rd Fighter Regiment – the Yen The (Peaceful Site)

925th Fighter Regiment – the Dong Nai (a province in South Vietnam)

927th Fighter Regiment – the Lam Son (Blue Hill)

917th Combined Air Regiment – the Dong Thap (a province of South Vietnam)

918th Air Transport Regiment - the Hong Ha (historical name of the Red River)

Other Units

370th Air Division - the Hai Van (Way of the Ocean Clouds)

371st Air Division – the Thang Long (the Imperial name of Ha Noi)

372nd Air Division - the Le Hoi (founder of the Le Dynasty, 1428-1528)

937th Fighter Bomber Regiment – the Hau Giang (a province of South Vietnam)

The Commanding Officers of the VPAF

Colonel Luyen Dao Dinh, C-in-C, Political Commander

Lieutenant Colonel Nguyen Ngoc Do, Senior Assistant Deputy Commander

Lieutenant Colonel Chu Duy Kinh, Assistant Commander

Lieutenant Colonel Tran Hanh, Assistant Deputy Commander

Lieutenant Colonel Tran Minh, Assistant Deputy Commander

Lieutenant Colonel Luong Huu Sat, Assistant Deputy Commander

Lieutenant Colonel Chu Mao, Commander of Political Department

Lieutenant Colonel Ho Dat, Commander of Logistics

Lieutenant Colonel Do Huu Nghia, Commander of Technical Department

North Vietnamese air war doctrine

Unlike many other fighter pilots from the West where individual instincts and action play a large part in combat, North Vietnamese pilots had their actions largely dictated to them by their control, especially before May 1972.

The VPAF realized from the very beginning that the air war over North Vietnam would always be more political than military. The VPAF had very inexperienced pilots and, in general, were no match against the better trained and equipped Americans, so they devised tactics to prevent the Americans from accomplishing their missions instead of shooting them down in the more traditional custom. The Red Baron's statement that 'a fighter pilot's duty is to shoot down the enemy and everything else is nonsense' did not apply to the VPAF.

The VPAF would appear before the Americans in squadron strength but only use the intercept flight to attack the Americans (from behind if possible), firing with their cannon. The F-4s would be forced to take on the MiGs and then be unable to continue with their mission or to escort the slower fighter-bombers to their targets. The covering flight would then enter the fray and pick off the slower fighter-bombers when the opportunity arose.

The North Vietnamese fighter pilot cannot be viewed as an independent entity: instead he worked in close co-operation with the ground control units who would tell him if an intercept was permitted, how long he should stay in the combat area, and the number of times he would be allowed to fire. The reason for this strict approach was that SAM units in any area would fire on all aircraft in the area: MiGs lingering in the combat area were in danger of being shot down by their own side.

APPENDIX 4   The North Vietnamese pilots

The recruitment of North Vietnamese pilots was based more on ideological grounds than academic ability. According to Nguyen Van Minh of the Vietnamese Army Historical Branch, all candidates had to fulfill certain fixed criteria. In the early years all candidates had to prove a military record fighting the French for independence: this was to make certain of their devotion to the Communist cause. Furthermore, nearly all candidates had to be serving officers from the Army or Navy. These requirements made the average age of a North Vietnamese pilot (at 27 years) higher than most countries. There was also a very high emphasis placed on physical fitness, but once a candidate had overcome these initial hurdles, then his ambition to become a fighter pilot would have been within his grasp. Going by North Vietnamese figures from the Historical Branch, about 95 per cent of those selected for training qualified as pilots. The flow of pilots throughout the war was about twelve pilots per month reaching operational status.

Any recruit without at least a grade five education (junior high) had to acquire another year's theory on mathematics and physics before going on to flying training. The second generation of North Vietnamese pilots (1970 to 1975) was given a higher level of education and the average age fell to 23 years as the ideological criterion was less stringently applied: it has been discovered that pilots with too much 'nationalistic zeal' tended to be over-confident, resulting in unnecessary losses. The average North Vietnamese was not as educated as the average American of his age and obviously there was a much smaller population base from which to choose. However, the criteria used by the North Vietnamese were more than vindicated when such pilots took on and, on many occasions, shot down their more educated and better-equipped enemy

Fighter aircraft of North Vietnam and their US opposition

The Vietnamese had only two main types of fighter aircraft to deal with the Americans, the MiG 17 and the renowned MiG 21. Until the middle of 1966 the MiG 17 was the mainstay of the Vietnamese fighter force. It was a single-seat fighter, more of 1950s vintage than the 1960s. It was subsonic, flying at a speed of 711 mph, and had a combat range of 915 miles. It was about 55 per cent slower than the F-4 Phantom and less sophisticated, and it did not carry any missiles (at this time). The 'Fresco' (as the MiG 17 was known by the Americans) had some saving features, such as the single 37mm cannon and the two 20mm cannon which were absolutely lethal in close-quarter combat, as many Americans found out. It could also out-turn an F-4 and it was simpler to fly and maintain, which suited the VPAF. The MiG 17 was also able to take a lot of punishment, as Nguyen Nhat Chieu recalled. 'I was once hit seven times in a MiG 17 and still managed to fly back to my base in Kep in one piece.' The real defect of the MiG 17 during the Vietnam war was the pilot, often inexperienced and often flying into combat to take on the American veterans of the Korean War and even some from the Second World War. To compound matters for the North Vietnamese, they faced odds of 4, 5 or even 6 to l.

From 1965 the VPAF would use the MiG 17F clear-weather fighters from the Soviet Union and Shenyangs from China. Later in the war they would receive MIG 17PFUs, from which the cannon had been removed and replaced by AA-1 air-to-air missiles, but by then they were very obsolete and used as ground-attack aircraft.

The MiG 17 was the staple equipment of the 921st, 923rd and 925th Fighter Regiments during the early part of the war

before the MiG 21 took over as the main VPAF fighter. However, the author has discovered by talking to North Vietnamese pilots that the MiG 17 was not the preferred aircraft if the MiG 21 was available. Pham Ngoc Lan remembers that 'most of us would dream of the day we could fly the MiG 21 instead of the MiG 17'.

The later fighter used by the North Vietnamese was the MiG 21. The 'Fishbed', using its NATO code name, was used in more countries than any other fighter in history and was the most numerous jet fighter in aviation history. This classic aircraft became the backbone of the VPAF from 1966 to 1980, and is still used by the it today. Like all Soviet-made fighters of the day it was light, agile and cheap, and had a top speed of 1,386 mph, which was comparable to the F-4 Phantom, the best American fighter. Its basic armament was two 23 mm cannon and two ATOLL heat-seeking air-to-air missiles. The main types operated by the VPAF were the MIG 21F 'Fishbed C', a clear-weather fighter, the MIG 21PF 'Fishbed D', the MIG 21PFS 'Fishbed E' and the MIG 21PFMA which had heavier armament. In the hands of the 921st, 923rd and the 927th Fighter Regiments, the MiG 21 accounted for 70 per cent of all air-to-air kills during the war. Contrary to popular belief, most North Vietnamese pilots did not prefer the MiG 17 to the MiG 21. This belief may stem from propaganda of the time that the North's pilots were inferior and could fly only less sophisticated aircraft. Ace pilots such as Nguyen Van Bay did, in fact, approve of the MiG 17 (with which he claimed all his seven victories) but only because many pilots like him never flew the MiG 21 in combat with American aircraft.

The other fighter used in small numbers (about fifty being delivered) was the MIG 19 'Farmer'. This aircraft was not as widely used as other types owing to its very short range (425 miles), and it was quickly superseded as a supersonic interceptor by the MiG 21. It was a single-seat fighter capable of reaching speeds of 900mph. It appeared in late 1969 and was armed with three 30mm cannon. It was allocated to the 925th Fighter Regiment, scoring only seven victories before it was withdrawn from service in June 1972 due to heavy losses and low serviceability.

Mikoyan-Gurevich MiG-17F - Basic specifications

Crew: One
Length: 11.36 m (37 ft 3 in)
Wingspan: 9.63 m (31 ft 7 in)
Height: 3.80 m (12 ft 6 in)
Wing area: 22.6 m² (243.2 ft²)
Empty weight: 3,930 kg (8,646 lb)
Loaded weight: 5,354 kg (11,803 lb)
Max takeoff weight: 6,286 kg (13,858 lb)
Powerplant: 1× Klimov VK-1F afterburning turbojet,33.1 kN with afterburner (7,440 lbf)

PERFORMANCE
Maximum speed: 1,144 km/h at 3,000 m (711 mph at 10,000 ft)
Range: 1,080 km, 1,670 km with drop tanks (670 mi / 1,035 mi)
Service ceiling: 16,600 m (54,500 ft)
Rate of climb: 65 m/s (12,795 ft/min)
Wing loading: 237 kg/m² (48 lb/ft²)
Thrust/weight: 0.63

ARMAMENT
1x 37 mm Nudelman N-37 cannon (40 rounds total)
2x 23 mm Nudelman-Rikhter NR-23 cannons (80 rounds per gun, 160 rounds total)
Up to 500 kg (1,100 lb) of external stores on two pylons, including 100 kg (220 lb) and 250 kg (550 lb) bombs or fuel tanks.

Mikoyan-Gurevich MiG-21 - Basic specifications

Crew: One
Length: 15.76 m (51 ft 8 in)
Wingspan: 7.15 m (23 ft 5 in)
Height: 4.12 m (13 ft 6 in)
Wing area: 23 m² (247.5 ft²)
Empty weight: 5,350 kg (11,800 lb)
Loaded weight: 8,726 kg (19,200 lb)
Max takeoff weight: 9,660 kg (21,300 lb)
Powerplant: 1× Tumansky R-25-300 afterburning turbojet, 70 kN (15,700 lbf)

PERFORMANCE
Maximum speed: 2230 km/h (1,385 mph) (Mach 2.1)
Range: 450-500 km (280-310 mi)
Service ceiling: 19,000 m (62,300 ft)
Rate of climb: 225 m/s (23,600 ft/min but with 50 per cent fuel and two AA-2 'Atoll' missiles, the MiG-21 can reach 58,000 feet [19,000 meters] in one minute, under favorable weather circumstances)
Wing loading: 379 kg/m² (77.8 lb/ft²)
Thrust/weight: 0.84

ARMAMENT
One centerline twin-barrelled GSh-23 23 mm cannon (PFM, MF, SMT, and Ibis variants) or one single-barrelled NR-30 cannon (F-13 variant).
Up to 2,000 kg (4,400 lb) of air-to-air and air-to-ground weapons on two or four underwing hardpoints, depending on the variant. Early machines carried two Vympel K-13 (AA-2 'Atoll') air-to-air missiles under the wing pylons. Late models carried two K-13 and two fuel tanks under the wing pylons or combinations of four K-13 infrared- and radar-guided missiles. The Molniya R-60 (NATO reporting name AA-8 'Aphid') was also used on multiple pylons. Most aircraft carried a single 450 L (119 US gal) fuel tank on the centerline pylon.

THE MAIN FIGHTER OPPOSITION

McDonald Douglas F-4 Phantom

F-4D - As against previous versions, the F-4D showed new technology in improved radar, weapons and navigation instruments. Widely used in the Vietnam War.

F-4E - This version was designed to fill many roles for the U.S Air Force, including air support, close support for ground troops and interdiction-interference with enemy movements. Pilots of the F-4D had complained that they had missed many chances to shoot down enemy MIGs at close range because the F-4D was armed only with missiles. The E version begun in 1967 answered this critiscism by coming equipped with internal 20-mm guns for close work against enemy aircraft and additional fuel cells to improve flying time.

Specifications (F-4E)

GENERAL CHARACTERISTICS
Crew: Two
Length: 63 ft 0 in (19.2 m)
Wingspan: 38 ft 4.5 in (11.7 m)
Height: 16 ft 6 in (5.0 m)
Wing area: 530.0 ft² (49.2 m²)
Airfoil: NACA 0006.4-64 root, NACA 0003-64 tip
Empty weight: 30,328 lb (13,757 kg)
Loaded weight: 41,500 lb (18,825 kg)
Max takeoff weight: 61,795 lb (28,030 kg)
Powerplant: 2× General Electric J79-GE-17A axial compressor turbojets, 17,845 lbf (79.6 kN) each
Zero-lift drag coefficient: 0.0224
Drag area: 11.87 ft² (1.10 m²)
Aspect ratio: 2.77
Fuel capacity: 1,994 US gal (7,549 L) internal, 3,335 US gal (12,627 L) with three external tanks
Maximum landing weight: 36,831 lb (16,706 kg)

PERFORMANCE
Maximum speed: Mach 2.23 (1,472 mph, 2,370 km/h) at 40,000 ft (12,190 m)
Cruise speed: 506 kn (585 mph, 940 km/h)

Combat radius: 367 NM (422 mi, 680 km)
Ferry range: 1,403 nmi (1,615 mi, 2,600 km) with 3 external fuel tanks
Service ceiling: 60,000 ft (18,300 m)
Rate of climb: 41,300 ft/min (210 m/s)
Wing loading: 78 lb/ft² (383 kg/m²)
Thrust/weight: 0.86
Lift-to-drag ratio: 8.58
Takeoff roll: 4,490 ft (1,370 m) at 53,814 lb (24,410 kg)
Landing roll: 3,680 ft (1,120 m) at 36,831 lb (16,706 kg)

ARMAMENT
1x 20 mm M61 Vulcan gatling cannon, 639 rounds
Up to 18,650 lb (8,480 kg) of weapons on nine external hardpoints, including general purpose bombs, cluster bombs, TV- and laser-guided bombs, rocket pods, air-to-ground missiles, anti-runway weapons, anti-ship missiles, targeting pods, recce pods, and nuclear weapons. Baggage pods may also be carried. External fuel tanks of 370 US gal (1,420 L) capacity for the outer wing hardpoints and either a 600 or 610 US gal (2,310 or 2,345 L) fuel tank for the centerline station can be fitted to extend the range.
4x AIM-7 Sparrow in fuselage recesses plus 4x AIM-9 Sidewinders on wing pylons.

A fully armed Phantom F-4D of the 555th Tactical Fighter Squadron, 432nd Tac Recon Wing at Udorn Royal Thai Air Foce Base with LORAN 'towel rail' aerial on fuselage spine. (Jerry Scutts)

An F-4E of the 34th TFS, 388th TFW from Korat. Fuselage stripes denoted the wing CO's aircraft; many wing Phantoms carried the shark's mouth until higher authority ordered their removal. (Jerry Scutts)

Radar Bombing: led by an RB-66 Destroyer, USAF F-4C Phantoms drop bombs on a military target in North Vietnam. Using radar equipment to pinpoint their targets, the high-flying aircraft were not hampered by clouds or adverse weather. Numerous missions of this type were flown when inclement weather obscured targets in North Vietnam. (Jerry Scutts)

US Air Force Sgt. Robert E. Sloan (right) and Sgt. Vincent M. Glasener of the 559th Tactical Fighter Squadron at Cam Ranh bay Air Base, South Vietnam, adjust the support mechanism on an F-4 bomb rack, December 1968. The rack holding the general purpose bombs is a standard fit TER - triple ejector rack. (Jerry Scutts)

A USAF technician fits tail fins to AIM-7 Sparrow air-to-air missiles. (Jerry Scutts)

A flight of USAF F-4C Phantom fighter-bombers refuel from a KC-135 tanker aircraft before making a strike against Communist targets in North Vietnam. The Phantoms are fully loaded with 750 lb general purpose bombs and rockets. (USAF)

Port side view of an RF-4C Phantom II with auxiliary fuel tanks in flight, August 1968. The aircraft was assigned to the 192nd Tactical Reconnaissance Group, Nevada Air National Guard. (U.S. Air Force photograph by Sgt. Mark L. Comerford)

Robin Olds, commander of the 8th Tactical Fighter Wing, Southeast Asia in 1967, preflights his F-4C Phantom. Col. Olds shot down four enemy MiG aircraft in aerial combat over North Vienam. (USAF)

Head-on view of a Phantom F-4C. (USAF)

F-105D Thunderchief of the 357th TFS, 355th TFW out of Takhli RTAFB. Note 'daisy cutter' fuse extender on the 750 lb bombs for maximum anti-personnel effect. (Jerry Scutts)

Right: The versatile 'swing wing' F-111 entered the Air Force inventory in 1967. The aircraft provided many firsts among weapons systems. It was the first production aircraft with variable swing wings that could be swept back or brought forward to increase efficiency. It also had the first terrain-following radar, allowing it to fly at night at high speeds and low altitudes, as well as the first crew escape module. The aircraft was one of the more controversial aircraft ever to fly, yet it achieved one of the safest operational records of any aircraft in Air Force history. (USAF)

A trio of F-105Ds of the 333rd TFS, 355th TFW from Takhli take on fuel from a 'Young Tiger' KC-135A Stratotanker. (Jerry Scutts)

Three F-5As, armed with 750 lb bombs, are shown in the revetment area at Bien Hoa Air Base, South Vietnam, 31 January 1966. (USAF)

F-100 Super Sabres in their revetment area at Bien Hoa Air Base, South Vietnam, 31 January 1966. (USAF)

B-52 Stratofortress dropping bombs in the 1960s. (USAF)

On the flight line, U.S. Air Force technicians prepare a McDonald RF-101 Voodoo for a photo-reconnaissance mission. Overhead, a Fairchild C-123 Provider takes off on another assault airlift sortie, providing an air bridge to an outpost in South Vietnam. High above, a Cessna O-1E 'Bird Dog' returns after pointing out Viet Cong targets to pilots of strike aircraft. 6 January 1967. (USAF)

The A-7D was a single-seat, tactical close air support aircraft. Although designed primarily as a ground-attack aircraft, it also had limited air-to-air combat capability. It was derived from the basic A-7 originally developed for the U.S. Navy. The first A-7D made its initial flight on 5 April 1968, and deliveries of production models began on 23 December 1968. When A-7D production ended in 1976, 459 had been delivered to the U.S. Air Force. (USAF)

APPENDIX 6

Other US aircraft types in use in Vietnam

TYPE	CREW	SPEED	RANGE	FIXED WAEPON
A-4 Skyhawk	1	(673 mph, 1,077 km/h)	2,000 miles	2 x 20 mm
A-6 Intruder	2	(648 mph, 1,040 km/h)	3,200 miles	None
A-7 Corsair	2	(698 mph, 1,123 km/h)	715 miles	1 x 20 mm
A-37 Dragonfly	2	(300 mph, 480 km/h)	900 miles	1 x 7.62 minigun
AT-28D Trojan	2	346 mph	1,060 miles	None
B-52 Stratofortress	8	(650 mph, 1,000 km/h)	4,480 miles	1 x Vulcan
B-57 Canberra	2	Mach 0.79 (598 mph, 960 km/h)	950 miles	8 x .50 calibre
F-8 Crusader	1	Mach 1.86 (1,225 mph, 1,975 km/h)	450 miles	4 x 20 mm
F-100 Super Sabre	1	(864 mph, 1,390 km/h)	1,500 miles	4 x 20 mm
F-105 Thunderdhief	1	Mach 2.08 (1,372 mph, 2,208 km/h)	780 miles	1 x 20 mm Vulcan
F-111 Aardvark	2	Mach 2.5 (1,650 mph, 2,655 km/h)	1,330 miles	1 x 20 mm Vulcan

Main Air-to-Air Missiles used in Vietnam

TYPE	ASPECT	RANGE	WEIGHT
AIM-4 Falcon	Rear	11 miles	145 pounds
AIM-7D Sparrow	All	50 miles	450 pounds
AIM-9B Sidewinder	Rear	3 miles	155 pounds
AIM-9D Sidewinder	Rear	11 miles	170 pounds
AA-2 ATOLL	Rear	3 miles	155 pounds

American air war doctrine

The air war in Vietnam from the American point of view has been explored in many books, articles and journals. Even a book such as this which portrays the Vietnamese view needs to implant some of that common knowledge to provide the reader with a sense of the purpose behind the bombings of North Vietnam, the creation of artificial Rules Of Engagement and the bombing halts that appeared just when it would seem that the bombings were working.

A sustained air war only started in early 1965. The American aims were to cripple the so-called 'strategic industries' of North Vietnam and to interrupt its lines of communication. The air war was sustained because the Americans wanted to show the North Vietnamese that by 'misbehaving' and supporting the Viet Cong in the South, there would be a price to pay. If the North Vietnamese had showed signs of conforming to US requirements, the bombings would have been halted.

The US air war against North Vietnam therefore had a three-point approach:

1 To force North Vietnam to end its support of the Viet Cong.
2 To show the weak democratic government in the South that they were not alone.
3 To create a position of advantage whereby the US government could manufacture a permanent democratic state in the South.

The US government divided the air campaign over North Vietnam into five phases. The first phase commenced in April 1965 and was directed mainly against North Vietnam's transportation system. The second phase lasted for only one month from 29 June 1966 to the end of July 1966, and destroyed 70 per cent of North Vietnam's storage capacity. The third phase started in the spring of 1967 and was aimed at previously no-go areas, such as strategic targets in populated cities like Ha Noi and Haiphong. The fourth phase began on 1April 1968 and was called 'Rolling Thunder': this was only halted by the changing political circumstances in the US. The last phase was a continuation of the war but was more of a defensive nature on the part of the US, with punishment as the objective rather than outright victory.

For the North Vietnamese and American pilots, the air war had three time zones or campaigns: the Rolling Thunder campaign from 2 March 1965 to 3 October 1968; the Linebacker raids from 8 May 1972 to 18 October 1972; and the third phase from 18 December 1972 to 29 December 1972.

APPENDIX 8   Rules of Engagement

The United States was never legally at war with North Vietnam: because of this a complex set of rules of engagement had to be memorized by all pilots. Any breach of such rules could result in severe consequences, even court martial for American air crews. The rationale behind this was to stop any 'innocent civilians' being killed. The pilots were not allowed to hit SAM sites or MiGs on the ground under any circumstances. It was hard for such pilots to follow instructions when it was those very MiGs and SAMs that were killing their fellow airmen and servicemen. What should be considered is whether any such acts of revenge were made without sufficient reason. For example, the Vietnamese did not have the raw materials to make their own weaponry. All such equipment was supplied by China and the Soviet Union throughout the war. Many American pilots were therefore of the opinion that the North Vietnamese MiGs should be attacked and destroyed on the ground. The shortcoming of this idea was that any MiGs destroyed would merely be replaced by new ones without real loss to the VPAF.

If, however, the radar sites allowed the MiGs up into action, then the Americans would have the opportunity to destroy the aircraft and kill the pilots (possibly the North's raw material). It is possible that the desire to hit aircraft on the ground evolved from older pilots with experience from World War Two, who flew over Luftwaffe airfields destroying aircraft that the Third Reich had used up time and raw materials to build.

Route packages and exclusion zones

The US strategists divided Vietnam into six route packages. The higher the route number, the closer the US pilot was to the North's capital, Ha Noi (route 6 covered Ha Noi and Haiphong), and the closer he would be to the MiGs.

Route package 6 was sub-divided into two sectors, 6A and 6B. In routes 1and 2 the MiGs of the VPAF did not claim any American aircraft shot down during the whole war. In route 3 they shot down at least five American aircraft: in route 4 they shot down eight: in route 5 at least fourteen aircraft were downed and in route 6, they accounted for another 71.

The USAF was given the responsibility of covering route packages 1, 5 and 6 B. There were areas around Ha Noi and Haiphong that were no-go areas for all military aircraft except when given express permission on a mission basis. The US government did not want to antagonize the international community still based in that area by destroying their property and killing their citizens – most of the foreign community members were in central Ha Noi so a 10-mile exclusion zone was made. (The bombing of the Chinese Embassy in Belgrade in 1999 and the problems it caused for the US government serves to highlight the reason for this zone.) A similar four-mile zone was made around Haiphong since almost all ships in the harbour were non-Vietnamese, mainly coming from the Eastern Bloc and China.

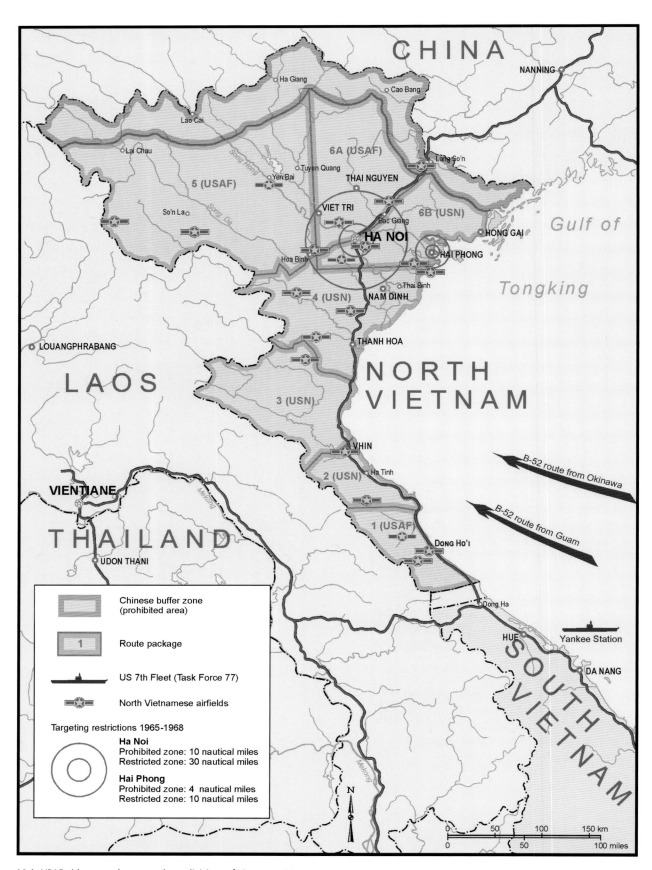

CHINA

NANNING

Ha Giang

Cao Bang

Lao Cai

Lai Chau

6A (USAF)

Lang So'n

5 (USAF)

Tuyen Quang

Yen Bai

THAI NGUYEN

So'n La

Song Hong

Song Da

VIET TRI

Bac Giang

6B (USN)

HONG GAI

Gulf of

HA NOI

HAI PHONG

Hoa Binh

Thai Binh

Tongking

4 (USN)

NAM DINH

LOUANGPHRABANG

THANH HOA

LAOS

NORTH
VIETNAM

3 (USN)

VIENTIANE

VHIN

B-52 route from Okinawa

Ha Tinh

2 (USN)

B-52 route from Guam

THAILAND

1 (USAF)

DONG HO'I

UDON THANI

Mekong

Dong Ha

HUE

Yankee Station

SOUTH

DA NANG

Mekong

VIETNAM

N

	Chinese buffer zone (prohibited area)
1	Route package
	US 7th Fleet (Task Force 77)
	North Vietnamese airfields

Targeting restrictions 1965-1968

Ha Noi
Prohibited zone: 10 nautical miles
Restricted zone: 30 nautical miles

Hai Phong
Prohibited zone: 4 nautical miles
Restricted zone: 10 nautical miles

0   50   100   150 km
0   50   100 miles

Main VPAF airbases and route package divisions of Vietnam, 1965-1973

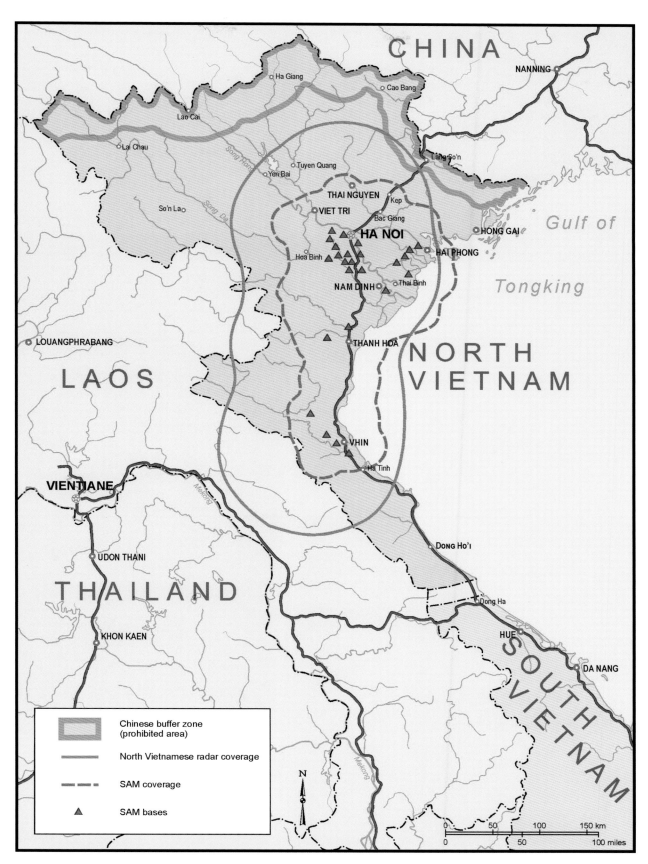

CHINA

NANNING

Ha Giang

Cao Bang

Lao Cai

Lai Chau

Song Hong

Lang So'n

Tuyen Quang

Yen Bai

THAI NGUYEN

Kep

So'n La

Song Da

VIET TRI

Bac Giang

HA NOI

HONG GAI

Gulf of

Hoa Binh

HAI PHONG

NAM DINH

Thai Binh

Tongking

THANH HOA

LOUANGPHRABANG

NORTH

LAOS

VIETNAM

VHIN

Ha Tinh

VIENTIANE

Mekong

Dong Ho'I

UDON THANI

THAILAND

Dong Ha

KHON KAEN

HUE

SOUTH

Chinese buffer zone
(prohibited area)

North Vietnamese radar coverage

SAM coverage

▲   SAM bases

DA NANG

VIETNAM

N

50   100   150 km

0   50   100 miles

Principal radar sites and extent of radar coverage, 1972

TABLE 1 North Vietnamese officer ranks

	VPAF RANK	ENGLISH EQUIVALENT	INSIGNIA	
1.	Dai Tuong	Senior General	4 Gold stars	
2.	Thuong Tuong	General	3 gold stars	
3.	Trung Tuong	Lieutenant General	2 gold stars	
4.	Thieu Tuong	Major General	1 gold star	
5.	Dai Ta	Senior Colonel	4 silver stars and 2 silver pipes on shoulder boards	
6.	Thuong Ta	Colonel	3 silver stars and 2 silver pipes on shoulder boards	
7.	Trung Ta	Lieutenant Colonel	2 silver stars and 2 pipes on shoulder boards	
8.	Thieu Ta	Major	1 Silver Star and 2 pipes	
9.	Dai Uy	Senior Captain	4 silver stars and 1 pipe on shoulder boards	
10.	Thuong Uy	Captain	3 silver stars and 1 pipe on shoulder boards	
11.	Trung Uy	Senior Lieutenant	2 silver stars and 1 pipe on shoulder boards	
12.	Thieu Uy	Lieutenant	1 silver star and 1 pipe on shoulder boards	
13.	Chuan Uy	Warrant Officer	1 silver pipe on shoulder boards	

Note:

1. All General shoulder boards were edged with gold piping

2. The rank of Chuan Uy has no direct equivalent in English but loosely translated means 'Aspirant'.

In the VPAF this rank is not strictly a full officer rank, but the US equivalent is a Second Lieutenant.

Complete VPAF Combat Losses (262 in total)

TABLE 2

RANK	NAME	AGE	KIA
Warrant Officer	TRINH VAN HOA	28	1.5.1964
Lieutenant	NGUYEN XUAN TINH	29	1.5.1964
Senior Lieutenant	LE MINH HUAN	27	4.4.1965
Lieutenant	TRAN NGUYEN NAM	31	4.4.1965
Senior Lieutenant	PHAM GIAY	31	4.4.1965
Senior Lieutenant	TRAN VAN THUY	31	23.4.1965
1ST. Lieutenant	LE TRONG LONG	31	17.6.1965
Lieutenant	NGUYEN VAN LAI	30	20.6.1965
Lieutenant	NGUYEN CUONG	32	10.7.1965
1ST Lieutenant	PHAN THANH NHA	33	10.7.1965
Warrant Officer	TRA VAN AT	29	7.10.1965
Lieutenant	NGUYEN XUAN CANH	30	7.10.1965
Lieutenant	PHAM VAN KY	28	7.10.1965
Warrant Officer	VO XUAN KHANH	23	7.10.1965
Warrant Officer	HOANG VAN NGOAN	24	7.10.1965
Lieutenant	PHAM NGOC ANH	25	7.10.1965
Lieutenant	NGUYEN VAN THO	26	7.2.1966
Lieutenant	NGUYEN SY HIENG	31	24.7.1966
Senior Lieutenant	TRAN TAN DUC	30	30.4.1966
Senior Lieutenant	TRAN TRIEM	31	13.7.1966
Lieutenant	TA VAN THANH	24	24.7.1966
Captain	PHAM THANH CHUNG	32	18.8 1966
Lieutenant	NGUYEN KIM TU	22	22.8.1966
Captain	NGUYEN VAN BIEN	32	29.9.1966
Senior Lieutenant	DANG VAN HUNG	30	22.11.1966
Lieutenant	LUU DUC SI	25	4.12.1966
Lieutenant	NGUYEN KIM TIEN	30	19.12.1966
Lieutenant	TA VAN CHEN	27	19.12.1966
Lieutenant	NGUYEN MINH LY	24	19.12.1966
Warrant Officer	LE CON SON	23	19.12.1966
Captain	NGO DUC MAI	29	3.6.1967
Senior Lieutenant	DONG VAN DE	27	6.11.1967
Captain	PHAN VAN BAN	34	6.11.1967
Lieutenant	NGUYEN NGOC TIEN	24	7.11.1967
Lieutenant	LE BA CUONG	30	7.11.1967
Lieutenant	NGUYEN XUAN SINH	24	7.11.1967
Lieutenant	VU HUY LUONG	25	26.3.1967
Senior Lieutenant	NGUYEN XUAN NHUAN	26	3.4.1967
Lieutenant	VU XUAN DUOC	25	20.4.1967
Warrant Officer	NGUYEN VAN KHAM	26	24.4.1967
Senior Lieutenant	TRAN THIEN LUONG	25	26.4.1967
Lieutenant	NGUYEN VAN KHANH	30	1.5.1967

RANK	NAME	AGE	KIA
Lieutenant	NGUYEN BA DICH	30	1.5.1967
Captain	NGUYEN VAN NHIEU	25	2.5.1967
Senior Lieutenant	NGUYEN THE HON	26	14.5.1967
Lieutenant	NGUYEN VAN PHI	26	19.5.1967
Captain	TRAN MINH PHUONG	33	19.5.1967
Senior Lieutenant	PHAN THAN TAI	29	19.5.1967
Captain	VO VAN MAN	28	19.5.1967
Lieutenant	NGHIEM DINH HIEU	27	20.5.1967
Warrant Officer	CHU VAN PHUNG	27	21.5.1967
Lieutenant	NGUYEN TRONG OANH	33	26.5.1967
Senior Lieutenant	NGUYEN GIA KHUNG	22	26.5.1967
Lieutenant	PHAN TAN DUAN	23	3.6.1967
Captain	TRAN HUYEN	32	5.6.1967
Senior Lieutenant	HOANG VAN KY	28	5.6.1967
Lieutenant	TRUONG VAN CUNG	27	5.6.1967
Lieutenant	DO BUU	32	20.7.1967
Lieutenant	NGO SI NGHI	26	20.7.1967
Captain	BUI DINH KINH	34	10.8.1967
Senior Lieutenant	HA BON	25	20.8.1967
Lieutenant	LE VAN PHONG	25	23.8.1967
Captain	TRAN NGOC SIU	31	30.9.1967
Lieutenant	TRAN SAM KY	23	30.10.1967
Captain	NGUYEN HUU TAO	34	6.11.1967
Senior Lieutenant	NGO DOAN NHUNG	27	18.11.1967
Senior Lieutenant	NGUYEN DINH PHUC	23	19.12.1967
Lieutenant	NGUYEN HONG THAI	26	19.12.1967
Captain	PHAN VAN TUC	30	31.12.1967
Lieutenant	LE XUAN KICH	31	12.1.1968 +
Captain	PHAM THANH TAM	34	12.1.1968 +
Senior Lieutenant	TRAN SI TIEU	35	12.1.1968 +
Lieutenant	PHAM VAN PHAN	26	12.1.1968 +
Senior Lieutenant	TRAN HUU Quy	33	12.1.1968 +
Captain	PHAN NHU CAN	30	12.1.1968 +
Captain	HA VAN CHUC	30	19.1.1968
Lieutenant	NGO PHUONG CHAU	26	7.2.1968 +
Senior Lieutenant	PHAM KE	33	7.2.1968 +
Lieutenant	NGUYEN MINH	26	7.2.1968 +
Warrant Officer	NGUYEN VAN TE	28	7.2.1968 +
Lieutenant	NGUYEN VAN MAN	25	7.2.1968 +
Captain	NGUYEN TRIET	35	9.2.1968 +
Senior Lieutenant	NGUYEN PHI HUNG	26	9.7.1968 +
Lieutenant	HO VAN TIEP	32	12.2.1968 +
Lieutenant	LUU VAN TUYEN	32	12.2.1968
Senior Lieutenant	PHAM THANH BA	31	12.2.1968
Warrant Officer	DINH TIEN NGAC	28	12.2.1968 +
Lieutenant	PHAM DINH PHU	26	12.2.1968 +
Lieutenant	NGO VAN LUYEN	29	12.2.1968 +
Lieutenant	NGUYEN VAN CONG	28	12.2.1968 +
Lieutenant	MAI VAN THUONG	31	12.2.1968 +
Lieutenant	NGUYEN DINH HOI	32	12.2.1968 +
Lieutenant	NGUYEN VAN NUNG	31	2.2.1968 +
Senior Lieutenant	VO MINH CHUNG	31	12.2.1968 +
Lieutenant	LE VAN AN	32	12.2.1968 +
Lieutenant	TRAN VAN TU	33	12.2.1968 +
Captain	BUI DINH VAN	35	12.2.1968 +
Lieutenant	LE HUU DAC	27	12.2.1968 +
Captain	NGUYEN VAN BANG	37	12.2.1968 +
Lieutenant	HO DINH HAC	32	20.4.1968
Lieutenant	VO NGO QUYEN	24	30.4.1968
Lieutenant	NGUYEN VU KHOA	26	30.4.1968

RANK	NAME	AGE	KIA
Senior Lieutenant	TRINH DUC THANG	28	30.4.1968
Warrant Officer	NGUYEN DUY THANG	28	30.4.1968
Lieutenant	LE VAN HANH	30	30.4.1968
Senior Lieutenant	DINH VAN HA	26	23.5.1968
1ST Lieutenant	NGUYEN PHI HUNG	26	9.7.1968
Lieutenant	VU HONG THAI	31	17.7.1968
Senior Lieutenant	DINH VAN MINH	29	17.7.1968
Warrant Officer	NGUYEN HUU NGHIEM	26	17.7.1968
Senior Lieutenant	LE SY DIEP	24	29.7.1968
Warrant Officer	NGUYEN VAN HOA	23	4.2.1969
Senior Lieutenant	NGUYEN QUANG SINH	29	4.3.1969
Senior Lieutenant	DUONG TRUNG TAN	31	13.9.1969
Lieutenant	PHAM DINH TUAN	32	28.3.1970
Lieutenant	PHAM THANH NAM	22	28.3.1970
Lieutenant	BUI DINH DOAN	23	6.4.1970
Major	LE QUANG TRUNG	36	6.4.1970
Lieutenant	LUONG DUC TRUONG	24	9.3.1971
Warrant Officer	NGUYEN VAN TRUAT	28	24.4.1971
Lieutenant	TRAN VAN MAO	30	30.5.1971
Senior Lieutenant	NGUYEN QUOC HIEN	28	30.5.1971
Senior Lieutenant	NGUYEN DONG TRIET	34	30.5.1971
Senior Lieutenant	NGUYEN VAN KHANH	28	18.12.1971
Senior Lieutenant	NGUYEN VAN TAM	34	2.2.1972
Senior Lieutenant	NGUYEN TRONG TIEN	27	2.2.1972
Warrant Officer	VU HUU DIEN	31	3.3.1972 +
Major	PHAN ANH THO	45	3.3.1972 +
Senior Lieutenant	BUI VAN LONG	27	3.3.1972 +
Senior Lieutenant	NGUYEN VAN PHONG	35	3.3.1972 +
Lieutenant	BUI THE TAN	33	3.3.1972 +
Senior Lieutenant	CAO VAN TUYEN	40	3.3.1972 +
Major	LE TRONG HUYEN	36	3.3.1972 +
Senior Lieutenant	PHAM VAN MAO	31	3.3.1972 +
Senior Lieutenant	HOANG IOH	25	6.3.1972
Warrant Officer	NGUYEN DUC KHAI	38	26.4.1972
Lieutenant	NGUYEN VAN BAY	29	6.5.1972
Senior Lieutenant	NGUYEN KHAC GIAM	36	7.5.1972
Lieutenant	LE VAN TUONG	24	10.5.1972
Senior Lieutenant	CAO SON KHAO	27	10.5.1972
Lieutenant	LE DUC OANH	28	10.5.1972
Lieutenant	TRA VAN KIAM	27	10.5.1972
Lieutenant	NGUYEN VAN NGAI	25	10.5.1972
Senior Lieutenant	VO SY GIAP	27	11.5.1972
Lieutenant	NGUYEN VAN DIEN	27	23.5.1972
Senior Lieutenant	VU VAN DANG	29	23.5.1972
Lieutenant	NGUYEN XUAN MINH	25	26.5.1972
Senior Lieutenant	NGUYEN VAN LUNG	33	31.5.1972
Lieutenant	NGUYEN XUAN MINH	25	26.5.1972
Senior Lieutenant	NGUYEN VAN LUNG	33	31.5.1972
Captain	PHAM TRONG VAN	Unknown	26.1972
Lieutenant	NGUYEN VAN PHUC	26	11.6.1972
Senior Lieutenant	PHAM NGOC TAM	28	27.6.1972
Lieutenant	VU VAN HOP	24	8.7.1972
Senior Lieutenant	NGUYEN NGOC HUNG	27	8.7.1972
Captain	DANG NGOC NGU	33	8.7.1972
Lieutenant	HOANG THE THANG	23	11.7.1972
Lieutenant	NGUYEN THE DUC	22	18.7.1972
Senior Lieutenant	NGUYEN NGOC THIEN	27	10.8.1972
Lieutenant	NGUYEN THANG DUOC	22	21.8.1972
Warrant Officer	NGUYEN VAN THUAN	29	2.9.1972
Lieutenant	NGUYEN VAN TUE	25	13.10.1972

RANK	NAME	AGE	KIA
Senior Lieutenant	NGUYEN HUU TUONG	30	20.12.1972
SeniorLieutenant	NGUYEN HONG HAI	33	20.12.1972
Senior Lieutenant	HOANG TAM HUNG	24	28.12.1972
Captain	VU XUAN THIEU	27	28.12.1972
Lieutenant	PHAM VAN NIEN	44	5.1.1973
Captain	HOANG CONG	32	8.1.1973
Senior Lieutenant	LUU KIM NGO	28	12.1.1973
Senior Lieutenant	NGUYEN VAN HUNG	28	19.1.1973
Lieutenant	NGUYEN VAN HONG	24	29.3.1973
Lieutenant	TRIEU TIEN LE	27	20.7.1973
Senior Lieutenant	PHAN THANH LIEM	38	8.3.1974 +
Senior Lieutenant	TRAN NGOC LAC	38	8.3.1974 +
Senior Lieutenant	LE VAN DAN	34	8.3.1974 +
Warrant Officer	BUI THE VIET	27	8.3.1974 +
Senior Lieutenant	LE TRUYEN	31	8.3.1974 +
Senior Lieutenant	TRUONG CONG THANH	27	1.5.1975
Lieutenant	THAI DOAN HO	25	29.6.1975
Warrant Officer	NGUYEN QUANG TRUNG	26	25.1.1975 +
Senior Lieutenant	PHAM HUU HOANG	27	25.1.1975 +
Senior Lieutenant	BUI DINH LUONG	38	25.1.1975 +
Lieutenant	LE DUY KHOAN	25	25.1.1975 +
Senior Lieutenant	NGUYEN VAN HIENG	20	25.1.1975 +
Senior Lieutenant	NONG VAN PHUC	31	25.1.1975 +
Senior. Lieutenant	PHAN DUC TOAN	30	15.7.1975
Senior Lieutenant	HOANG MAI VUONG	28	15.7.1975
Senior Lieutenant	NGUYEN NGOC TIEP	33	15.8.1975
Senior Lieutenant	TRONG VAN NHUNG	42	21.12.1975 +
Senior Lieutenant	NGUYEN TIEN YENG	39	27.12.1975 +
Senior Lieutenant	TRUONG VAN NHUNG	42	27.12.1975 +
Lieutenant	DAO DUC BAO	Unknown	27.12.1975+
Lieutenant	PHAN VAN THANG	26	27.12.1975 +
Lieutenant Colonel	CAO THANH TINH	44	4.8.1976
Lieutenant	HOANG XUAN LAM	29	17.9.1976
Senior Lieutenant	LE VIET THUYET	36	7.12.1976
Senior Lieutenant	DO XUAN CU	35	27.1.1977 +
Senior Lieutenant	NGUYEN HUU TU	35	27.1.1977 +
Major	HOANG NGOC TRUNG	47	27.1.1977 +
Warrant Officer	NGUYEN VAN SONG	36	27.1.1977 +
Senior Lieutenant	NGUYEN VAN TRAC	41	27.1.1977 +
Senior Lieutenant	NGUYEN THE HUNG	32	1.10.1977
Warrant Officer	NGUYEN MINH AN	26	19.4.1978
Warrant Officer	VU DINH NGHI	22	9.6.1978
Senior Lieutenant	PHAN VIET TAN	28	8.8.1978
Lieutenant	LAM VAN CHI	31	8.8.1978
Lieutenant	PHAM NHU TRI	26	11.8.1978
Captain	NGO DUY THU	31	29.11.1978
Senior Lieutenant	BUI VAN KY	27	29.11.1979
Captain	TRAN SANG	38	4.1.1980
Lieutenant	TRINH VAN HOA	27	10.2.1980
Senior Lieutenant	NGUYEN NANG NGHIA	34	20.2.1980
Senior Lieutenant	TRINH HONG THU	25	19.4.1980
Lieutenant Colonel	DO VAN LANH	32	9.7.1980
Colonel	DINH TON	44	14.11.1980
Warrant Officer	NGUYEN DUC TUAN	24	27.6.1981
Lieutenant	NGUYEN VAN VINH	28	9.7.1981
Captain	NGUYEN VAN SINH	38	10.7.1981
Senior Lieutenant	NGUYEN VAN DAU	31	10.9.1981 +
Major	BUI THANH LIEN	32	2.9.1981 +
Senior Lieutenant	NGUYEN XUAN MAU	31	22.9.1981 +
Captain	DOAN LE	38	28.9.1981 +

RANK	NAME	AGE	KIA
Senior Lieutenant	KHUAT DUY LUONG	23	28.9.1981 +
Lieutenant	PHAM VAN THOAN	20	28.9.1981 +
Senior Lieutenant	CAO SON HUNG	25	28.9.1981 +
Senior Lieutenant	DANG DINH LE	25	28.9.1981 +
Senior Lieutenant	NGUYEN DINH DONG	27	28.11.1981
Warrant Officer	HOANG VAN KHAI	23	11.2.1982
Senior Lieutenant	NGUYEN XUAN AN	29	21.10.1982
Major	DUONG DINH NGHI	33	5.12.1982
Senior Lieutenant	NGUYEN TRAN DAI	35	22.2.1984
Senior Lieutenant	NGUYEN MANH HUN	28	22.2.1984
Senior Lieutenant	NGUYEN HUU CUONG	28	22.2.1984
Senior Lieutenant	PHAM NGOC HUNG	25	5.6.1984
Senior Lieutenant	LE VAN SON	24	8.10.1984
Senior. Lieutenant	NGUYEN KIM SON	25	12.2.1986
Senior Lieutenant	NGUYEN VIET HONG	24	9.5.1986
Senior Lieutenant	TRAN THANH BINH	26	9.6.1986
Senior Lieutenant	NGUYEN XUAN TRUONG	30	24.9.1986
Major	MAI VAN SACH	38	30.10.1986
Captain	LE QUANG THUONG	28	12.2.1987
Captain	LE HONG KHOI	26	12.2.1987
Senior Lieutenant	HOANG THANH NGHI	26	12.2.1987
Senior Lieutenant	PHAM VAN LICH	25	20.4.1987
Captain	VUONG HUU QUY	39	16.9.1987 +
Senior Lieutenant	NGUYEN QUOC HOE	28	16.9.1987 +
Senior Lieutenant	TRIEU MINH SON	27	16.9.1987 +
Senior Lieutenant	NGUYEN NGOC VAN	27	16.9.1987 +
Senior Lieutenant	NGUYEN XUAN LOAN	28	16.9.1987 +
Senior Lieutenant	NGO KHAC SU	25	16.9.1987 +
Lieutenant Colonel	DAO HUU NGOAN	51	16.9.1987 +
Senior Lieutenant	PHAM ANH DUNG	24	22.10.1987
Major	NGUYEN DUC LAM	42	5.5.1988
Captain	PHAM QUANG HIEN	35	5.5.1988
Captain	VUONG THIET BINH	31	10.7.1989
Captain	HOANG QUANG THAI	27	15.8.1989
Lieutenant Colonel	LE KHUONG	45	15.8.1989
Senior Lieutenant	BUI ANH TUAN	26	28.9.1989
Major	NGUYEN VAN THINH	41	10.11.1989
Captain	NGUYEN DANG CHUC	32	19.12.1989
Captain	CHU VAN DOAN	30	19.12.1989
Senior. Lieutenant	NGUYEN QUANG SAU	29	19.12.1989
Warrant Officer	PHAM VAN THAO	24	18.7.1990
Lieutenant	TRAN HA	24	21.4.1992

+ Denotes Bomber and transport aircrew killed together in the same crash.

Note: Dates that the pilots were shot down and killed always tally with official Vietnamese dates of death.

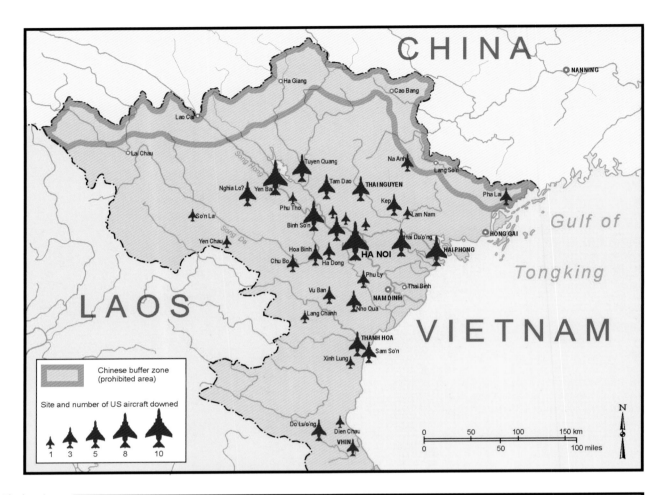

Above: The locations show the crash sites of main US fighters shot down from 1965-1972.

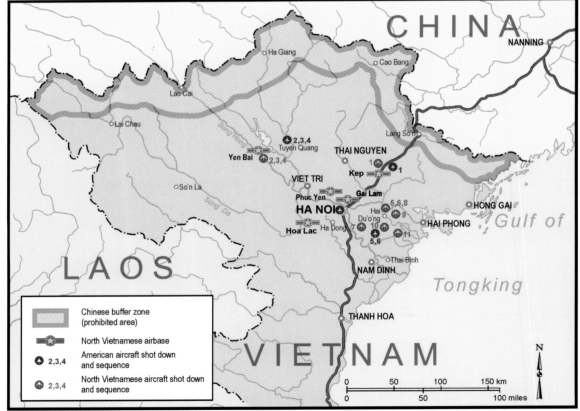

Location of North Vietnamese and American aircraft shot down on 10 May 1972. All claims shown relate only to both sides during the day's battles.

Estimated VPAF MiG and pilot strength

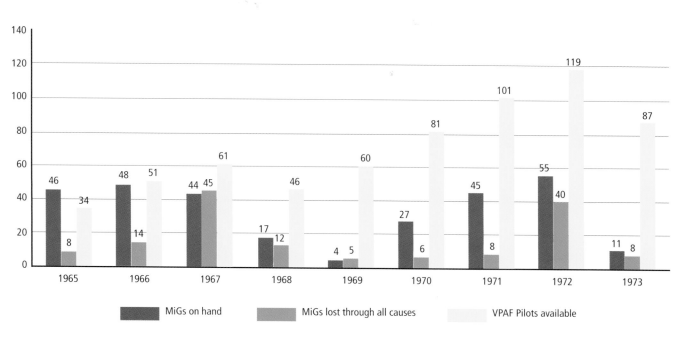

On a yearly average, 30 to 40 MiGs were supplied to North Vietnam. Primary and secondary evidence suggests that, on average, 24 to 30 pilots reached active status on a yearly basis. At the time of writing, supply figures of MiGs and exact number of pilots trained is still classified information in Vietnam.

Comparison of US claims and VPAF pilot and MiG losses

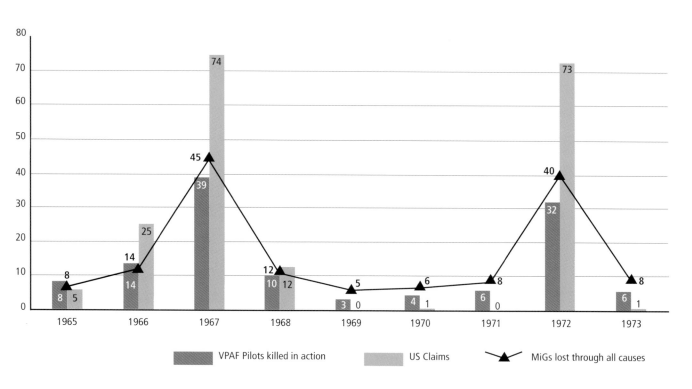

A comparison of US claims and VPAF pilot and MiG losses. The above figures are based on known US and Vietnamese data.

TABLE 3   MiG and Pilot data

A = Date
B = MiGs on hand
C = MiGs lost through all causes
D = Pilots available,
E = Pilots killed in action
F = US claims

A	B	C	D	E	F
1964	35	2	36	2	0
1965	45	8	34	8	5
1966	48	20	51	14	25
1967	44	45	61	39	74
1968	17	12	46	10	12
1969	4	5	60	3	0
1970	27	6	81	4	1
1971	45	8	101	6	0
1972	55	40	119	32	73
1973	27	2	105	0	0
1975	43	6	129	4	0

The North Vietnamese received on average 30 to 40 MiGs each year from their allies. The primary oral evidence indicates that about 24 pilots reached active status on a yearly basis.

Some of the above data are working averages and varied from year to year. The author has collated this information partly from official figures and interviews conducted with living aircrew.

At the time of writing, exact supply figures of MiGs and pilot training numbers are still regarded as highly classified in Vietnam (if such documents exist). The author is of the opinion that the above table is the most accurate study done that is available for public scrutiny.

VPAF kills from 3 May 1962 - 12 January 1973

TABLE 4

A = NAME
B = 1/4 KILL
C = 1/2 KILL
D = FULL KILL
E = UNMANNED KILL
F = HELICOPTER KILL
G = TOTAL

	A	B	C	D	E	F	G
1.	Bui Duc Nhu	0	0	1	0	0	1
2.	Bui Thanh Liem	0	0	1	0	0	1
3.	Bui Van Sui	0	3	0	0	0	3
4.	Cao Thanh Tinh	2	0	0	0	0	2
5.	Dang Ngoc Ngu	0	0	7	0	0	7
6.	Dinh Ton	0	0	2	0	0	2 1 at night
7.	Do Hang	0	2	0	0	0	2
8.	Do Van Lanh	0	0	4	0	0	4
9.	Dong Van De	0	0	2	0	0	2 double kill
10.	Dong Van Song	1	4	0	0	0	5
11.	Duong Truong Tan	0	3	0	0	1	4
12.	Ha Van Chuc	0	0	1	0	0	1
13.	Ha Bon	3	0	0	0	0	3
14.	Ha Vinh Thanh	0	0	2	0	0	2
15.	Han Vinh Tuan	0	0	1	0	0	1
16.	Ho Van Quay	0	0	2	0	0	2
17.	Hoang Ngoc Ti	0	0	1	0	0	1
18.	Hoang Quoc Dung	0	0	1	0	0	2
19.	Hoang Tam Hung	0	0	1	0	0	1
20.	Hoang The Thing	0	0	1	0	0	1
21.	Hoang Van Ky	5	0	0	0	0	5
22.	Lam Van Lich	0	0	0	0	2	2
23.	Le Kien	0	0	1	0	0	0
24.	Le Minh Huan	0	0	1	0	1	2
25.	Le Hai	4	0	2	0	0	6 Possibly 7
26.	Le Thanh Dao	0	0	6	0	0	6 Joint top 923 FR Ace
27.	Le Trong Huyen	0	0	4	0	0	4
28.	Le Trong Long	0	0	2	0	0	2
29.	Le van Phong	1	0	0	0	0	1
30.	Le Van Tuong	0	0	1	0	0	1
31.	Le Xuan Di	0	2	0	0	0	2
32.	Luong Duc Truong	0	0	1	0	0	1
33.	Luu Duc Si	0	0	2	0	0	2
34.	Luu Huy Chao	2	0	1	0	0	3
35.	Mai Duc Thai	2	0	0	0	0	2
36.	Mai Van Cuong	0	0	8	0	0	8

	A	B	C	D	E	F	G
37.	Ngo Ba Dich	6	0	1	0	0	7
38.	Ngo Duan Hung	0	0	1	0	0	1
39.	Ngo Duc Mai	0	0	3	0	0	3
40.	Ngo Duc Tho	0	0	1	0	0	1
41.	Ngo Duy Thu	1	0	2	0	0	3
42.	Ngo Van Phu	0	0	1	0	0	1
43.	Nguyen Ba Khang	0	0	2	0	0	2 1 night kill
44.	Nguyen Bien	0	0	1	0	0	1
45.	Nguyen Dang Kinh	0	2	4	0	0	6
46.	Nguyen Dinh Phu	0	0	2	0	0	2
47.	Nguyen Doc Soat	1	0	5	0	0	6
48.	Nguyen Hang So	0	0	1	0	0	1
49.	Nguyen Hay Diet	0	0	1	0	0	1
50.	Nguyen Hong Nhi	0	0	6	2	0	8 two double kills
51.	Nguyen Hong Son	0	0	1	0	0	1
52.	Nguyen Hong Thai	0	0	1	0	0	1
53.	Nguyen Hung Son	0	0	1	0	0	1
54.	Nguyen Huu Tao	0	0	1	0	0	1
55.	Nguyen Kiem Tiem	0	0	1	0	0	1
56.	Nguyen Ngoc Do	1	0	0	5	0	6
57.	Nguyen Ngoc Ngu	0	0	1	0	0	1
58.	Nguyen Ngoc Ti	0	0	1	0	0	1
59.	Nguyen Nhat Chieu	0	0	6	0	0	6
60.	Nguyen Manh Tung	0	0	1	0	0	1
61.	Nguyen Minh Ly	0	0	1	0	0	1
62.	Nguyen Nhung	0	0	1	0	1	2 First Helicopter kill
63.	Nguyen Hong Viet	0	0	1	0	0	1
64.	Nguyen Phi Hung	0	0	3	0	0	3
65.	Nguyen Phuc Ninh	0	0	2	0	0	2
66.	Nguyen The Hon	6	0	0	0	0	6
67.	Nguyen Tiem Sam	4	0	2	0	0	6 Joint top 923 FR Ace
68.	Nguyen Van Ba	0	0	1	0	0	0 1 Piston engine kill
69.	Nguyen Van Bay	4	0	3	0	0	7 10 kills? First Ace
70.	Nguyen Van Bay	0	0	1	0	0	1 the younger
71.	Nguyen Van Coc	0	0	7	2	0	9 13 kills? Top Ace
72.	Nguyen Van Dien	0	1	0	0	0	1
73.	Nguyen Van Lai	0	0	1	0	0	1
74.	Nguyen Van Minh	0	1	2	0	0	3
75.	Nguyen Van Nghia	0	0	5	0	0	5
76.	Nguyen Van Vuong	0	0	0	1	0	0 Last VPAF air kill
77.	Nguyen Vinh Tuong	0	0	0	1	0	0
78.	Pham Hung Son	0	0	3	0	0	3 Top 925 FR Ace
79.	Pham Ngoc Lan	0	0	2	0	1	3 First VPAF air kill
80.	Pham Ngoc Tam	0	0	1	0	0	1
81.	Pham Phu Thai	0	0	1	0	0	1
82.	Pham Thanh Ngan	1	0	0	7	0	8
83.	Pham Trong Van	0	0	1	0	0	1
84.	Pham Tuan	0	0	1	0	0	1
	First night kill (B-52) and later became a Cosmonaut						
85.	Phan Dinh Tuan	0	0	1	0	0	1
86.	Phan Thanh	1	0	0	0	0	1
87.	Phan Thanh Tai	0	0	1	0	0	1
88.	Phan Thanh Truong	2	0	1	0	0	3
89.	Phan Trung Van	0	0	1	0	0	1
90.	Phan Van Tuc	4	0	1	0	1	6
91.	Ta Van Chen	0	0	1	0	0	1
92.	Tran Manh	0	0	1	0	0	1
93.	Tran Triem	0	0	2	0	0	2
94.	Tran Huyen	1	1	0	0	0	2

TABLE 4

	A	B	C	D	E	F	G
95.	Tran Van Phuong	0	0	0	0	1	1
96.	Tran Viet	0	0	3	0	0	3 All F-4s.
97.	Tranh Hanh	0	0	1	0	0	1
98.	Tran Ngoc Xia	0	0	1	0	0	1
99.	Truong Ton	0	0	1	0	0	1
100.	Vo Van Man	4	0	2	0	0	6 2ND Ace by 30 secs.
101.	Vu Dinh Rang	1	0	1	0	0	2
102.	Vu Duc Hop	0	0	1	0	0	1
103.	Vu Huy Luong	0	0	1	0	0	1
104.	Vu Ngoc Dinh	0	1	3	0	0	4
105.	Vu Xuan Thieu	0	0	1	0	0	1 Night kill (B-52)

Total = 261 kills

Vietnamese officials have admitted to the author that there is an official list of 126 pilots who share 319 kills. However, this list is still classified in Vietnam.

The North Vietnamese did not distinguish between shared kills and full kills in the same way back-seat pilots were credited with victories by the Americans during the same period.

Vietnamese Sources

Diary of the Air Defence Units of North Vietnam. 1983. V.P.A. Publishing House, Ha Noi.

Le Thanh Chon, 1990. *Nine Layers of the Clouds.* Ho Chih Minh Press.

History of the VPAF Vols. I, II and III. 1980. V.P.A. Publishing, Ha Noi.

Interview with Miss Ngo Th Kim Dung, Assistant Director VPAF Museum on 23-25 September 1999.

Interview with Nguyen Minh Tam. Director N-52 Musuem interviewed 24 September 1999.

Interview with Nguyen Nhat Chieu, Major General VPAF (Retired) on 26 September 1999.

Interview with Nguyen Van Bay, Colonel VPAF (Retired) on 27 September 1999.

Interview with Pham Ngoc Lan, Major General VPAF (Retired) on 28-29 September 1999.

Interview with Nguyen Minh Tam, Director, Army Historical Branch on 30 September 1999.

Interview with Le Thanh, Painter, Christmas Bombing witness 31 September 1999.

Le Thiet Hung, Chief Ground Controller (Thang Log) officer interview by Vietnamese: sources and date unknown.

Pham Tuan, ex-VPAF fighter pilot interviewed by Vietnamese sources, date unknown.

Duoung Ba Khang, ex-VPAF fighter pilot interviewed by Vietnamese sources, date unknown.

Vu Dang Rang, ex-VPAF fighter pilot interviewed by Vietnamese sources, date unknown.

Other Sources

Air War Study Group, The Air War in Indochina. Beacon Press Boston.

Airplane Vol.6 Issue 66 1990, History of Aviation MiG 15/17. Aerospace Publishing Ltd.

Dunnigan, James F. 1999. *Dirty little secrets of the Vietnam War,* ST. Martins Press New York.

Dorr, Robert F and Bishop, Chris 1996. *Vietnam War Debrief.* Aerospace Publishing Ltd.

Drendal, Lou. *Air to Air combat in the Vietnam War.* Squadron Signal Publications.

Gordon, Yefim. 1982. *MiG 15* 4+ Publications NA.

Grandonlini, Albert, 1998. *Armour of the Vietnam War.* Concord Publications.

Heiri Stapfer, Hans, 1992. *MiG 17 Fresco in Action.* Squadron Signa Publications.

Heiri Stapfer, Hans 1994. *MiG 19 Farmer in Action,* Squadron Signal Publications.

Linn, Don and Spering, Don 1993. *MiG 21 Fishbed, Aircraft no.* 131. Squadron Signal Publications.

McCrea Micheal. 1975. *USN, USMC AND USAF Fixed Wing loss and damage SEA 1962-73.*

Mesko, Jim. 1987. *South Vietnamese Air Force 1945-1975.* Squadron Signal Publications.

Morris, Jeremy, USN Captain (Retired). E-Mail conversation. 20/4/2000.

Murray, Williamson. 1996. *The Luftwaffe, 1933-44: Stragedy for Defeat.* Air University Press, Alabama.

Oliver, David. 1990 *MiG Dynasty,* Airlife Publishing Ltd. UK

Redemann, Hanns 1991. *Innovations in Aircraft Constructions.* Schiffer Publications.

Rendall, Ivan 1999. *Rolling Thunder Jet Combat from World War II.* The Free Press New York.

Sakai, Saburo. *Samurai.* 1996. Distributed by Simon and Schuster.

Smith, John. T. 1998. *Linebacker Raid. The Bombing of North Vietnam.* Arms and Armour.

Souder, J. B. USN Commander (Retired). E-Mail conversation on 21/4/2000.

Summers, Harry G. Jnr. 1995. *Historical Atlas of the Vietnam War.* Swanston Publishing Ltd.

Summers, Harry G. Jnr. 1999. *The Vietnam War Almanac,* Preside Press.

Taylor, Michael 1990. *Encyclopedia of Modern Military Aircraft,* Published by Bison Books.

Toperczer, Istvan. 1998. *Air War Over North Vietnam.* Squadron Signal Publications.

Toliver, Raymond and Constable, Trevor 1997. *Fighter Aces of the USA.* Schiffer Publications.

VC/NVA Clothing and Equipment 1969. Air University Library, Maxwell Air force base, Alabama.

Wings of Fame. 1998. VOL. 11 Aerospace Publishing. *World Air Power Journal.* Vol. 16 Spring 1994 Aerospace Publishing.